Automotive UPHOLSTERY & INTERIOR Restoration

Fred Mattson

CarTech®

CarTech®

CarTech®, Inc.
838 Lake Street South
Forest Lake, MN 55025
Phone: 651-277-1200 or 800-551-4754
Fax: 651-277-1203
www.cartechbooks.com

© 2017 by Fred Mattson

All rights reserved. No part of this publication may be reproduced or utilized in any form or by any means, electronic or mechanical, including photocopying, recording, or by any information storage and retrieval system, without prior permission from the Publisher. All text, photographs, and artwork are the property of the Author unless otherwise noted or credited.

The information in this work is true and complete to the best of our knowledge. However, all information is presented without any guarantee on the part of the Author or Publisher, who also disclaim any liability incurred in connection with the use of the information and any implied warranties of merchantability or fitness for a particular purpose. Readers are responsible for taking suitable and appropriate safety measures when performing any of the operations or activities described in this work.

All trademarks, trade names, model names and numbers, and other product designations referred to herein are the property of their respective owners and are used solely for identification purposes. This work is a publication of CarTech, Inc., and has not been licensed, approved, sponsored, or endorsed by any other person or entity. The Publisher is not associated with any product, service, or vendor mentioned in this book, and does not endorse the products or services of any vendor mentioned in this book.

Edit by Wes Eisenschenk
Layout by Monica Seiberlich

ISBN 978-1-61325-331-1
Item No. SA393

Library of Congress Cataloging-in-Publication Data
Names: Mattson, Fred, author.
Title: Automotive upholstery and interior restoration / Fred Mattson.
Description: Forest Lake, MN : CarTech, [2017]
Identifiers: LCCN 2017010581 | ISBN 9781613253311
Subjects: LCSH: Automobiles–Upholstery. | Automobiles–Interiors. | Automobiles–Conservation and restoration.
Classification: LCC TL256 .M38 2017 | DDC 629.2–dc23
LC record available at https://lccn.loc.gov/2017010581

Written, edited, and designed in the U.S.A.
Printed in China
10 9 8 7 6 5 4 3

Title Page:
Upon inspection of the new carpet set, the model reveals that some of the chalked lines need to be straightened and some additional trimming must be done before any sewing can happen. Addressing these issues now gives the carpet a better fit when it is installed.

Back Cover Photos

Top:
The locations of the armrest mounting holes are measured and transferred to the new door panel. Through-holes are cut in the new door panel with a 1/2-inch hole punch. These access holes make the attachment of the armrest hardware easier.

Middle:
The new seat cover has been steamed and inspected. The new seat cover looks just like the original when it was new. With the addition of the front accessory aprons screwed in place, the front seat is complete and ready to be installed in the car.

Bottom Left:
A piece of scrap panel board is used to size the bottom edge of the cleat. The metal is hammered over the edge of the panel board and then sized for a secure fit. It is easy to overwork the metal on small flanges like this, which causes the piece to warp.

Bottom Right:
The chrome was good on this medallion, so I opted to restore it instead of replacing it. After a thorough cleaning, the color on the medallion was restored with a fine artist brush and adding a high-gloss paint to the surface a drop at a time.

DISTRIBUTION BY:

Europe
PGUK
63 Hatton Garden
London EC1N 8LE, England
Phone: 020 7061 1980 • Fax: 020 7242 3725
www.pguk.co.uk

Australia
Renniks Publications Ltd.
3/37-39 Green Street
Banksmeadow, NSW 2109, Australia
Phone: 2 9695 7055 • Fax: 2 9695 7355
www.renniks.com

Canada
Login Canada
300 Saulteaux Crescent
Winnipeg, MB, R3J-3T2 Canada
Phone: 800 665 1148 • Fax: 800 665 0103
www.lb.ca

CONTENTS

Acknowledgments 4
About the Author 4
Introduction 5

Chapter 1: Tools of the Trade 6
Pres-N-Snap Setter 7
Hog-Ring Pliers 8
Steamer 8
Door-Clip Tool 8
Window- and Door-Crank Tool 8
Headliner Tuck Tool 9
Regulator 9
Scissors 9
Staple Lifter 10
Hammer 10
Pegboard 10
Workbench 14
Supply Sources 16
Shop Supplies 16
OEM Materials 19

Chapter 2: Seat Restoration 21
Seat Cover Panels 22
Seat Removal 22
Disassembly 24
Coil Springs 27
Seatback Supports 32
Zigzag Springs 32
Trim Panels and Seat Skirts 33
Seatback Panels 37
Robe Cords 38
Patterning 41
Material Orientation 43
Panel Inserts 44
Rear Apron Panel 45
Welt Cord 46
Listings 46
Seat Cover 47
Seat Cushion 49
Seat Cover Installation 51
Outside Backs 53
Final Assembly 53
Seat Cover Build Without a Pattern 55
Pleated Seat Cover Alignment 64

Chapter 3: Door Panels 65
Material Choices 66
Deconstruction 67
Door Panel Cleat Fabrication 69
Creating a New Door Panel 70

Door Panel Assembly 75
Door Panel Installation 80
Planning and Layout 85
Panel Construction 87
Installation 93

Chapter 4: Armrests 94
Armrest Replacement 94
Console Restoration 99
Fabrication 106

Chapter 5: Headliner 112
Inspection 113
Create a Headliner 115
Bow Measurement 115
Headliner Prep 115
Windlace 115
Headliner Installation 116
Dome Light 117
Sun Visor 127
Package Tray 142

Chapter 6: Carpet 151
Project Assessment 152
The Pad 153
Carpet Measurements 154
Sewing 160
Carpet Installation 163

Chapter 7: Convertible Top 166
Inspection and Evaluation 166
Removal and Adjustment 167
Header Bow Servicing 172
Frame Servicing 174
Frame Painting 175
Pad Installation 176
Rear Tack Rail 178
Well Liner 179
Rear Curtain 180
Top Fitment 182
Prior Damage Repair 187
Hydraulic System Servicing 188
Tack Rail Reconditioning 189
Double-Blank Curtain 190

Source Guide 192

ACKNOWLEDGMENTS

I would like to acknowledge Don Hanson, Russel Peterson, and Lon Burris for the opportunity to work on their projects and share them with you, the enthusiast.

Most of all I thank the one who saw the potential in me as a child, my grandmother, Rose, who taught me how to thread a needle and sew buttons.

ABOUT THE AUTHOR

Fred Mattson began working on car interiors as a teenager in the 1970s by hand stitching inserts into his own 1969 Oldsmobile and working on the cars of several friends in his neighborhood.

Soon after opening a full-time upholstery business in 1980, Fred's auto trimming career expanded to sewing car interiors for many prestigious upholstery shops and restoration specialists in the metropolitan area of the Twin Cities, in Minnesota.

Having earned the nickname "Fearless," Fred works his magic on hopeless projects, restoring them to factory condition by fabricating missing parts and reconditioning the potentially hopeless.

Fred now restores vintage American cars. His clients have won numerous awards and trophies and credit their wins to the high quality and correctness of detail of their interiors and convertible tops.

INTRODUCTION

My goal for writing this book is to pass along some knowledge and spark interest in vintage car restoration. It is my intent to leave you with enough information to take on a project and complete it with confidence and success.

Through years of research and conversations, I have learned a trade that has brought me much joy and pain. Learning about the evolution of the automobile and then applying that knowledge to the restoration of these wonderful works of art gives me much satisfaction. Turning junk into gems is a fulfilling endeavor. I wish you the joy of being a part of the auto trimmer trade.

Except For . . .

The one phrase I hear all the time from car enthusiasts is "except for." My seats are in excellent condition . . . except for this one seam that is split. The top on my car is like new . . . except for the rear window that is yellow and difficult to latch. My car is perfect . . . except for the mouse hole in the headliner.

What I know for sure is, the seat springs are broken, the foam has deteriorated, and the burlap foundation is dry rotted. When the convertible top binding is cracking and it is almost impossible to latch, it is time for a whole new top. Oh, and a mouse hole means a nest and a lot of mouse dirt is lurking just overhead.

Just because a car interior looks good, doesn't mean that it is serviceable. After 45 years or more of use, compounded by exposure to the elements, everything inside the car needs extensive repair and replacement. Factor in animal and insect infestations, and you have a smelly, filthy mess that is crying out to be replaced with clean and fresh materials.

Most car owners believe that restoring their car's interior will be really expensive. Well, it is expensive if you go about it the wrong way. You can save money on restoring the interior of your car if you know a few things.

Why Restore the Interior

The interior makes up one third of the car. The engine is one third and the body and paint are one third. Unfortunately, the interior doesn't get one third of the budget and often becomes an afterthought when it comes to your restoration dollars. As the driver, you will spend a lot of time sitting inside the car. Why wouldn't you want a nice, comfortable interior?

The value of your car increases dramatically if the interior is in prime condition. An old, worn-out, and damaged interior only detracts from the value of the car.

You can save money by restoring your interior yourself, if you are smart about it. Knowing your limitations and preplanning make all the difference in any restoration. Do not start buying stuff just because it is a "good" deal. Online "box" houses do not care what you buy; they just want you to buy. It is up to you to know exactly what type of car you are working on; purchasing the wrong parts can be an expensive mistake.

Changes cost money. Redoing something because you changed your mind about it costs money. Moreover, if you find yourself in over your head after purchasing interior materials, hiring the wrong trimmer will cost you money.

Working with a true professional gets you the best products for the best price. They also know how to properly install the interior components. If you are a hands-on person looking to restore a dream car, this book will help guide you in the right direction. Any task can be accomplished in many ways, but there is only one way to restore a cars' interior: the right way.

CHAPTER 1

TOOLS OF THE TRADE

Tools are designed to help you do a better job. Cheap tools are often made poorly and do not operate as smoothly as they should. They often fail prematurely, which can cause damage to your work or injury to you. When a tool breaks it usually is replaced with another, and this frequent replacement gets expensive. For these reasons, off-brand or cheap tools are usually not good choices for the professional. Higher-grade tools made with precision and quality cost you less in the long run because they help you save time working on your projects and achieve professional results. You also get a lot more use out of a professional-grade tool.

It is always a good practice to put your tools away when you are finished using them. You will work more efficiently in a neat workplace, with less time wasted searching for a desired tool. It is also important to keep your tools clean and in working order. As you work on a project, your tools become covered in glue and dirt. Take the time to properly service your tools. Wipe them off when they get dirty and keep them oiled and sharp. With a little care, your tools will stay serviceable for a long time.

Tools can be expensive and take a lifetime to acquire. If you do make a living with your tools, make a habit of not loaning your tools to others as they tend to come back broken or not at all. I know only one thing for sure, and that is, if you take care of your tools, they will take care of you.

As with any specialty trade, upholstery requires some unique tools that can make each job easier to accomplish. Every shop should have the basic tools found in any toolbox (i.e., screwdrivers, socket set, hex wrenches) to perform the everyday tasks of auto upholstery. Upholstery-specific hand tools that are essential to the trade include hog-ring pliers, staple and tack lifters, heavy-duty scissors, and my favorite tool, the regulator. Although not required, a walking-foot sewing machine, foam saw, and steamer are nice to have.

Most auto trim suppliers have the professional tools you need. Basic tools such as hog-ring pliers and scissors are not very expensive and will serve you for a long time. Entry-level tools range from $12 to $40 per tool, but as your auto trim needs grow, acquiring tools that make the job easier will appeal to you. They will save you time and can earn you more money.

Organizing your tools is not a science but a matter of convenience. Access to any tool should be

The HooVer Pres-N-Snap tool is the most efficient way to install snaps and grommets in upholstery materials. Not only does it save you time, it installs snaps professionally without crushing or denting the cap. The tool is available at almost any professional upholstery supplier and comes complete with three sets of setting dies.

effortless. Many shops store theirs in overfilled toolbox drawers, and they waste precious time hunting for the right tool. Specialty racking devices are available to help sort sockets and wrenches by size and type.

Keeping all your screwdrivers organized in one drawer can be simplified by just opposing the screwdriver handles: Have the straight-blade screwdrivers point to the right and the Phillips screwdrivers point to the left. This tip alone will save you a lot of time when you are looking for a certain screwdriver.

Specialty tools can be stored in a drawer with similar tools and so on.

Not all tools need to be state of the art. Using a lesser tool may work just fine when you are just starting out in the upholstery trade. For example, an electric knife can be used to cut foam if you cannot afford a foam saw. Another example is a gravity-fed cup gun to spray glue. They work well for most shops and are available at a low cost. A cup gun requires very little maintenance, whereas a pressurized spray pot is great for large jobs and is more convenient to use, but the cost and cleanup are much more substantial.

Sometimes you find yourself needing to accomplish a task and you just don't have the right tool to do the job. Unfortunately, that special tool sometimes does not exist. Well, you just can't buy everything, so modifying or fabricating a tool for that specific task is necessary. For example, I needed a long, thin, but rigid stuffing tool. Such a tool is not available in a catalog or online, so I took a simple piece of bar stock that I had in my scrap pile, rounded the end, and polished it smooth to make a great stuffing tool. You will find that the longer you work in the auto upholstery trade, the more creative you become, and overcoming problems soon becomes second nature to you.

Pres-N-Snap Setter

One tool that I could not do without is the HooVer Products Pres-N-Snap setter. This tool sets you back about $130, which sounds like a lot for just one tool, but it does a professional job of installing snaps without crushing or denting the cap on the snap. This alone saves you money by not wasting materials, and it also saves time (i.e., makes you more money) by allowing you to install a snap in just one squeeze,

---

Sample Tools List

The list of tools that you use in the upholstery trade can be long. Building a tool set takes time and could cost hundreds of dollars if you tried to get them all at once. Start simply with the very basic hand tools and pick up other hand tools and power tools as you need them.

Please note that the following list is far from complete and not all of them are needed to begin work on a project.

Hand Tools
- Screwdrivers: assorted Phillips, slotted, Torx (The use of a magnetic-tip handle gives you the freedom to carry fewer tools around by providing more variety in a single tool.)
- Hammers: tack hammer, ball-peen, body hammers (A rubber mallet or dead-blow hammer is also quite handy to have.)
- Socket set: basic set 1/4-, 3/8-, 1/2-inch-drive standard and metric, Torx
- Pliers: slip-joint, needle-nose, Vise-Grips
- Allen wrenches: standard and metric
- Scissors: 6-, 8-, 10-, 12-inch; snips, seam ripper (Having several pairs of scissors is a good idea because they do get dull and using a sharp pair makes your work much easier.)
- Staple lifter
- Door panel tool
- Door handle tools
- Headliner tuck tool
- Regulators
- Assorted hole punches
- Wire cutter: 7- and 9-inch, bolt cutters
- Hog-ring pliers: straight, angled
- Rulers: 36-, 48-, and 72-inch tape measures
- Utility knife (Always have plenty of blades on hand.)
- Bench vise
- Workbench

Power Tools
- Walking-foot sewing machine
- Steamer
- Drill motor: 3/8-, 1/2-inch
- Heat gun
- Air compressor
- Staple gun: electric, pneumatic, mechanical
- Glue gun: foam, contact cement, hot glue
- Rotary tool
- Foam saw

CHAPTER 1

unlike the manual setter that comes free with some snap kits.

Hog-Ring Pliers

Different types of hog-ring pliers are available and each has its own purpose. Originally the hog-ring pliers were used in agriculture to ring the nose of hogs to keep them from rooting and destroying the land. Other uses for hog-ring pliers range from food processing to sealing sausage casing to industrial usage in chain link fences. Hog-ring pliers look like regular pliers but are notched at the tip to hold a wire hog ring while clamping it tight.

A quality hog-ring tool is made from cast iron with long handles to allow for a tight and complete cinch of the hog ring. The professional hog-ring tool costs about $30 to $35 and will last you a lifetime. The cheap hog-ring pliers that come with a seat kit are most likely made from round stock and riveted together. They typically are short in length, which makes crimping a hog ring more difficult, causing the hand to fatigue quickly,

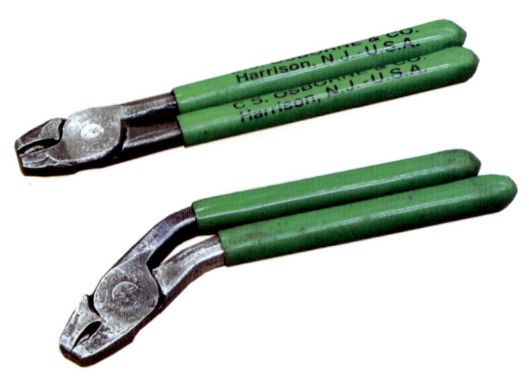

Hog-ring pliers are essential to the auto upholsterer. Several shapes and styles are available to reach into difficult areas. Professional-quality hog-ring pliers can properly install a hog ring with ease and serve you for many years without failing.

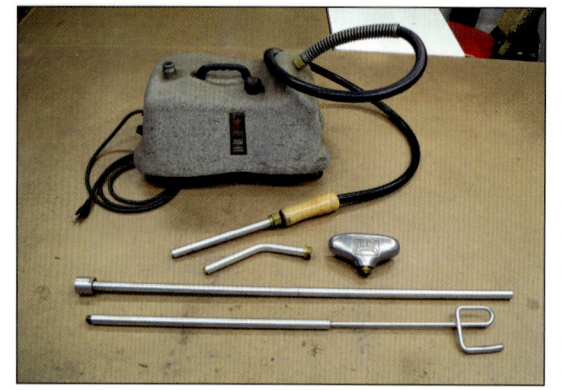

Use the steamer to remove wrinkles in upholstery materials as well as to help with pattern making. Professional-grade steamers such as this Jiffy model J-4000 will last a long time in the shop because they are built to withstand the rough service they are bound to see. Interchangeable heads make this model even more useful.

and they usually last only a few dozen crimps before they fall apart.

Steamer

The use of a steamer to remove wrinkles and small imperfections is essential to the upholstery trade. Several models of steamers are available for upholstery and each has its own strengths. Some have a dedicated purpose while others use different heads for specific applications. Hands down, the most versatile and durable auto upholstery steamer on the market today is the Model J-4000A manufactured by the Jiffy Steamer Company. This steamer unit has interchangeable heads on a 7½-foot hose and they are great for different applications. The 6-inch flat-iron head is used for general steaming and pattern making; the straight-tube head is perfect for steaming the hard-to-get-to spots on convertible tops.

Door-Clip Tool

Removing door panels is an easy task when you use the right tool. Some people use a screwdriver for this job and end up scratching the door and causing damage to the door panel while they are trying to free it from the door.

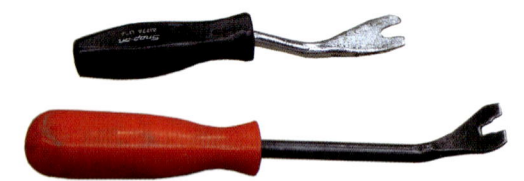

A variety of door panel tools are available for purchase and most are relatively inexpensive. The tool works on leverage to lift the fastener from the door. Long and short versions of the panel clip tool are useful to gain access to tight situations.

Getting under the panel fastener and lifting it without damaging the door panel is what this tool is all about. Many different lengths of panel tools, as well as plastic panel tools, are available to accommodate any task. These manual tools use simple leverage to get under the fastener and lift the panel safely from the door. The forked end of the tool is slid under the fastener and then the clip is pried out, releasing the panel without damaging it or the car.

Window- and Door-Crank Tool

It has always been a chore to remove the window and door cranks from a panel, but using the correct device speeds the job and prevents harm to you or the door panel. Early Ford cars used a 1/8-inch-diameter

8 AUTOMOTIVE UPHOLSTERY AND INTERIOR RESTORATION

Using the correct tool makes removal of a window and door crank much simpler. The upper tool is for early GM cars that have a small spring clip. Later-model cars used a larger clip that is pushed out of the handle using the middle tool. Ford used a small pin that is difficult to access without the special fork tool shown at the bottom.

pin to hold the crank to the regulator post. The pin is accessed by depressing the decorative escutcheon and pushing the pin out. Using the correct pin removal tool makes this operation simple.

GM cars used a small "C" spring clip in its early models and it is removed with clip pliers. Later models used a larger spring clip and that was removed by sliding the handle clip tool between the escutcheon and the crank to push out the clip.

Headliner Tuck Tool

Getting a headliner to settle into place is a breeze when you use the correct tuck tool. The tuck tool is made of spring steel with a wooden handle. The blade of the tool is blunt and rounded on the corners to prevent damage to the headliner material or molding you are working with and is available with a thin or heavy version to suit the task at hand.

The thin-blade tool can push the headliner material under and into the tightest places, leaving the out-

This tuck tool is essential for the installation of a suspended headliner. The wide blade is great for lifting rubber window molding without causing damage. The top tool has a thicker blade for lifting and prying and the lower tool has a thinner blade for tucking headliner material into tight places.

side of the headliner wrinkle free and snug; the heavy-duty blade works well for lifting the rubber moldings around the windows so that glue can be applied underneath.

Other versions of this tool are also available and are used in the same manner. Always choose the tool that is right for your specific needs.

Regulator

This is my personal favorite tool of all. The unlimited uses of this long, needle-like tool are remarkable. The pointed end can locate and align trim screw holes in garnish moldings and it can make perfect holes in panels for accent trim to be applied. The flat end is useful for applying glue or tucking material into unreachable places.

The tool is called a regulator because it was originally designed for furniture upholstery. After the fabric was applied over the cotton stuffing on the arm, cushion, or backrest of a chair, the regulator was inserted into the chair from the backside so that the cotton stuffing could be moved and repositioned into the corners, evening out the stuffing. This brought on the term of "regulating" the cushion.

Regulators are available in different sizes (ranging from 8 to 10 inches in length) and types. They can be found with a plastic or wooden handle.

It is easy to lose these when you are working on an interior because they seem to hide in the most unobvious places. They are not expensive, so I buy them four or five at a time. Once you start using a regulator, you will never be without this tool.

Scissors

Heavy-duty scissors are an essential tool for the upholstery shop. It is important to get the right size scissors for the task you are performing. Many types and uses for scissors exist and making the proper choices will save you money. The lightweight, plastic-handled scissors are not well suited for upholstery use. They fatigue your hand and the blades are too thin for heavy cutting. Maintenance is almost impossible due to the fact that they are riveted together and difficult to resharpen. Although they may be inexpensive, replacing them when they are worn out ends up costing more than buying good scissors in the first place.

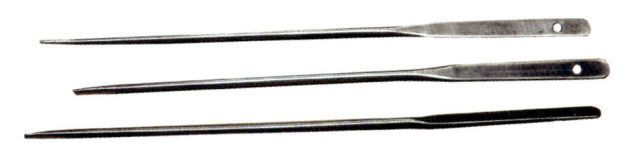

This 10-inch steel regulator is my personal favorite tool. It can be used on every job to help with assembly by locating hidden screw holes, aligning components, and tucking material into tight places.

AUTOMOTIVE UPHOLSTERY AND INTERIOR RESTORATION

Professional-quality scissors are a must for any trim shop. The variety of scissors makes specific jobs easier. From the top is an 8½-inch straight-handle industrial that is used for precision cutting, an 8⅛-inch bent-handle inlaid blade for the sewing machine, a 10-inch bent-handle inlaid for general-purpose cutting, a 10-inch bent-handle wide blade for cutting panel board and heavy materials, and a 12-inch bent-handle knife edge for cutting carpet and heavy materials.

The brand of scissors that I prefer to use in my shop is made by Wiss. The general size of scissors used every day is a 10-inch bent-handle. They work great for cutting leather, vinyl, and panel board. For carpet I use a bent-handle 12-inch knife-edge scissors. They cut through carpet like it was paper. At the sewing machine, I have used 8⅛-inch bent-handle scissors for trimming tread.

Overall I have a dozen or more scissors that I keep in rotation so that I'm always using sharp scissors. The professional-grade scissors last and can be repaired and sharpened to new condition many times. I have three scissors in service now that are more than 35 years old and they still work great.

Staple Lifter

Removing staples and tacks is not one of the tasks that anyone enjoys. Fighting a stubborn fastener only

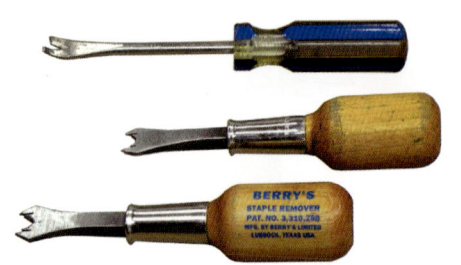

If you ever replace a convertible top, you need a good staple lifter. Tack and staple removers are available in many styles and they all seem to work fine. The best staple remover in my opinion is the Berry's staple remover. It fits in your hand perfectly and it removes the toughest staples with ease.

makes it more frustrating. A generic tack lifter is useful but not the go-to tool. The best tool I've found is the Berry's staple remover. Ask anyone who has used one and he or she will tell you that it works. It lifts even the most difficult tacks, staples, and small nails. Its unique wooden handle design just fits into your hand comfortably and removes the tough staples and tacks with almost no effort.

Hammer

A wide range of hammers is available, each designed for a specific job. Choosing the right one for the task at hand will give you professional results.

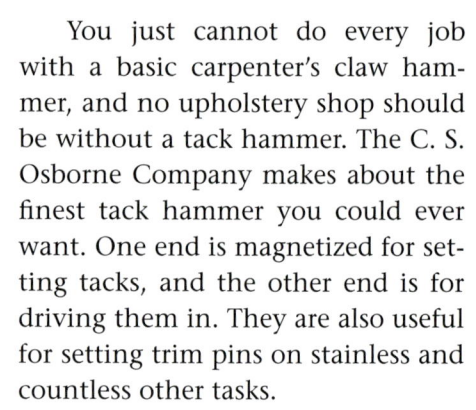

You just cannot do every job with a basic carpenter's claw hammer, and no upholstery shop should be without a tack hammer. The C. S. Osborne Company makes about the finest tack hammer you could ever want. One end is magnetized for setting tacks, and the other end is for driving them in. They are also useful for setting trim pins on stainless and countless other tasks.

A soft mallet is handy for setting wire-on welt and persuading door panel clips into place without marring the surface of the panel.

A machinist hammer (ball-peen) is useful for setting rivets and hammering a hole punch through panel board. I have several sizes and weights of machinist hammers for these tasks.

Because you are working on cars, it only makes sense to have some body hammers for straightening and shaping metal. A wide-tip pick hammer is great for repairing flared-out screw holes in the tack rail of a convertible.

Pegboard

Pegboard comes in 4 x 8–foot sheets and is available in different thicknesses. I prefer the 1/4-inch thick because it does not warp and

An assortment of hammers to handle any task that comes up. From left to right: dead-blow, interchangeable head, 32-ounce ball-peen, 12-ounce ball-peen, magnetized tack, soft-tip tack, split-tip tack, general body, and wide-tip pick hammer.

holds the pegboard hooks better. I also prefer the heavy-duty pegboard hooks instead of the standard hooks. The option is up to you.

Every room has some empty wall space, and by applying pegboard to a bare wall, you can conveniently store the tools that you use every day. This is a low-cost solution to free up floor space, allowing you to work more efficiently. Imagine what tools you would like to have hanging on the wall ready for use on that next project. The wall must be measured to determine the size to cut your pegboard. Make the pegboard as large as possible from the start. Don't worry if you cannot fill it up right away; eventually you will.

Make a reference line for aligning the bottom of the pegboard by using a long level. This helps you when mounting the pegboard to the wall. Keeping the pegboard straight and even allows the tools to hang right on the pegboard hooks. The use of all-purpose screws to apply furring strips to the wall as a foundation for the pegboard is a good choice. The furring strips are cut from 1/4-inch plywood and they are 1¼ inches wide and run the length of the pegboard. The furring strip prevents the pegboard from sinking into the wall.

Use hot glue to attach 3/8-inch nuts to the pegboard to work as a standoff providing a gap between the wall and the pegboard. This way you do not lose any extra peg holes once the pegboard is on the wall. The location of the wall studs is transferred to the backside of the pegboard so that you know where to glue the standoff nuts. When the pegboard is set into position on the wall, the 3/8-inch nuts should land on top of the furring strip backer that is already on the wall.

Hot glue a 3/8-inch nut over an existing hole on the backside of the pegboard as a standoff so that it allows enough space for a pegboard hook to be inserted. The nut only blocks one hole as a furring strip covers up many. The pegboard is aligned to the wall with the nuts contacting the furring strips. A broad-head cabinet screw is inserted through the hole with the nut behind it to secure the pegboard to the wall. The screws are snugged up but are not overtightened.

Dust off the surface of the pegboard and give it a coat of primer and two topcoats of topcoat paint to protect the surface of the pegboard from wear. White is a good color because it highlights your tools and makes them easier to select. Pegboard hooks are inserted into the holes of the pegboard and tools can now be hung up. The best advantage of pegboard storage is the ability to rearrange the hooks so that the tools you use most often are ready and at your fingertips.

Installing Pegboard

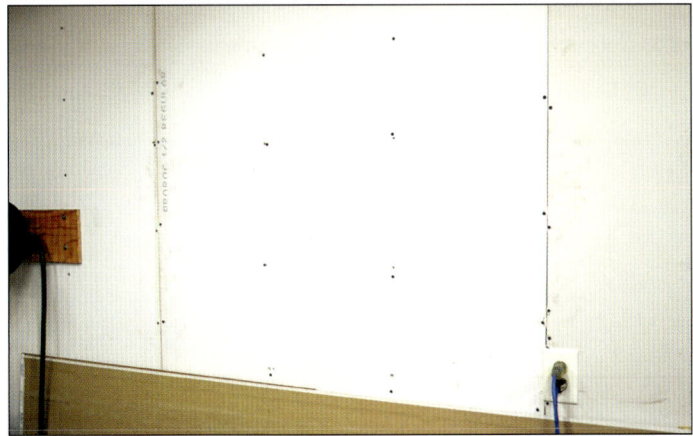

1 *Because floor space is always at a premium for storage racks and toolboxes, consider your shop walls a wealth of ample space for tool storage. By using pegboard to hang tools and supplies, you not only gain easy access to them but also find that this is a low-cost storage solution. Pegboard also gives you the freedom to change or rearrange items as your needs change, making it much more useful than a drawer or shelf.*

2 *You need to know how much wall space to cover with pegboard. Measure your wall to determine the dimensions of pegboard you require. Measure the pegboard and mark where it needs to be trimmed. Cut the pegboard to the desired wall size.*

3 *The pegboard should be hung level on the wall. Use a long level to make a mark on the wall as a reference baseline to fit the pegboard to.*

4 *Cut furring strips 1¼ inches wide and the width of your pegboard from 1/4-inch plywood and attach them to the wall with all-purpose screws. Use the furring strip as a backer so that the pegboard standoffs do not sink into the drywall. The pegboard covers over all of this. The length of the mounting screw needed is determined by the thickness of your materials, i.e., 1/2-inch drywall + 1/4-inch furring strip = 3/4-inch material depth + 3/4-inch penetration depth = 1½-inch screw.*

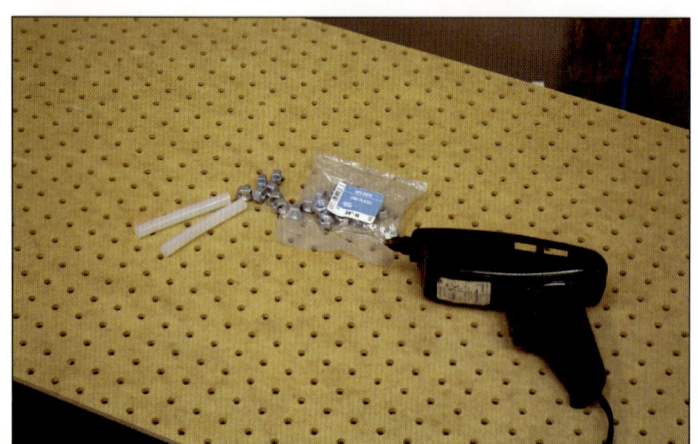

5 *Before mounting the pegboard to the wall, measure and locate the wall studs, transfer the stud locations onto the backside of the pegboard, and then hot glue some 3/8-inch nuts to the backside of the pegboard at the marked stud locations for a standoff. Glue the nuts over a hole in the pegboard so that a screw can go through the hole and nut. Space the nuts about 12 inches apart.*

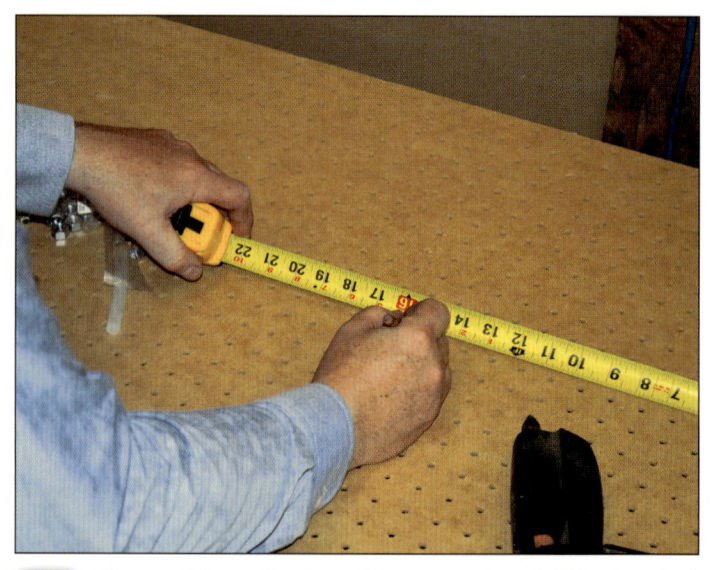

6 *You could use furring strips as a standoff instead of the spacer nuts, but you lose a lot of useful holes if you do. The 1/4-inch pegboard is rigid enough and it spans between the studs in the wall just fine.*

TOOLS OF THE TRADE

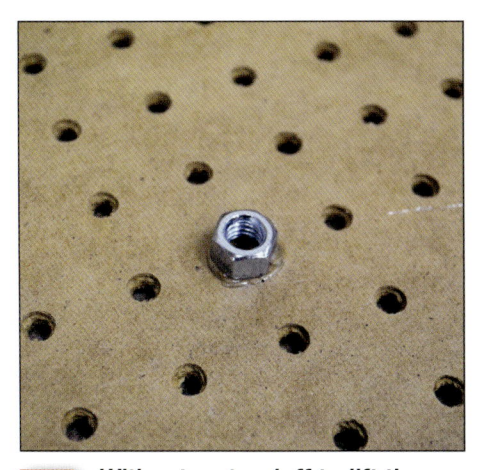

7 *Without a standoff to lift the pegboard from the surface of the wall, you don't have enough room behind the pegboard to insert the peg hooks.*

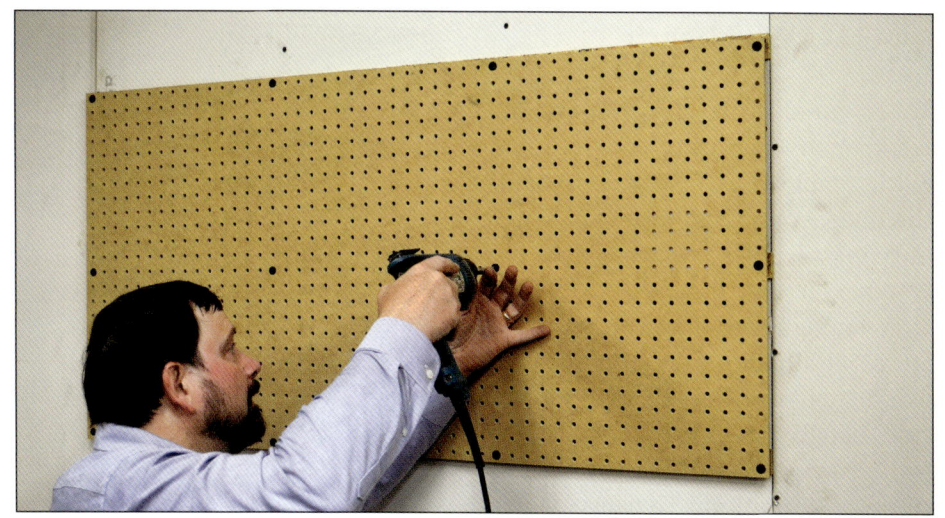

8 *Use broad-head cabinet screws to mount the pegboard to the wall. Insert the screw in the hole that is backed by the nut standoff and screw it into the wall without overtightening.*

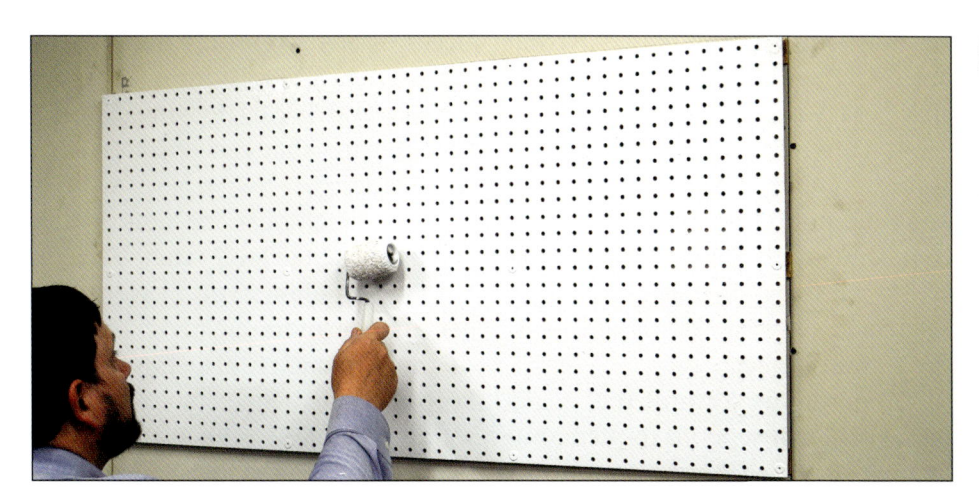

9 *When the pegboard is securely mounted to the wall, give it a good coat of primer and then two coats of paint to protect it for many years of service.*

10 *When the paint is dry, you can start hanging your tools up for easy access. Add peg hooks and rearrange them as necessary.*

AUTOMOTIVE UPHOLSTERY AND INTERIOR RESTORATION

CHAPTER 1

Workbench

Essential to every shop is the workbench, or as some may call it, a cutting table. If you are serious about the trade, you just cannot work without one. Every project touches the workbench and having one that is large enough for your projects is not always attainable. You can purchase a workbench and assemble it, but the store-bought benches lack in size and features due to manufacturing and shipping limitations. They just do not have all the features it takes to satisfy an active upholstery shop's needs.

Folding tables are useful for some things, but they are generally not rigid enough for most projects. Working on a wobbly surface is unsafe for you and the project you are working on. Some trimmers like a bench that is movable, but unless you have a huge warehouse space, a movable workbench is just not practical. Adding castors on a bench is something of a preference, but the thought of chasing a bench around does not appeal to me.

Some trim shops have a bench that is built around and incorporates the sewing machine. This gives the trimmer support for materials that are being sewn together as well as space to lay out and cut patterns.

It is essential that a bench is sturdy enough to stand on its own and hold up to the weight and stress of pushing and pulling. My solution is to build my own benches from scratch to the size I desire and with the features I need.

Some of the features that make my workbench superior to premanufactured workbenches are that it can be customized to fit the individual needs of any workshop. Because the workbench is built from common lumber and hardware, there are no special parts that can break or need to be ordered.

The height can be adjusted to a comfortable level that reduces fatigue and allows you to work longer and be more creative. The legs of the workbench also interlock to keep the workbench stable and rock solid. This allows the bench to be placed anywhere in the shop without anchoring it to a wall or the floor.

The workbench is an essential part of any shop. My design is very sturdy with a lot of room for material layout and patterning as well as assembly of projects. Underneath is plenty of storage room for materials and upholstery supplies.

Building a Workbench

I have compiled the plans for you to construct your own table. Feel inspired to make any changes that work best for you.

Bench Frame

Begin by making the frame of the workbench.
From two 2 x 4 x 96, cut the rails to a length of 96 inches.
From two 2 x 4 x 96, cut four stiles to a length of 45 inches.
From two 2 x 4 x 96, cut four legs to a length of 36 inches. (The height of the table can be adjusted to suit your personal needs.)
The stiles are let in 1½ inches from the ends of the rails and the middle stiles are placed at 32 inches on center from the end of the rails. They are secured with two 2½-inch deck screws through the rail into the ends of the stile.

The legs are placed into the outside corners of the frame and are attached by drilling two 3/8-inch holes diagonally from each other through the leg and end stile. The 3/8-inch carriage bolts are inserted through the holes and secured by a flat washer, a split-lock washer, and nut. Tighten with a ratchet wrench.

Measure the distance between the legs. From one 2 x 4 x 96 cut two lock stiles to a length of 38 inches long so that it fits snugly between the legs. Secure the locking stile to the end stile with 2½-inch deck screws.

14 AUTOMOTIVE UPHOLSTERY AND INTERIOR RESTORATION

TOOLS OF THE TRADE

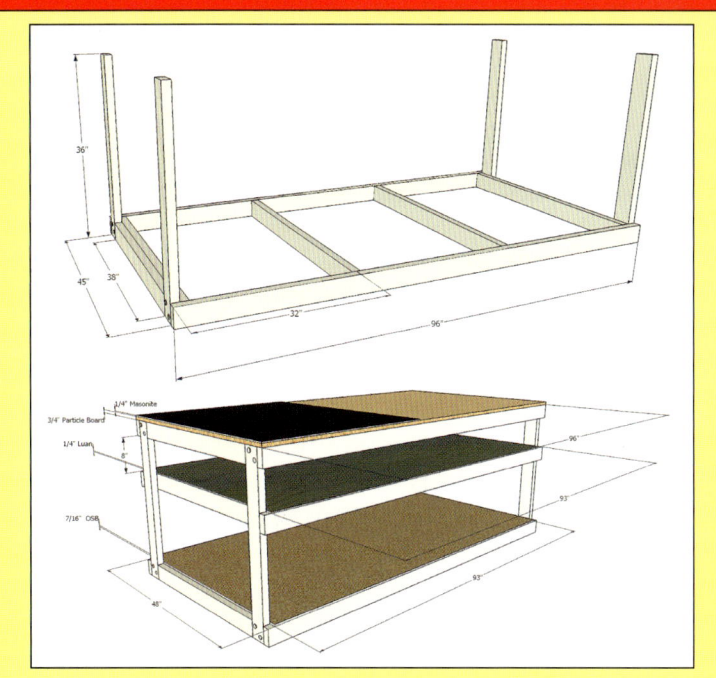

This 3-D drawing shows some measurements and the overall design of the workbench. Standard construction materials are used in this simple-to-assemble workbench. Any of the features can be customized to fit the needs of any shop.

Turn the table over so that it is standing on its legs and repeat the process to create the base of the table.

Panel Board Shelf (optional)

From two 2 x 4 x 96, cut the rails to a length of 96 inches.
From two 2 x 4 x 96, cut four stiles to a length of 45 inches.
Measure 8 inches down from the bottom of the top rail and make a mark for the top of the shelf rail.
Attach the rail to the leg with 2½-inch deck screws.
On each end, attach a stile to the rail with 2½-inch deck screws.
The middle stiles are fitted horizontally at 32 inches on center and are secured with 2½-inch deck screws.

Decking

The bottom deck is covered in 7/16-inch-thick oriented strand board. Trim the 48 x 96–inch sheet to 48 x 93 inches.
Put the sheet in place and secure it to the rails and stiles with 1¼-inch deck screws. Do not use black phosphor drywall screws because they are too brittle.
The panel board shelf is covered with 1/4-inch-thick

Materials
- (17) 2 x 4 x 96 Dimensional lumber
- (1) 3/4 x 48 x 96 Particle board
- (1) 7/16 x 48 x 96 Oriented strand board
- (1) 1/4 x 48 x 96 Luan plywood
- (16) 3½ x 3/8 Carriage bolts
- (16) 3/8 Nuts
- (16) 3/8 Flat washers
- (16) 3/8 Split lock washers
- (1 pound) 1¼ Deck screws
- (1 pound) 2½ Deck screws
- 9/16 Staples

Tools
- Circular saw
- Chop saw
- Drill motor
- 3/8 Drill bit
- 1/8 Drill bit
- Ratchet wrench and sockets
- Screw driver
- Staple gun
- Tape measure

It is important to note that there are variations in the actual size of dimensional lumber. These variations can be +/- 3/32 inch and the measurements given represent the ideal size for the cut pieces. Please measure your actual lumber and make size adjustments accordingly before cutting any materials.

Luan plywood. Trim the 48 x 96–inch sheet to 48 x 93 inches.
Position the cut sheet of Luan plywood and secure it to the rails and stiles with 9/16-inch galvanized staples.
The top of the workbench is covered with a 3/4 x 48 x 96–inch sheet of high-density particle board. Place the sheet and secure it to the rails and stiles with 1¼-inch deck screws. To prevent the particle board from breaking, it is necessary to predrill a 1/8-inch hole for the deck screw. The heads of the deck screws need to be flush with the surface of the particle board. Chamfer the hole to countersink the head of the deck screw.
The working surface of the workbench is covered with a 1/4 x 48 x 96–inch sheet of tempered Masonite hardboard. This sheet is not fastened down so that it can be easily replaced as it gets worn from cutting and gluing. ∎

CHAPTER 1

You also have ample room under the workbench for storage of upholstery materials. Adding a panel board shelf can double storage space.

One of the best features of my workbench is the replaceable work surface. A sheet of 1/4-inch tempered hardboard or Masonite is placed on top of the workbench, providing a durable and yet yielding work surface. After many projects, when the surface of the workbench becomes dirty, scarred, and uneven, the worn tempered hardboard can be easily lifted off and replaced.

Supply Sources

Every project needs raw materials to create a finished product, and obtaining these materials can be a challenge. One source is your local fabric or hobby store. However, these generic materials do not hold up to the climate changes and abuse that a car interior faces. Automotive vinyl and fabrics are UV coated to prevent fading, bleaching, and chalking. They are also heavier in weight and designed specifically for durability.

Auto upholstery supply houses will have most of what you need for your project. They generally sell wholesale to the trade only, but you may be able to find an exception.

Auto trim suppliers can be found on the Internet by a simple search for "auto upholstery supplies." It's a good idea to call or visit the supplier before you order. They can be a lot of help to find you what you need for your project.

I am very fortunate to live in a city that has several upholstery suppliers nearby. Fabric Supply in Minneapolis and Pyramid Trim Products in St. Paul have been my go-to sources for upholstery supplies since 1980.

Because I live near my suppliers, I can get what I need right away. Being able to see and feel the products helps me obtain items that I may otherwise not know exist. Picking up my upholstery materials saves on shipping costs as well. Going to see the supplier takes time away from working on a project, but the relationships I have built with them is priceless.

Shopping online for products can be overwhelming. You have a lot of choices, but not all of the products offered are of the quality you may be looking for. Brand-name parts and supplies are usually consistent in quality, but house brands vary due to the suppliers' ability to secure more of any given part. Also beware of seconds. These are materials with small flaws or surface defects and they are not suitable for use in a restoration. They are great for patterning and can save you money if you can work around the flaws. Seconds are often available from your supplier and are usually offered at a discounted price.

Shop Supplies

Every shop should keep on hand several things that you need for every job. Common products to have on hand are thread, glue, and hog rings. Building an inventory of hardware and supplies takes time and money.

Buying in bulk saves you money in the long run, but it is not uncommon to buy what you need as you need it. You can always try and network with other trimmers close by and split the cost of buying bulk items. Everyone saves money, and you build relationships too.

Here are some common supplies that you should have on hand at any given time.

Thread

Upholstery thread comes in many sizes and types. Nylon thread is generally used for auto upholstery. It has a high strength and durability that allows it to move with the material.

Polyester thread is well suited for outdoor applications such as marine and canvas work. If sunlight is a big factor, then this is the thread to use.

Monofilament is a clear nylon thread used when color matching is an issue. Topstitching for quilting is a good example of when you do not want the thread to show.

Thread comes in many colors to match with OEM vinyl and fabrics and it is available in 4-, 8-, and 16-ounce spools. Choosing the correct size of the thread is determined by what you are sewing. Standard upholstery thread is #69 and heavier contrast thread is T-270.

An assortment of thread is always good to have. Each project receives a matching thread and some get a heavy contrast thread. Here is an assortment of colors in #69 nylon and polyester. The natural and black contrast threads are T-270.

AUTOMOTIVE UPHOLSTERY AND INTERIOR RESTORATION

TOOLS OF THE TRADE

Among the most common supplies used in the trimmer trade are automotive hog rings. You'll use the sharp wire fasteners to attach seat covers securely to the frame of the seat. Professional hog-ring pliers are essential for crimping the hog rings correctly.

Fastening fabric and vinyl to the car and to interior trim panels used to be done with tacks. Stapling the materials in place has replaced the older method. Staples have proven to hold better and are much faster to use than tacks.

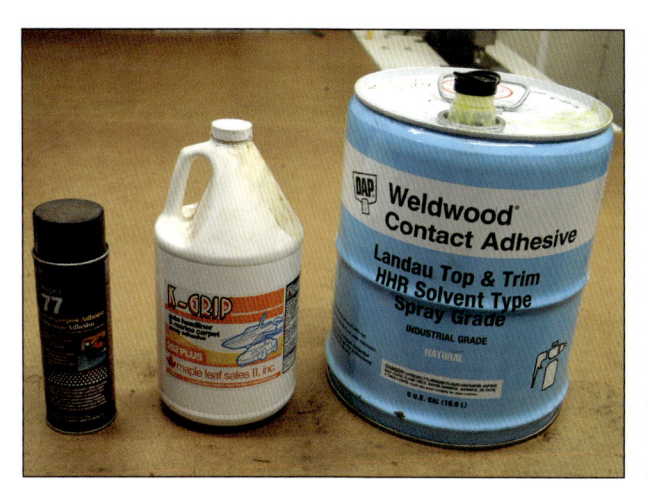

Using the correct adhesive for the task at hand saves you a lot of frustration. Aerosol cans are convenient, but they can get expensive. Foam requires an adhesive that binds it and does not harm it. Contact cement is a great all-around glue; you can purchase it in large quantities to save money.

Hog Rings

Absolutely the one product to keep on hand in the shop is hog rings. Hog rings are C-shaped metal wire with very sharp angle-cut ends that can pierce through materials to securely hold the material in place. Crimping with hog-ring pliers closes them. These metal fasteners are typically purchased by the pound or can be obtained in 25-pound or more containers. Hog rings are the go-to fastener for attaching seat covers to the frame of a seat. Hog rings are also used to connect Marshall springs and attach burlap and foam to the springs of the seat.

Staples

Tacks were the standard upholstery fastener to attach materials to the wooden frame of the car. Postwar cars were built out of metal, and fiber tack strips were installed to allow for the attachment of the upholstery. Staples replaced tacks because they are faster and a more efficient way to attach materials. They also cause less damage to the tacking surface than tacks.

Staples are available in many different sizes and types. The crown of a staple is the part that spans between the legs. The crown determines the width of the staple and the legs determine the size, or depth, of the staple.

Choosing the correct staple for a job is important. The staple needs to hold the material in place without the crown going through the material. Generally, a wide metal staple is used in auto upholstery because it holds vinyl and fabrics without damaging the material. If you are working with fabric, a fine wire staple works well.

Staples are made in different materials for specific applications. Galvanized and stainless steel are good choices for auto and marine use because they do not rust with exposure to moisture.

Adhesives

Many different adhesives are used in auto upholstery and each type has a specific use. The key to getting a good bond is to have your surfaces clean and oil free. It is not the adhesive's fault if it fails because of poor preparation, but using the correct product does matter. Be sure that you know that the parts you are trying to glue together are compatible. Some surfaces react to the adhesive you are using by melting or lifting the paint. Always follow the directions on the label of the can.

Aerosol spray cans provide the convenience of use, but the down side is the cost per can is not practical for most shops and they usually do not have the holding power required for the task at hand, especially when working with heavy materials such as carpet.

AUTOMOTIVE UPHOLSTERY AND INTERIOR RESTORATION   17

CHAPTER 1

Foam and fabric adhesives are typically available in clear or red. They are lightweight and great for bonding seat foam because they do not harm or react against the foam. Foam adhesives can be found in economical 1-gallon bulk containers for brushing or spraying as well as in aerosol cans.

I have found that the most useful glue is contact cement. DAP Weldwood makes an HHR (high-heat resistant) that provides excellent adhesion for headliners and carpets. It is available in 1- and 5-gallon cans. This adhesive can be applied by brushing or it can be sprayed with a cup gun or spray pot connected to an air compressor. It is well suited for auto upholstery work and, after the glue has cured, it is usually unaffected by temperature changes.

Burlap

Burlap is a product that is said to have 101 uses; in auto upholstery it is used as a foundation component. Always keep plenty of burlap in inventory; it is used on every seat project to cover and tension the seat springs, which gives support to the cotton and foam materials that pad the seat.

Burlap is a strong woven material that is available in natural jute and synthetic fibers. Most auto trim suppliers offer both types of burlap for sale by the cut yard, but because of its low cost it is most economical if purchased by the roll.

Cotton

Another must-have in the shop is cotton for seat padding. Real cotton is graded on the purity of the processed product. It has seeds, stems, and other debris in it and processing real cotton is cost prohibitive. Before the use of cotton, upholsterers used horsehair and straw to pad furniture and the seats of cars. Modern cotton is a synthetic blend of cotton fibers and spun polyester. It is much cleaner and easier to work with than the natural cotton batting that once was used. Synthetic cotton is sold by the pound and your best value is to buy it by the half bale (3 rolls).

Denim

Upholstery denim is a tightly woven fabric that is a durable and low-cost material that is high in

Often used but never seen, denim is used in auto upholstery to make listings and panel fillers, saving money on seat cover material that does not show. The durable nature of denim is well suited for upholstery because it is a strong low-cost material.

Burlap is made from the fibers of the jute plant and is a durable and strong natural material that is the main foundation material for covering and tensioning springs in every car seat. This material is one of the items you should keep in inventory. Because of its low cost, it is best to purchase it by the roll.

Synthetic cotton batting is used to pad the cushion of a car seat and it is available in rolls. When purchased from an auto trim supply house, cotton is sold by the pound and is put up in rolls for convenient use. This product is easy to use and well suited for the auto industry.

TOOLS OF THE TRADE

strength. Denim is used primarily to save money in auto upholstery by substituting it for the expensive cover materials that do not show, such as for listings, stretchers, and filler panels. Many colors and widths are available. I usually have two neutral colors on hand to complement the project that I am working on at the time.

Muslin

Muslin is a low-cost, lightweight, woven-cotton fabric that is used as a cover material for seat padding and it is also a common sewing backer that can be added to the back side of sew foam to hold the stitching when pleating an insert.

Muslin can be purchased in rolls or bolts (flat folded). If you purchase a bolt of muslin, I suggest that you unfurl it and put it up on a roll to relieve the wrinkles. It is also much easier to work with when it is flat and smooth. Muslin is available in many different widths as well as bleached or unbleached. Bleached muslin is much whiter than the unbleached, which is a natural off-white in color. Another difference is the thread count of the material; it can be higher in the bleached version.

Some trimmers use muslin for patterning or mocking up a seat cover because the material is so inexpensive.

Cheesecloth

One product that I use a lot of is cheesecloth. This is an open-weave cotton fabric that is used to cover the cotton batting, keeping it in place so that the cotton does not pill and bunch up as the seat upholstery is pulled over the cotton when it is being installed. The cheesecloth does not interfere with the look of the seat cover, but merely enhances the seat cover installation process. Without the cheesecloth covering the cotton padding, the finished seat cover can appear lumpy and uneven.

OEM Materials

If you are looking for original fabrics, vinyl, and leather, a great place to start your search is your local auto trim supplier. They may have the original OEM Detroit Fabric books to help you find the desired color and material type you need for your restoration.

Online searches can also aid you in finding original materials for the year and model of your project. If you have a piece of the original material to send a supplier, they can do a search for you and get you an exact match. They may also be able to help you locate other hard-to-find interior materials to complete your project. Be careful of online sellers of vintage auto upholstery materials. Some of them charge you up front for the product you desire and then take months to deliver them. Be sure to ask when the items that you ordered will be shipped for delivery and what their return policies is if the materials you ordered are not what you expect them to be.

Leather

The auto industry has used leather for interior seating from the early 1900s. Leather is considered a

Cotton muslin is a commonly used backer material for sewing and pleating seat inserts. Its lightweight nature does not cause wrinkling of the top material and it provides a solid foundation for sewing, which keeps the stitches from pulling out.

Auto upholsterers use cheesecloth as a cover material to protect the cotton padding of the seat from becoming lumpy and bunching up when the seat cover is installed. Do not overlook the usefulness of cheesecloth. It is inexpensive and makes your seat covers look better.

CHAPTER 1

Nothing speaks louder than real leather when it comes to luxury seating. Leather has been used in auto interiors from the very first cars and is considered a premium upholstery material. This natural product is available in full and half hides and in many colors and grains to complement your projects.

Vinyl is a durable choice for automotive seating because of its ability to withstand rain, temperature, and heavy use. Available in a wide variety of colors and grain, vinyl is more versatile than natural leather and can be embossed with patterns and company logos.

The 1950s and 1960s brought many color and design choices. Seats were covered in beautiful woven hard cloth that added uniqueness to the interior of each car. These fabric examples represent just how different the patterns and colors can be.

premium upholstery material choice because it has proven to be very durable due to its natural ability to withstand the effects of rain, sunshine, and extreme temperatures. The outer seat and door coverings in open cars were generally fashioned from leather. Leather is a natural product coming from the hides of cattle, and it is preserved through a tanning process that allows it to remain soft and supple. Different grades are available for the upholstery trade with a wide choice of colors and textures.

Vinyl

Prior to the 1940s, the vinyl material that was used in auto interiors was actually an oilcloth. This material was made from a coating of boiled linseed oil applied over a close-woven cotton duck cloth. Although it was waterproof, it was not very durable. When it was exposed to sunlight and heavy use, the surface cracked and deteriorated with age. A more stable product later replaced oilcloth; it was made from a composite of a knit fabric backing and an expanded polyvinyl chloride (PVC) plastic coating. Sometimes referred to as pleather (plastic leather), this has evolved into the modern vinyl that we know today. Vinyl is manufactured to a standard width of 54 inches and is sold by the running yard.

Modern embossing has given manufacturers the ability to create patterns and logos in the vinyl, which enhances the look of the material and gives styling to cars, which nature cannot do.

Woven Fabrics

Before the onset of synthetic fabrics in the 1940s, car interiors were trimmed in fabric woven from natural fibers such as wool, cotton, and linen (made from flax). Cotton and linen are derived from plants and wool is made from animal hair. Weather conditions are harsh on an interior and durability has a lot to do with the materials chosen by car manufacturers. The materials also had to be attractive and comfortable to the touch. The most durable and versatile material available at the time was wool. Thanks to its ability to be dyed and woven into many different patterns and textures, it was the logical choice for upholstery. Different types of wool fabric have been used on seat covers and door panels; the most common are broadcloths and mohair.

Broadcloth was typically made from wool and was easy to tailor into seat covers. Durable and yet economical, it was the standard upholstery material used in car interiors until the early 1950s.

Mohair is made from the hair of the Angora goat. It is best known for its high luster and sheen, giving it a velvety look. Although it is extremely durable, it is also soft to the touch, making it a perfect auto upholstery material.

In the mid-1950s, automakers started using ornate woven hard cloths on seats and door panels. These fabrics brought a new look to the interior, making it more elegant and distinctive. This body cloth was made from blends of synthetic fibers, such as nylon, polyester, and rayon. The result was a polished-looking material with beautiful brocade patterns, stripes, and textures that are not only durable, but they are available in many complementary colors to the car's exterior paint.

CHAPTER 2

SEAT RESTORATION

The main focal component of an auto interior is the driver's seat. Its purpose is to provide a safe and comfortable place for the driver to operate the car. Over many years of evolution, the driver's seat has changed in style, comfort, and safety.

Early seats consisted of a hand-crafted wooden frame with coil springs that were covered in leather, linen, or wool fabric. After many years of service, these seat covers have worn through, exposing the springs, horsehair, cotton, and burlap that had been supporting the cover and providing comfort.

Seats in this condition do not necessarily need to be replaced. They were built with raw materials and basic woodworking joints, so repairing a distressed seat frame and springs can be restored to original condition with a lot of patience, time, and basic woodworking skills.

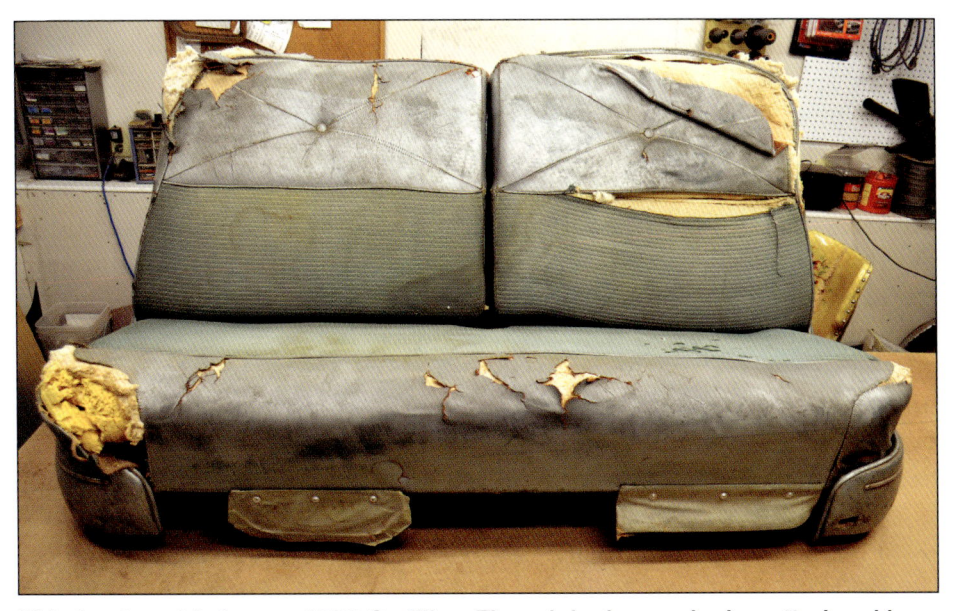

The post-war car era began fabricating seats with metal frames and zigzag springs. These frames were mass produced by stamping out components from sheet metal and spot welding the pieces together, making the frame stronger and very durable. The springs were covered with burlap and employed a latex rubber pad for comfort. Because of the abundance of man-made materials, manufacturers were now able to mass-produce the seat coverings from broadcloth, leather, and vinyl. This allowed many variations in style and features.

In the early 1960s, the challenge of restoring a seat became more difficult for trimmers to reproduce when manufacturers began to emboss vinyl with patterns and logos. The process of dielectrically embossing vinyl involves expensive equipment. The average trimmer typically does not invest money to acquire the tooling or the time learning the process to produce one-off seat covers. Sewing the patterns into the vinyl used to be the only way an upholsterer could get the general look of an original embossed piece. Fortunately today many manufacturers can do the embossing of these patterns and once again these seats can be restored to original condition.

This front seat is from a 1952 Cadillac. The original cover is dry rotted and in need of a complete restoration. The owner bought the car when it was already disassembled and the repaint process had been started in a non-original color. I will re-create this seat in a period-correct red.

AUTOMOTIVE UPHOLSTERY AND INTERIOR RESTORATION

CHAPTER 2

The market today offers many ready-made reproduction seat covers and interior kits. A lot of these interior kits use generic materials that are not correct in color, texture, and fit. The tailoring on some of these seat covers and interior kits fits well, but many do not fit. This is why a professional upholsterer should install these kits so that alterations can be made to the panels and seat covers to make the finished job look good. A lot of time and effort can go into fitting and re-fitting these kits, and it is for these reasons I prefer to make the interior panels and seat covers from scratch.

The goal of a restoration is to have a new seat that looks like the original, but an original-style seat cover is based on the choice of materials, pattern, and design used for the restoration. Some of the original materials used in vintage cars are no longer available, so a substitution of modern materials must be made. Products chosen for the restoration should be similar in characteristics to the original materials in look, feel, and performance. One product that is not available today is the thin cotton coach wadding used in almost every component of an interior. Coach wadding is no longer produced, leaving the trimmer to substitute a felt underliner to cushion the fabric from the subsurface of wood or sheet metal.

Seat cover materials produced today are more durable and colorfast than their vintage counterparts. The modern synthetic fibers being produced are also softer and more comfortable than the vintage woolen fabrics, yet they are very close in appearance to the originals.

The look of a new interior in a classic automobile can vary considerably. A custom tailored interior is suitable for a highly modified street rod but just does not have the right look if you are going for a vintage restoration. The seat pattern can be the basic design or upgraded to the deluxe interior of a higher-level model. Most manufacturers produced base model cars, which were more affordable but limited in accessories and options. The base model had a very simple interior covered in wool broadcloth and a rubber mat covering the floor. Deluxe models were equipped with more luxury and upgraded options. Door panels and plush seat covers of mohair with wide pleats was a common design along with woven carpet on the floors. Whether the seat cover is plain or fancy, you are striving for a *period correct* restoration, meaning that the interior reflects the vintage of car.

Seat Cover Panels

A seat cover is made up of many individual panels and each panel has a name and purpose. Knowing what to call them helps with the design and assembly of the seat cover.

The face panel of the seat is called an insert. Inserts can be plain, pleated, or made up of decorative patterns. Raised panels called bolsters surround the insert. The insert and bolsters make up the top and/or front of a seat cover. Around the outsides of the seat are panels that make up the boxing. The face panel is attached to the boxing by sewing them together. The seam may be trimmed with a covered welt cord, a single top cap stitch, or a decorative double stitch called a French seam.

The front seatback cushion has an outside back cover that is either sewn to the seatback cover or it may have a metal shell–type back that is covered with matching seat material. The seatback outside cover may also have a robe cord attached.

A denim sleeve is sewn along the outside edges of the cover. This sleeve is referred to as a listing; inserted into the sleeve is a listing wire that will be hog ringed to the seat frame.

Overall, the seat cover is assembled in a sequential order by creating subassemblies and joining them to create a complete seat cover.

Seat Removal

The first thing that you need to do is to remove the seat from the car and put it up on the bench. Early-model seats have a frame that the seat cushions are set into. This seat frame is called a sleigh. The upholstered cushions simply lift out of the frame starting with the bottom cushion, and then the backrest can be lifted off the frame.

Postwar cars had seatbacks that were assembled to the lower frame as one unit. Many of these bench seats had skirts to hide the seat tracks and backrest pivot arms, while robe cords graced the backs of the front bench seat. All these extra fittings make the bench seats exceptionally heavy and awkward to move, so the simplest and safest way to remove the front seat from the car is to disassemble the seat by section while it is still in the car.

Before the seat can be unbolted from the floor, the seat-bottom skirts and aprons need to be removed to gain access to the anchor bolts holding the seat to the floor. Remove the countersunk washer trim screws with a #2 Phillips screwdriver and disconnect the power seat actuator

SEAT RESTORATION

from the seat by removing the bolt that connects the power ram to the seat frame.

The decorative side skirt is attached to the lower edge of the seat bottom with countersunk washer trim screws. Use a screwdriver to remove the trim screws and set the lower skirts aside. If there is a power-seat switch in the skirt, label and then disconnect the wires from the switch. Remove the switch from the skirt by removing the screws that hold it in place.

Pivot points for the seatbacks are under the skirts on each side of the seat bottom. A two-door car has a seatback that pivots forward, allowing the passengers to access the rear seat. Remove the spring clip by prying it off the pivot post. The center pivot point on this seat uses a long bolt to hold both inner arms in place. Simply loosen and remove the retaining nut and washer and remove the bolt. The backrest can now be removed from the seat bottom.

Many variations to these anchors are available depending on the manufacturer, make, and model. Some seat pivots use a cotter pin and others use a spring-clip pin through a hole in the pivot post. Other models are secured with an "E" clip fastener. Grab the fastener with needle-nose pliers and pull on the clip to remove it; now slide the backrest off the post and lift it out of the car.

Four-door cars do not have backrests that pivot. They are typically bolted directly to the seat bottom frame. Simply remove the bolts and lift the backrest off the seat bottom.

When you are down to the seat bottom, adjust the seat all the way to the rear and unbolt the front seat anchor bolts from the floor. Adjust the seat forward and then remove the rear anchor bolts. Now carefully lift and float the seat bottom out of the car. I find that it is easier to remove the seat through the passenger's door because it is not obstructed by the steering wheel. Place the seat components up on the workbench so they can be worked on much easier.

Removing a Seat

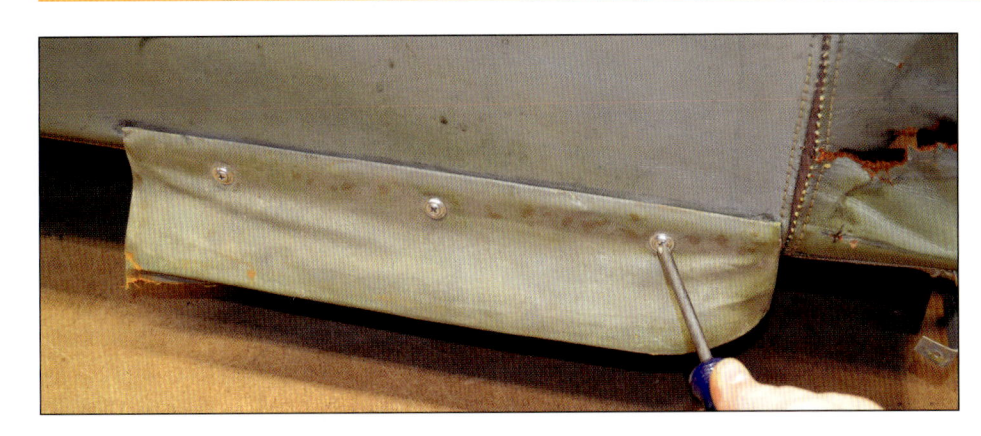

1 *A hydraulic ram under the seat provides power for the seat. Apron panels on the front of the seat cover the access to the under-seat accessories. The panels are removed from the frame by unscrewing them from the seat.*

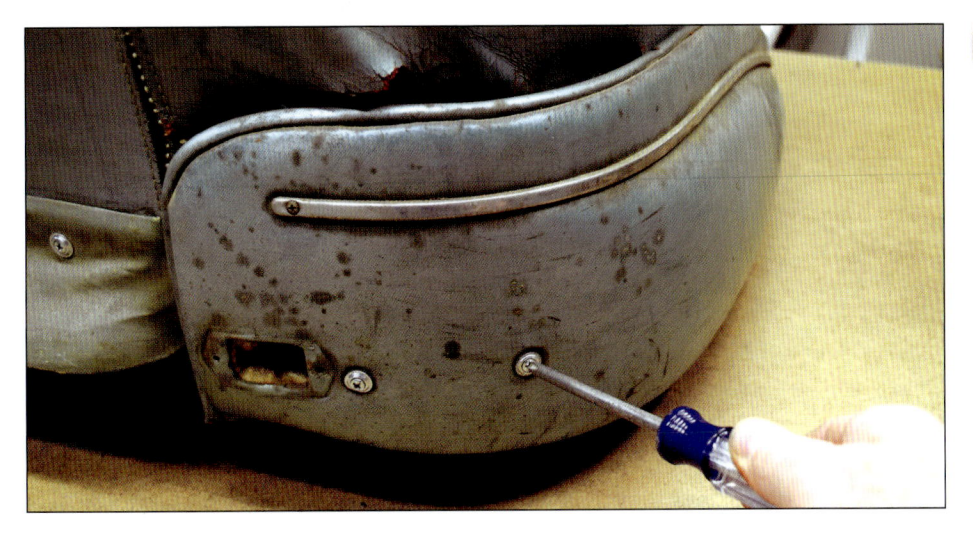

2 *Not only are the side skirts decorative, they are also functional. The side skirts conceal the seatback mounting hardware and pivot point. By removing the trim screws and skirt, you gain better access to the seat mounting bolts that hold the seat to the floor.*

CHAPTER 2

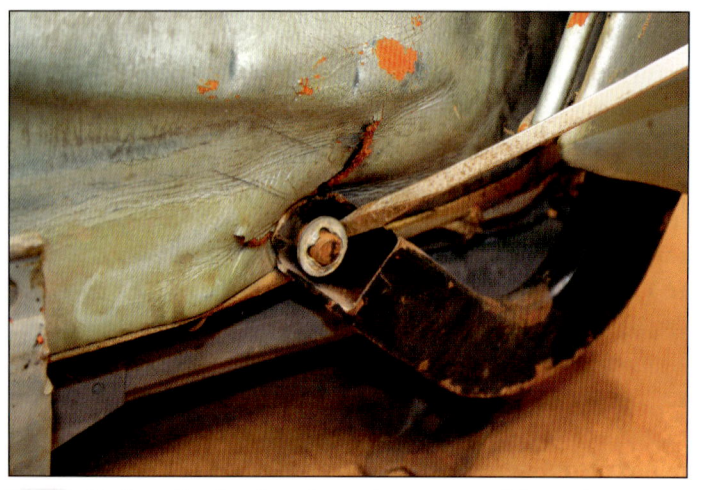

3 Before the backrest can be removed from the seat bottom, the spring retainer must be pried off the pivot post. The center pivot bolt must also be removed to release the inner pivot arms from the seat bottom.

4 The hardware used to assemble a seat varies by manufacturer and seat type. A two-door car has a split-back seat that pivots on a pin or bolt allowing passengers access to the rear seat. A spring clip and washer retain the seatback pivot arm to the frame.

Disassembly

Before you begin with the disassembly of an old car seat, I must remind you that it is very dirty and I strongly recommend that you wear protective eyewear and a dust mask to protect you from the dust, rust, and mouse dirt during the teardown process. Prolonged exposure to these elements can lead to long-term health problems.

Labeling and Bagging

Although car seats may be similar in basic design, they are often assembled with little differences that may create a challenge when you try to figure out how they come apart. Make notes as you disassemble the seat and take pictures as to how the hardware is attached so that you are able to correctly reassemble the seat later. Carefully label and bag small components to avoid confusion upon reassembly. Place all the parts in a container promptly after removal so that they do not get lost. The hardware will either be replaced or reconditioned before it is reinstalled on the seat.

Preserving the Cover Material

The key to making a good pattern is to preserve the old seat cover as much as possible. You can carefully remove the bottom seat cover without further damaging it by cutting the hog rings, pulling tacks, and unclipping the material from the frame.

Cutting the Hog Rings

There may be hidden or blind listings that secure bolsters to the seat frame. These are hog ringed to an anchor wire under the seat cushion and they are removed by cutting the hog rings to free the seat cover. After the cover has been cut free from the frame, lift it off and set the cover aside; you will get back to it once the frame is cleaned up. With the old seat cover removed and the seat padding exposed, you can now see the old support materials that cover the lower seat springs. These old support materials are dry-rotted, dirty, and have served their time. Replace them with fresh new materials upon reassembly.

Cut the hog rings that secure the old cotton, foam, and burlap covering the seat springs and discard all of it. All that should remain of the seat bottom are the springs; you will address them after you finish with the rest of the seat tear down.

Removing the Outside Shell

Working now with the seatback, the removal of the outside shell is done by removing the screws at the inside bottom of the seatback. If you encounter a problem with the release of the outside shell, look for additional screws or fasteners that may be hidden from view. Do not try to force the seat components apart as they may bend or break. Try pushing in and up, or sometimes a slight twisting motion frees a stuck component. If the seat has a robe cord on the outside back, it may be necessary to remove the trim bezel screws to get the back cover off. On most GM cars, you can release the robe cord by pushing the cord into the trim bezel and then giving it a quarter turn to pull it free.

After you have the seatback shell removed, cut the hog rings that are holding the listing wires of the old

SEAT RESTORATION

seat cover. Peel back the seat cover from around the seat frame and then carefully remove the seatback cover. Do not discard the old seat cover; it will be used as a pattern for the new backrest. Continue to remove the cotton and burlap that is covering the seatback springs by cutting away the hog rings that hold the old material in place. Discard all the dirty cotton padding and old, worn-out underlying burlap cover. The remaining seatback springs need to be refreshed. They are full of mouse dirt and the burlap casings are failing.

Disassembling a Seat

1 A single screw holds the center seatback bumper in place. The rubber bumpers are no longer useful and are replaced with new rubber pads. The base plate is also reconditioned and color matched to the new seat cover.

2 The hog rings are cut from underneath the seat frame, which releases the listing so that the old seat cover can be removed carefully with minimal damage to the old material. Having an original pattern allows you to re-create the new seat cover without guesswork.

3 A blind listing is revealed when the seat cover is pulled back. The hog rings holding the seat cover in place are to be cut free to allow the old seat cover to be removed from the seat frame. Use the old cover as a pattern to make a new one.

4 After 65 years of service, the foam padding and cotton in the seat has broken down completely and is no longer usable. The old padding and support materials will be removed from the seat frame and discarded.

AUTOMOTIVE UPHOLSTERY AND INTERIOR RESTORATION

CHAPTER 2

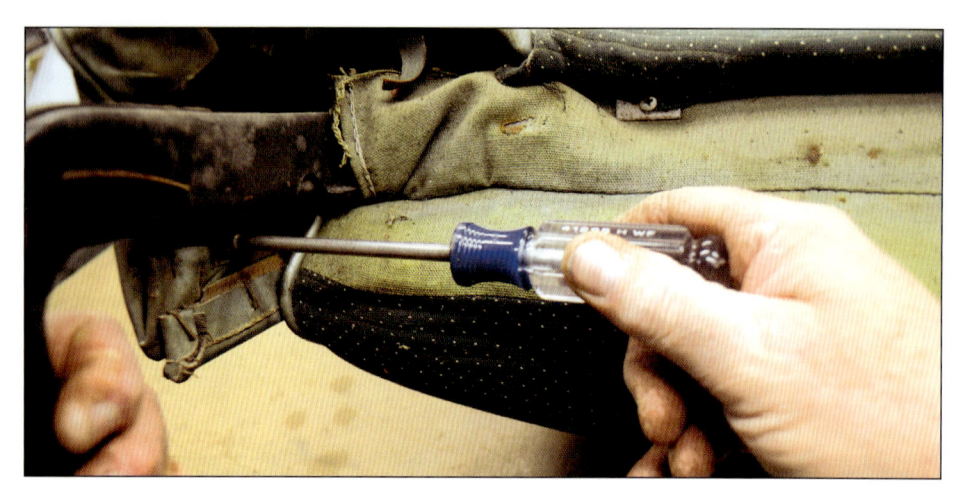

5 The outside seatback shell is removed from the backrest by removing the small screws that hold it in place on the backrest frame. The outside shell is stripped down and reconditioned with new padding and materials.

6 Additional screws are removed from the robe cord escutcheon and trim. The screws also help hold the outer seatback shell to the backrest frame. With the screws removed, the outside shell can be lifted off the backrest frame.

7 The hog rings are cut that hold the listings of the old seat cover to the seat backrest frame. The old backrest cover can then be removed carefully from the frame. By preserving the old cover, you end up with a better pattern for the new seat cover.

8 All the old cotton padding and burlap cover must be removed from the backrest. The hog rings that hold the cheesecloth-wrapped cotton are cut away from the seat frame so that the cotton can be discarded. The underlying burlap should also be thrown away.

26   AUTOMOTIVE UPHOLSTERY AND INTERIOR RESTORATION

SEAT RESTORATION

Coil Springs

Coil springs have been used for many years to give support and comfort to seating of all kinds. For springs to be effective, they need to work in unison to give proper support. If the springs work independently of each other, the result is lumpy and uneven support, making for a very uncomfortable seating experience. Taking the springs apart and putting them back together may seem overwhelming at first. You may feel that this is too much work and ask yourself, "What if I can't do it, then what?" Don't worry. I'll walk you through the process.

It is vital to the restoration of the seat to have a good and solid foundation for the seat cover. Tearing the springs apart and putting them back together may at first look impossible, but if you take it step by step, it is not hard to do at all and will give you a lot of satisfaction. You will appreciate knowing the job is done right and was not just patched up. The coil springs are re-cased in new burlap or denim. This gives the springs the correct tension for seating comfort and the durability to last for many more years. The seatback, too, is made of rows of coil springs that are sewn into burlap pockets that compress the springs to a predetermined tension.

Tensioner Removal

Begin working the springs by removing the tensioning burlap along the top and bottom of the springs. This piece of burlap limits the expansion of the springs. Having a small amount of tension on the springs as a unit gives the seat cover some definition. Label and save the tension burlap pieces so that new pieces can be made.

Spring Removal

The springs need to be removed from the seat frame so that they can be cleaned and re-cased. Cut all the hog rings that hold the springs along the edge wire of the spring frame. This frees the spring unit from the edge wire frame. A legend card can be created to map the position of tension rods and the rows of springs. Component location and measurements are taken and recorded on the legend card. This information helps when it comes time to rebuild the spring unit.

To get the springs out of the wire frame, you need to remove the edge wire clips from the tensioning rods and then mark and number the tensioning rod position with masking tape to aid in reassembly. To release the tension rods, carefully open the edge wire clips without destroying them. You will reuse the clips when the unit is put back together. If a clip is broken, a replacement clip must be fabricated from sheet metal. Remove the spring unit from the seat frame by lifting it out of the frame. Set the seat frame out of the way and begin to cut the hog rings holding the coils to each other. Do not cut the springs when removing the hog rings. Work on one row of springs at a time to prevent a mix-up of the spring placement. When a row of springs has been cut free, it should be numbered on the right-hand end of the row to identify its position and orientation. After the row has been numbered it can be set aside. Continue with the next row until all the rows of springs have been separated and numbered.

Double-Check Your Work

Before any further disassembly occurs, lay all the rows of cased springs out along with the other components that were removed and check them against the legend card you made. This way you begin to understand how they were assembled and it makes it easier for you to rebuild the spring unit. Make any corrections or add any additional information to

---

Seat Springs

Many different types of springs are used for seating support in car seats. The earliest cars used coil springs just like the ones used in furniture: rows of springs encased in burlap and padded with cotton. This was the technology at the time, and if it was good enough for grandma's parlor, well, then it must be good enough for the open road.

Many variations of the coil spring exist. Some are just helical coils with the same dimension from top to bottom. Double coil springs are tapered in the middle like an hourglass, and conical springs are cone shaped with a smaller coil at the bottom, growing progressively larger at the top just like a cone.

Postwar cars started to use the no-sag or zigzag springs in car seats because they were faster to install and cut the cost of manufacturing. By the mid-1960s, manufacturers had started using less metal in the seats, and the spring work began to get weaker. When fewer rows of springs are used the result is going to be a lot of broken springs. By the early 1970s the spring was replaced by a solid foam cushion. The foam used was very dense, and yet it made a comfortable seat cushion.

Keep Your Springs in Order

To remove the springs from the old casing, begin by cutting the stitching along the top of the casing and pull the spring out. Observe that the outside springs are sometimes a heavier gauge than the inside springs, so keep the springs in the same order that they were placed in the original casing. Flex and squeeze the springs to check for cracked or broken springs. Any spring component that is broken, worn, or rusted through must be replaced with a new part. Unfortunately, welding cannot repair a broken spring. The nature of a spring is to flex and, if you weld the metal, it draws the temper in the metal and it becomes brittle and prone to breaking, which brings me back to a broken spring.

Casing Measurements

After the springs are removed from the old casing, lay the casing out flat and carefully measure the overall height and width of each compartment. Also remember to measure the spacing distance between the spring compartments. These measurements allow you to accurately make the new spring casing.

Some compartments may have an extra seam in the bottom to add more tension to the spring. Record these measurements on the legend sheet as well. This will be your guide to help make sure that the springs are tensioned and spaced correctly when they are reassembled. Each row of springs is most likely different in height and by the number of springs it holds. Carefully measure and mark each row as you lay out the original pattern onto the new burlap. If your old casing measures 8 inches tall by 37 inches wide, mark the new burlap 16 inches tall by 37 inches wide. Then when you fold the strip in half it will be the correct size. Continue to mark the selvage on the ends of each row along with the closing allowance at the top. Include the tensioning seam along the bottom if needed. Now the new casing row can be cut out and sewn according to the original measurements.

Reinsert the Springs

Straighten any bent springs. Wire brush any rust off the springs to clean them before you insert the springs into their new pocket. It is easier to work with just one spring at a time. Compress the spring flat and insert it horizontally into the pocket of the burlap casing. Sew along the top of the casing to lock the spring into its new pocket. After all the springs are encased in burlap they must be turned to a vertical position and expanded. Rotate the spring inside the pocket until it is correctly positioned. Continue doing this until the row of springs are all turned and then set the row aside. Repeat this process until all the rows of springs have been restored. When all of the springs are re-cased, insert the back row of springs into the wire frame first and progress forward. Insert each tensioning rod in its correct position as you add rows of springs.

When all the rows of springs are in place, secure the tension rods to the edge wire with their clips. Hog ring the lower edge of the springs along the outside edges of the seat frame and then finish hog ringing the rows together just like they were. Do this one row at a time to prevent any missed springs. When you are finished with the top of the springs, turn the seat over and hog ring the bottoms of the springs in the same way as the top.

Reconditioning Coil Springs

1 *Several rows of coil springs make up the cushion system of the backrest. Being sewn into a burlap casing tensions the springs. Collectively, the springs work as a unit to provide comfort and support for the driver and passenger.*

SEAT RESTORATION

2 Each part of the spring system plays an important role. Along the top and bottom of the spring unit are tensioners that limit the amount of expansion of the springs. An edge wire frame contains the springs, allowing them to work as a unit.

3 The spring unit is attached to the edge wire frame with hog rings. Removing the hog rings to free the spring unit from the seat frame is the start of the rebuilding process. Parts removed are labeled for reassembly.

4 To keep track of all the parts and their positions a legend card is created. As pieces are removed their size and position are tagged with tape and recorded onto the legend card. Accuracy and detail are key elements to a successful spring unit rebuild.

AUTOMOTIVE UPHOLSTERY AND INTERIOR RESTORATION

5 With the spring unit on the workbench, it can be cut apart carefully. All the hog rings that connect the rows of springs are removed without cutting or damaging the coil springs. To keep the process simple, only work one row of springs at a time.

6 Each row of springs is numbered to identify its location and position. Knowing that the row number is on the right helps with the orientation of the row of springs as well as its position during the reassembly of the spring unit.

7 All the separated spring components are laid out and rechecked against the legend card. Good notes ensure a successful spring rebuild. Visualizing the placement of the parts also gives you confidence when it is time to reassemble the springs as a unit.

8 Springs are removed from the old canvas casing, cleaned, and checked for cracks. Each row of springs is different and some may be different in size and gauge. It is important to keep the springs in the original order they came in.

SEAT RESTORATION

9 Measurements are taken from the old burlap casing and recorded onto the legend card. Height, width, and overall length of the burlap are needed to reproduce the new casing. Variations in the spacing of the pockets should also be noted.

10 Spring tension is an important part of the rebuild. To create the correct spring tension, some pockets may be shorter than others. This measurement is also added to the legend card so that it can be sewn into the new casing.

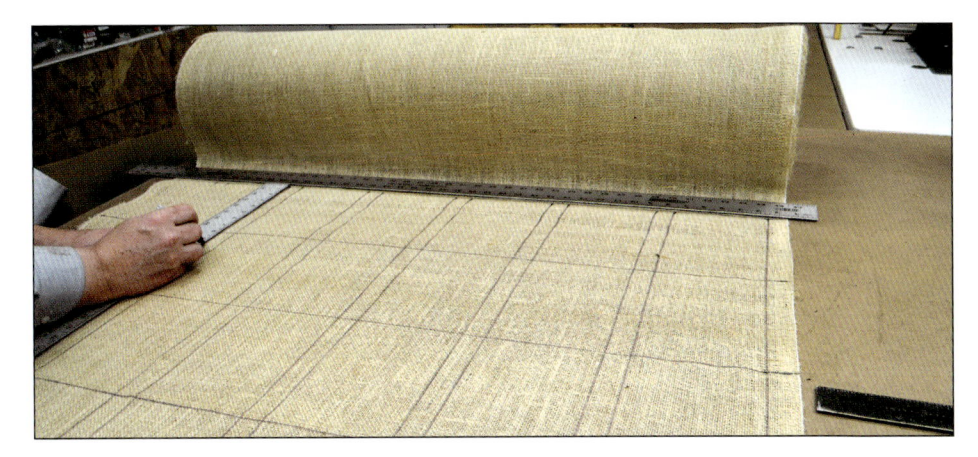

11 New spring casings are cut from burlap and marked according to the measurements taken from the original casing and recorded on the legend card. Individual pockets are then sewn into the new casings that divide and space each spring for proper alignment and tensioning.

12 Each spring is compressed and inserted into its pocket and then it is sewn closed. After the row of springs has been sewn in, the springs are turned and expanded vertically in their pocket. The rows of springs are now ready to be reinstalled into the edge wire frame.

AUTOMOTIVE UPHOLSTERY AND INTERIOR RESTORATION

CHAPTER 2

13 *Each casing of springs is hog ringed together one row at a time by following the legend card. Working in a methodical way ensures that no hog rings are skipped. Tension rods are secured in place and the edge wire frame is hog ringed to the outside edges of the spring unit.*

Seatback Supports

Now is a good time to address the mounting arm on the backrest of the front seat. The arm is a structural element to the seatback, and on a four-door car it is attached to the seat bottom with bolts and does not pivot. The backrest upholstery covers these supports, hiding them from view.

The design is different on a two-door car. The seat is designed to allow the backrest to be tilted forward for access to the rear seat. Because of this pivot action, the support arms are somewhat visible. The factory painted the metal arms to help them blend in with the upholstery, but their color choices were very generic.

The support arms need to be cleaned and any chips in the old paint should be sanded smooth before priming the metal. A complementary color can then be sprayed on the support arms and allowed to dry.

Zigzag Springs

The bottom seat frame of this project uses modern zigzag springs.

The backrest support arms are visible and they deserve to be cleaned up to look like new. Cleaning, sanding, and a good color coat make them fit in with the new seat cover that is installed over the freshly tensioned spring set.

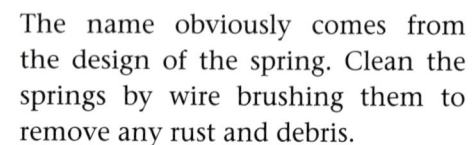

The name obviously comes from the design of the spring. Clean the springs by wire brushing them to remove any rust and debris.

Check for broken or loose springs and repair them as necessary. If the springs are rusty from mouse damage they need to be washed with a 50/50 solution of bleach and water before they are painted. Painting the springs seals them to keep them from smelling bad. The paint also helps prevent further corrosion. I use Rust-Oleum to paint the springs in my projects. What makes it a great paint is that it covers well and comes in rattle cans that are ready to use.

I don't recommend powder coating the seat springs. The powder coating does not like to be flexed as this cracks the coating, causing it to chip off.

The adjustable seat tracks must be serviced along with the lower seat springs. Clean the seat tracks and lubricate the roller bearings so that the track can move freely. It is not recommended to sand blast the seat tracks. Grit gets into the roller bearings and causes the seat tracks to grind and wear the bearings.

SEAT RESTORATION

This seat bottom frame is fitted with zigzag springs. These springs provide all the support necessary for a comfortable ride and yet they are easy to work on. The attached adjustable seat tracks give the seat the correct ride height and secure the frame to the floor of the car.

Decorative trim panels are used to hide unsightly components in the car. The small apron panels are stripped of their old cover material and the surface is cleaned and straightened in preparation for a new layer of upholstery.

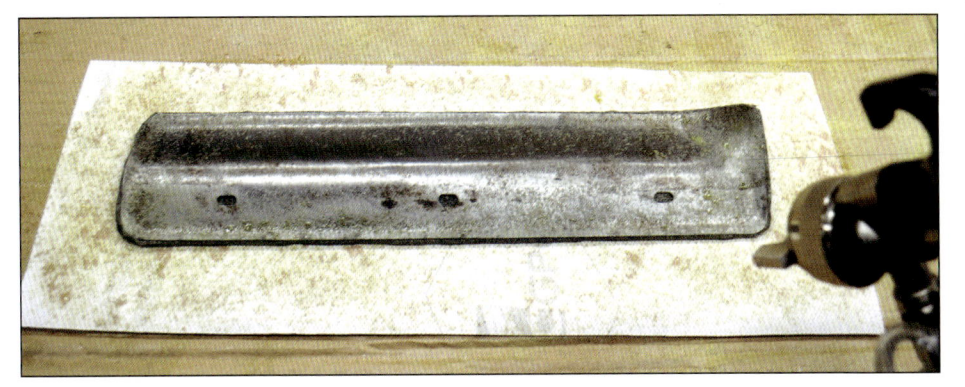

Adding a felt underliner material before the new vinyl cover is applied softens the surface of the metal. The new cover material is held in place by a coat of contact cement that has been sprayed onto the back surface of the material.

Trim Panels and Seat Skirts

Along the outsides of the seat are additional upholstered panels that conceal the raw edges and working elements of the seat. These decorative pieces need to be stripped and reconditioned before they can be reinstalled. Most of the panels are covered or wrapped with the same upholstery material as the interior. Some trim panels are metal or molded plastic and are painted to match the interior color scheme.

The simple flat apron panels are stripped down and the surface is cleaned. The metal is straightened and a felt underliner is applied to the face of the panel and trimmed to the edge. The underliner gives the panel a softer appearance when it is re-covered.

New vinyl is cut about 1 inch oversize of the panel to allow for the material to wrap around the backside of the panel. Glue is sprayed onto the backside edges of the panel and the overhanging vinyl material.

After the glue gets tacky the edges of the vinyl should be pulled taut as it is wrapped around the panel.

A little heat from a heat gun helps the vinyl conform to the panel when pulled around the corners. Press the vinyl into the glue to secure it to the panel. Trim off the excess vinyl that has bunched up on the backside of the panel.

Although seat skirts are mostly decorative, they do have a function: The seat skirt conceals the seat track and pivot point of the seatback. Some skirt panels have decorative chrome or stainless trim attached. This must be removed before the panel can be re-covered. First remove the inner liner of the skirt by lifting the staples holding it in place. The stainless trim

AUTOMOTIVE UPHOLSTERY AND INTERIOR RESTORATION

Wrapping the trim panels in vinyl gives the piece a nice, soft appearance. Applying a small amount of heat to the vinyl helps it to conform to the shape of the trim panel as it is pulled over the edge and glued into position.

A prominent feature of this era of car seat is the lower side skirt. This front skirt has a decorative band of stainless trim that helps the cover material contour to the profile of the skirt. The stainless trim is held in place by small pins and a trim screw.

is fastened to the skirt panel by small screws or tabs that are bent over to hold the trim in place. Remove any screws that may be holding the trim to the panel and from the backside of the panel carefully lift the tabs or pins that hold the trim in place. Try not to break off any of the fasteners or damage the trim when removing it from the panel.

The decorative stainless trim should be marked on the backside or with a piece of masking tape as to its orientation on the panel. Clean the stainless with #0000 steel wool to bring back its luster. Repair any broken mounting pins if necessary.

Cover Removal

The wrapped cover material of the panel is glued and/or stapled to the backside of the panels. These fasteners are lifted from the panel and then the cover material can be peeled off. Retain the old cover material so that it can be used as a pattern for the new panel cover.

Panel Cleaning and Prep

Under the upholstery material is usually thin cotton padding or coach wadding. Remove this by scraping it off with a putty knife and de-scaling the panel with a wire brush. Clean the surface of the panel with lacquer thinner to remove any residual glue and dust. The surface of the metal may be rusty and it should be sanded, primed, and painted to prevent it from further corrosion. If the panel is damaged or rusted out, proper repairs must be made before the panel can be re-covered. Replace the cotton coach wadding by gluing a felt underliner or foam-backed headliner material to the metal skirt. Wrap the padding around the edges of the skirt and trim the padding to fit.

Cut a new piece of vinyl about 2 inches oversize and set the skirt panel on the vinyl. Spray glue onto the backside edges of the skirt and around the vinyl cover material. Now stretch the vinyl over and around to the back of the skirt on the top and bottom edges. Add a couple of staples to hold it in place. Pull forward on the vinyl to remove any wrinkles and staple the vinyl to the front edge. Apply heat to the vinyl if necessary to help it stretch and lay smooth, and finish working the vinyl until it covers the skirt.

Welt Edging

Sew on a 5/32-inch welt to trim the upper edge of the skirt. Cut a vinyl strip 2½ inches wide for the welt cover. The extra selvedge material is stapled to the inside of the skirt. This decorative welt gives the skirt a finished appearance and it looks nice once the skirt is fit to the bottom of the seat, giving the skirt some extra definition.

Trim Installation

Before the stainless trim can be re-fit on the skirt the mounting holes need to be opened. From the backside of the skirt locate the trim mounting holes and with help from a regulator, poke through the surface of the vinyl to open the hole. Set the stainless trim in place by guiding the mounting pins through the holes in the vinyl.

Secure the stainless trim to the skirt by bending the mounting pins over with a tack hammer. Take care when bending the pins so that you do not break them off.

Cover over the staples and trim pins with a new inner liner made from a piece of panel board. Staple the liner in place.

Apply any other badges or trim pieces to the skirt. The skirts are finished and should be set aside until they are needed for the final assembly of the seat.

SEAT RESTORATION

Restoring Seat Skirts

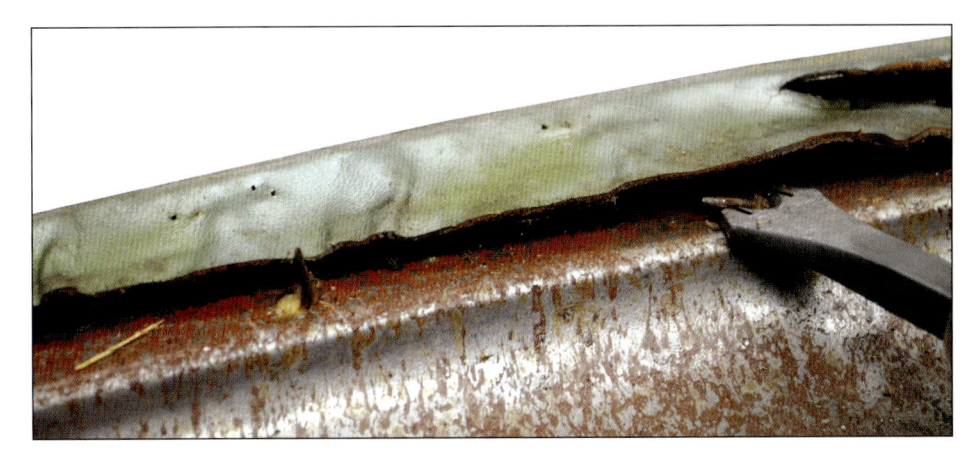

1 Before the skirt can be re-covered it is stripped of all the old upholstery materials. The inner liner of the skirt is removed along with all the staples holding the cover material in place. The old cover material is removed and used as a reference for the new cover.

2 Special care must be taken when removing the stainless trim from the trim panel. Lifting the mounting pins is a delicate job if you do not want to break them off. The pins are raised from the backside of the trim panel with a staple lifter.

3 The stainless trim piece is lifted carefully from the panel without bending it. Clean the stainless by wiping it down with a damp rag and polishing the surface with #0000 steel wool. The mounting pins are also straightened so that the piece can be reinstalled.

4 After the removal of the old cover material and coach wadding, the metal surface reveals some signs of corrosion. A light wire brushing and some sanding yields a clean surface for a new felt underliner to be glued in place.

AUTOMOTIVE UPHOLSTERY AND INTERIOR RESTORATION

CHAPTER 2

5 With the padding applied and trimmed, the outside of the skirt can now be wrapped in vinyl. An oversize piece of vinyl is cut and fit to the skirt. Glue is applied to the backside of the vinyl and inside edges of the skirt.

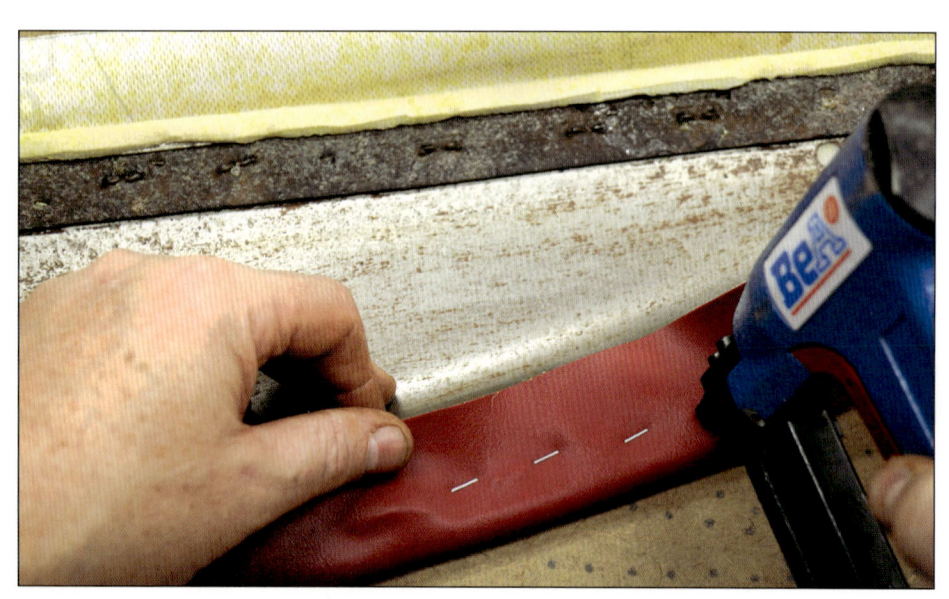

6 The vinyl is heated and stretched over the skirt and stapled along the backside to hold it in place. To get the vinyl to conform to the contours of the skirt's profile, additional heat is applied while the vinyl is pulled forward and worked around the corners.

7 A finishing touch is added to the skirt. The upper edge of the skirt is adorned with a decorative bead of welt. The welt on the outside edge of the skirt helps the skirt stand away from the seat cover boxing.

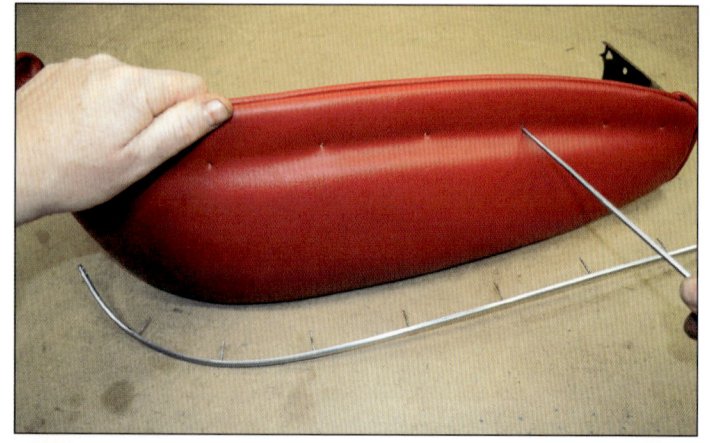

8 Replacing the decorative stainless trim on the skirt helps the vinyl keep tight to the surface. A regulator is used to pierce the vinyl, which then allows the mounting pins to easily pass through to the backside of the skirt.

AUTOMOTIVE UPHOLSTERY AND INTERIOR RESTORATION

SEAT RESTORATION

9 The stainless trim is secured in place on the skirt by gently tapping and bending the mounting pins over with a tack hammer. The staples and mounting pins are concealed on the inside of the skirt with a new inner liner.

10 The lower seat skirts are completed and ready to be installed. The seat trim makes all the difference in how finished the seat looks once it is installed in the car. These trim pieces are mostly decorative but worth the effort to make them new again.

Seatback Panels

The outside seatback also must be stripped down and reconditioned. Finish removing the robe cord from the inside of the seatback by removing the hook end of the robe cord from the spring-loaded tensioning retainer. The robe cord also needs to be restored. You will reuse some of its parts; set it aside until you address it later.

Remove the decorative welt cord from the edge of the seatback by lifting the staples that hold it in place. Continue around the shell, removing all the staples that are holding the cover in place. Peel back the edges of the old cover material and remove the cover from the shell.

With a putty knife, scrape off the cotton coach wadding that is on the seatback shell and clean the metal as you did with the skirts. Since coach wadding is no longer available, apply a layer of foam-backed headliner material or a felt underliner material to the seatback frame to replace the coach wadding.

Cut new vinyl and fabric for the seatback cover. Use the old cover as a guide to size the materials. Apply the materials in the reverse order that they were removed. Wrap the outside end cap with vinyl and glue or staple it in place. Begin with the long sides and then work the top and then the bottom. Apply a little heat to help the vinyl form around the corners of the shell.

Now work the fabric panel by blind tacking the inside edge of the upholstery fabric before it is pulled

Restoring the seatback shell requires that all old materials are stripped off. The hook end of the robe cord is disconnected from the tensioner that is located inside the shell. The old robe cord is set aside and saved for reconditioning.

Staples that are holding the decorative welt along the outer edge of the shell are removed, freeing the welt and upholstery material from the shell. The old upholstery materials can now be removed from the seatback shell.

AUTOMOTIVE UPHOLSTERY AND INTERIOR RESTORATION 37

CHAPTER 2

With the outside upholstery removed, you can see that the coach wadding has deteriorated and it must be scraped off the frame. Before the new felt underliner can be applied, the metal shell is wire brushed and cleaned.

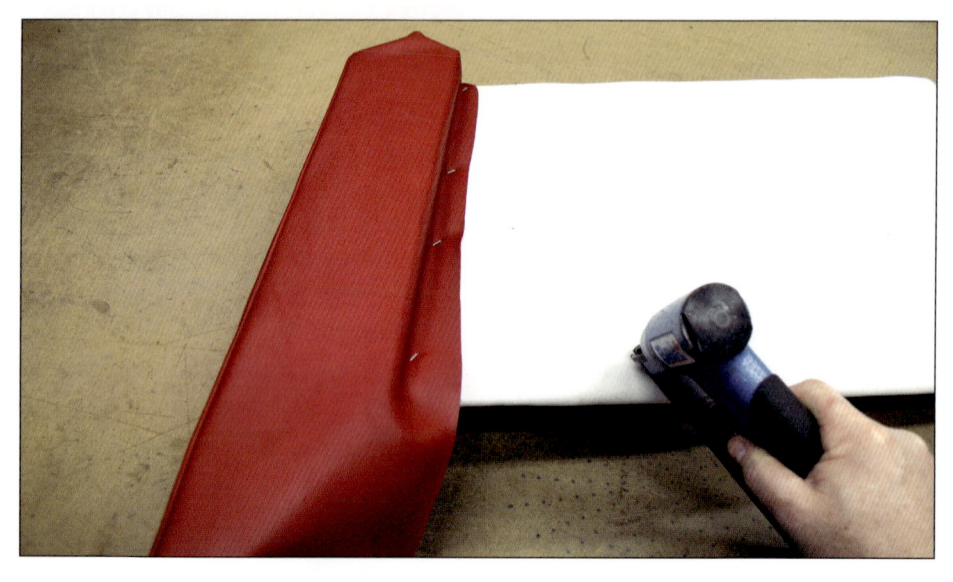

A fresh layer of felt underliner has been applied to the shell frame in preparation for the new cover materials. The new vinyl and fabric pieces are fitted to the metal frame by stapling, stretching, and gluing them in place.

to the outside and tacked in place. Work the top edge and then the bottom until all the wrinkles have been smoothed out of the material. Reapply the decorative welt along the outside edge of the shell with staples.

Robe Cords

Early-model cars did not have good heaters and the passengers in the rear seat used a "lap robe" to help keep their legs warm. Robe cords were attached horizontally across the back of the front seat and the lap robe draped over the cord, where it was stored out of the way when not in use. This project has a robe cord on each seatback. The robe cord is constructed of a metal chain inside a vinyl-covered rubber hose. Although the chain may be reusable, the original robe cord cover is usually dry rotted and must be replaced. Originally the core tube of the robe cord was made of rubber. The cost of rubber today is prohibitive, so I am opting to use a piece of PVC vinyl tubing instead. The new tube has a 1/2-inch outside diameter with a 3/8-inch inside diameter just like the original.

Size Measurement

To make the vinyl cover you need to know what size to cut and sew the cover material. To figure the width of the robe cord cover material, place two 1/2-inch strips of vinyl running parallel on top of the vinyl tubing. Now wrap a scrap strip of vinyl around the tubing and mark the point where it overlaps itself.

38   AUTOMOTIVE UPHOLSTERY AND INTERIOR RESTORATION

SEAT RESTORATION

This is the finished width of the robe cord cover.

Before cutting the material for the robe cord you also need to add an inch to the finished diameter, which gives you a 1/2-inch seam allowance along the edge. Now measure the length of the vinyl tube to get the final dimension of the cover material. Lay out the dimensions on the vinyl and cut the cover material to size.

Robe Cord Cover

The robe cord cover material is folded in half and is sewn face to face. To help with turning the cover right side out, lay a length of tufting twine on the inside of the casing. The end of the tufting twine is locked into the beginning stitches while you sew along the seam line. After the cover is sewn, a steady pull on the tufting twine helps invert the cord cover. It is helpful to use a screwdriver or blunt tool to aid in the turning of the robe cord cover. Care must be taken to avoid any damage to the vinyl cover material. Push the material inside itself and, with a steady pull on the tufting twine, the robe cord cover emerges inverted. Pulling too hard causes the material to bunch up and could pull the tufting twine free.

Remove the tufting twine from the cover by clipping it very close to but not cutting the stitches in the seam. Now insert the vinyl tubing into the cover and divide the seam allowance so that it lies flat against the vinyl tubing.

Before you insert the chain into the robe cord tube, remove one of the hooks attached to the chain to make the insertion easier. Hold the covered tube vertically by one end and insert the chain into the tube opening until it shows through the lower end. Now replace the hook on the end of the chain. The hook end of the chain is locked into place with a hog ring. This keeps the tube and cover from stretching when it is used.

The robe cord can now be attached to the seatback. Insert the robe cord through the trim ring and hook it into the spring anchor. Then, slide the outside end of the robe cord through the trim escutcheon and secure it when the cover is fitted to the seatback.

Rebuilding a Robe Cord

1 *The size of the robe cord casing is determined by mocking up the thickness of the material used to cover the vinyl hose. Just wrap a strip of material around the hose until it overlaps itself. This measurement is the diameter of the vinyl hose.*

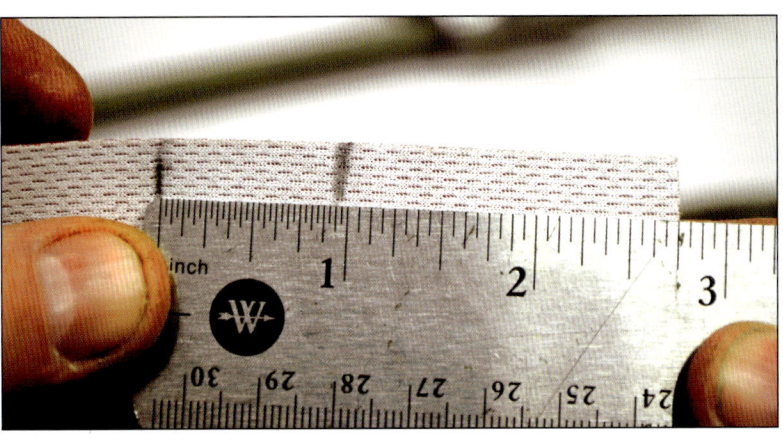

2 *Adding 1 inch for a seam allowance to the diameter of the robe cord tube gives you the width of the robe cord cover. A piece of vinyl material can now be cut to the correct width and length for the robe cord cover.*

AUTOMOTIVE UPHOLSTERY AND INTERIOR RESTORATION

CHAPTER 2

3 *To conceal the seam allowance of the robe cord it is sewn inside out. Before any sewing begins, the cover material is folded face to face and a length of tufting twine has been placed inside to help invert the cover material.*

4 *Pulling on the tufting twine rights the robe cord and allows the cover material to flow into the cord cover and come out turned. To get the turning process started, a small screwdriver can be very helpful.*

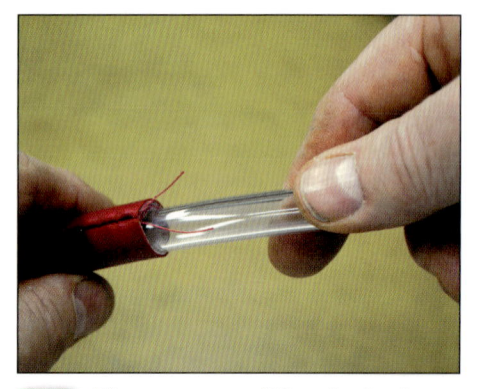

5 *The purpose of the vinyl robe cord cover is to dress up the chain and vinyl tube. A cut length of vinyl tubing is inserted into the robe cord cover. The vinyl tube splits the seam allowance, which then allows the cover to lie flat and smooth.*

6 *The key element to the robe cord is the internal chain and anchor hooks. These provide the strength needed to support the hanging lap robe. The chain is slid into the covered tube with a hook emerging from each end.*

7 *After the chain is fitted inside the vinyl tube, each end of the tube is hog ringed to the anchor hook. The hog ring secures the chain and tube in place and prevents the cover material from stretching or pulling apart with use.*

8 *The robe cord is the last element to be attached to the seatback shell. The robe cord is reconnected to the spring tensioner. The outer end of the robe cord is passed through a decorative escutcheon that covers the hook end of the robe cord.*

40 AUTOMOTIVE UPHOLSTERY AND INTERIOR RESTORATION

SEAT RESTORATION

Patterning

When making a pattern for a seat cover it is good to know that they are symmetrical in design. This means that the panels are the same left and right from the center. Therefore, if the driver's side is in bad shape, the passenger's side can be used as the pattern by turning it over and face down.

Another thing about front seats is that bucket seats and the backs on a two-door car are symmetrical as well and you should need to mark and disassemble only one of them. Leave one cover untouched for reference when you sew up and reassemble the seat. Make two sets of panels: one left and one right. Remember to turn the pattern upside down and mark that set with an X to distinguish it as the opposite seat cover.

It may also help if you make a sketch of the cover to remind you of how the seat was assembled. Label each panel so that you know what part of the seat it belongs to. Use this simple key when labeling the panels: A = front seat bottom, B = front seatback, C = rear seat bottom, D = rear seatback, T = top, L = left, R = right, I/S = inside, and O/S = outside.

Lay the old seat bottom cover out on the workbench and remove any remaining listing wires, hog rings, and staples that may be left over. Turn the seat cover inside out and with a marker begin to label each

A sketch of the old seat cover helps avoid confusion when it is time to reassemble the new seat panels. Before cutting the old seat covers apart, make sure that all the pieces are labeled to prevent any mix up of the pattern.

Make witness marks on the seams of the old cover before the seat panels are cut apart. This step saves you much frustration when it is time to sew the new panels back together. Knowing where a panel starts and ends is fundamental to a good pattern.

Breaking down the seat cover into a pattern is a matter of separating the panels; use a razor blade to cut the thread that holds the panels together. The thin, sharp blade works faster and more efficiently than scissors.

AUTOMOTIVE UPHOLSTERY AND INTERIOR RESTORATION

CHAPTER 2

Before the panels can be traced they are steamed flat so that they can be traced accurately onto the new upholstery material. The flattened panels are also trimmed and adjusted to correct for any distortions that may have formed.

panel of the seat cover with an "A" to indicate that the pieces are all from the front seat bottom.

The most vital part of making a pattern is panel alignment. Always make new witness marks along the seams of the old seat cover before you cut it apart. You also need to mark the start and end points of the panels. These witness marks help you accurately align the panels when you sew the panels of the new cover together.

Once the cover has been marked up, take a new razor blade, and carefully cut the seams of the old seat cover apart. The razor blade works better and faster than scissors. Cutting the dirty material quickly dulls the scissors and it is difficult to get into some seams with the larger blades.

Pay close attention to the order that the cover was assembled. The disassembly and reassembly of a seat cover follows a logical sequence.

The listings are sewn on last, but are the first to be removed. Look for the subassemblies of the seat cover. The covered welt cord that is sewn to the insert panel assembly separates the outside boxing panels. The insert subassembly is made up of bolsters and an insert panel. Make note of where the welt cord goes. All these little things matter, and sewing the seat together in the right order saves you time and frustration.

When you have finished with one seat section, move on to the front seatback, and mark all the panels with the letter "B," rear seat bottom with a "C," and rear seatback with a "D." Repeat the process of making the witness marks and then carefully cut it apart as you did for the seat bottom.

When all the old seat cover panels have been separated they need to be steamed flat. By using the flat iron head of the steamer and an ironing board, the individual pieces are flattened to make them ready for tracing.

After steaming the pieces for patterning it is not uncommon that you run across a panel that has become distorted. Most long lines are straight and over time they get stretched, pulled, and warped. If you try to sew

The original panel on this seatback boxing has been damaged and is in very poor condition. To make a usable pattern from the panel, masking tape is used to bridge the missing material of the panel. With a little trimming the piece is now traceable.

AUTOMOTIVE UPHOLSTERY AND INTERIOR RESTORATION

SEAT RESTORATION

up a cover with panels that are distorted, the finished cover does not look right or fit correctly. Before you cut the new panel from the material, you need to make adjustments to straighten out the panel.

You also need to cut off and remove the old seam allowance from the panel. The seam allowance that is found on the original panel is usually not a consistent size because of trimming after the cover was sewn. It is best to work with a given or known seam allowance to ensure that the panel fits correctly.

You can use any panels for patterning that have been damaged or have pieces missing by using masking tape to fill in the voids. Simply span the gap with masking tape on both sides of the damaged panel and trim the masking tape to the original profile of the panel. This method of repair gives you a traceable pattern for the new panel.

Material Orientation

Prior to tracing the panel pieces, check the direction of the nap on the material that you are working with and mark an arrow on the backside of the material with chalk to indicate the direction of the nap. Fabrics such as velvet, velour, and corduroy have standing fibers that are not quite vertical and when you rub your hand across the face of the material you can feel and see the difference in the directional flow.

Going with the nap has less surface resistance; going against the nap reveals a darker sheen and you will feel resistance. When laying out your panels, the nap should all run in the same direction. Generally, the nap should run down the back and forward on the seat bottom.

Just like with the nap on fabric, you need to be observant with the stretch of the vinyl. The vinyl has very little stretch going up the roll, but from side to side, or railroaded, the vinyl has a lot of stretch. A vinyl seat has to be able to move to prevent the vinyl from tearing when it's sat upon. A seat cushion tends to give more from side to side than up and down. The stretch of the vinyl should also move from side to side.

Another thing to consider about materials is the bias or diagonal of the material. When the material is cut at a 45-degree angle the nap becomes moot and this makes the best welt cover. The material will have seams where the strips are joined, but the nap looks correct when the seat cover is sewn. Cutting your seat panels correctly allows them to perform better and last longer.

The flattened panels are now ready to be traced onto the new

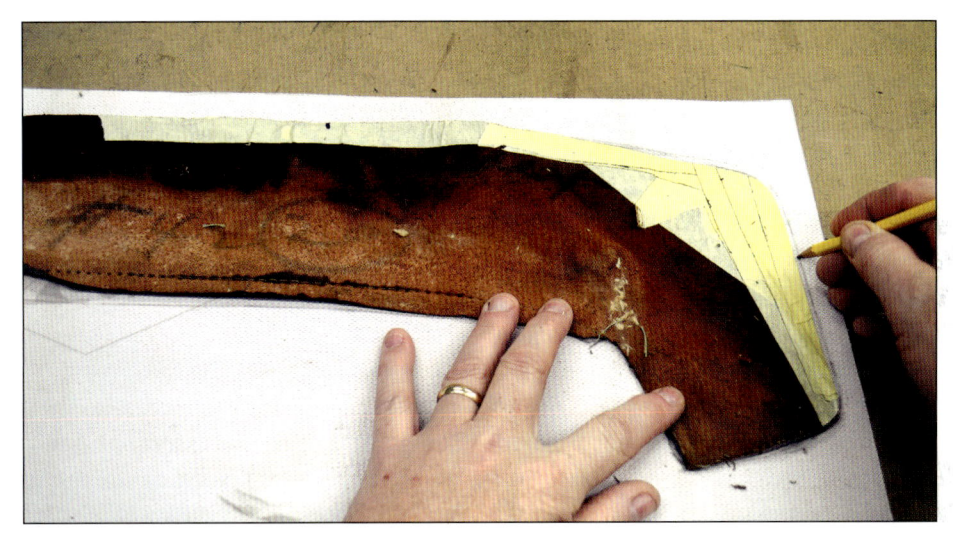

The profile of the pattern is traced onto fresh upholstery vinyl. A pencil is used for tracing because it does not smear or bleed into the material. Witness marks and other details about the panel are also transferred to the new material.

Before the new panel can be cut from the material, a seam allowance must be added. A ruler is used to add 1/2 inch to the outside of the sew line on the new panel. The panel is cut along the newly drawn line.

AUTOMOTIVE UPHOLSTERY AND INTERIOR RESTORATION

upholstery materials. Make sure that the workbench has been wiped down and is clean before you unroll any material.

Roll out the seat material with the backside up. Place the flattened panel face down on the material and trace around the panel with chalk or pencil. Avoid using ink pens or markers that may smear or bleed into the material. Transfer all the witness marks, notes, and start/end points onto the newly traced panel. Make sure that you also add the correct cover letter to the new panel to identify its orientation for assembly.

Trimmers use a seam allowance of 3/8 up to 5/8 inch. I prefer a 1/2-inch seam allowance when I sew. To create the seam allowance, measure 1/2 inch on the outside of the profile or sew line and make a small mark. Move the ruler a small distance and make another. Continue this process until you have a dotted line along the outside of the sew line of the panel. Cut out the new panel pieces following the dots and then set them aside for sewing.

Panel Inserts

The center section of the seat cushion is known as the insert, so called because it is "inserted" between the side bolsters of the seat cushion. Bolsters derive their name from the material that "borders" the insert. Seat boxing is what encases, or "boxes," the insert and bolsters.

Simple Version

The face panel or insert for the project is a simple fabric panel that is not pleated. The fabric for the insert is rolled out face down on the workbench. Check that the direction of the nap is running forward and place the old insert on top. Use chalk to trace the profile of the insert onto the backside of the new fabric. Transfer the witness marks and listing locations along with any other details. Measure for a 1/2-inch seam allowance before the panel is cut from the fabric.

Because this is a simple insert, the boxing and bolsters are sewn directly to the fabric insert without additional padding or backing materials.

Pleated Version

A variation to the plain panel insert is the pleated insert. The difference is that the pleated insert is made with a layer of sew foam. The bolster material was also created from sew foam to match the thickness of the pleated insert.

The new fabric for the insert has been rolled out onto the workbench and the old insert panel is placed on the fabric. The profile of the old insert is chalked onto the backside of the new fabric along with witness marks and listing locations.

To compensate for the thickness of the foam and sewing, a pleated insert panel begins with an oversize piece of material on top of a sheet of 1/2-inch sew foam. Vertical lines are drawn on the material with chalk to define the pleats.

SEAT RESTORATION

Pleat size is determined by the width of the seat. Divide the width of the insert by the size of the desired pleat and you have the number of pleats for the insert.

Example: 59 inches wide ÷ 3 inches equals 19.6 pleats. What this really tells you is that the seat insert has 17 pleats that were 3 inches wide and 2 end pleats of 4 inches (17 x 3 = 51, 8 ÷ 2 = 4). The end pleat varies depending on the pleat and insert size. Go with the wider end pleat over a smaller pleat.

The foundation of the pleated panel is a medium-dense sheet of sew foam covered by an oversized piece of the upholstery material. The insert panel material should be cut oversized to compensate for the foam thickness and allow for the sew lines when pleating the insert panel. I use a ratio of adding 1/8 inch per pleat on 1/2-inch sew foam plus 1 extra inch all around for margin. After the insert is sewn it measures correctly and still gives you a 1/2-inch seam allowance plus the margin for trimming.

After you determine the width of the pleats, chalk the vertical lines onto the fabric to indicate the sew line of the pleat.

To pleat the insert, the fabric and foam are sewn together to form a line or pattern in the material. Start with the center pleat and work your way to the outside. This method ensures that the insert fabric disperses evenly. Sew straight and even through the material by following the chalked guidelines on the fabric.

Once all the pleats have been sewn, lay out the pleated front seat bottom insert panel on the workbench and place the old insert panel on top. Square up the old panel and make sure that the pleated lines run true from top to bottom. Also check that the outer pleat measures the same on both ends of the insert.

Use chalk to trace around the perimeter of the old panel onto the new panel. Transfer all your witness marks and listing locations to the new insert panel. Sew along the newly traced perimeter line and then cut close to the stitching to trim away the unwanted material. This completes the making of the pleated insert.

Rear Apron Panel

Across the rear of the insert is an apron panel. This panel covers the back edge of the metal seat frame and may be made of carpet or a reinforced piece of vinyl or fabric. Bind the exposed edges of the carpet

The pleating in the insert panel is created by sewing the cover material to the sew foam. Long and straight even stitches are used to define the pleat in the insert panel. Sewing along the chalk lines makes the task quick and easy.

The pleated panel has been laid out face up on the workbench. The old insert was placed in position and the profile was chalked onto the new panel. The perimeter line is sewn and the edges trimmed to reveal the new pleated panel.

CHAPTER 2

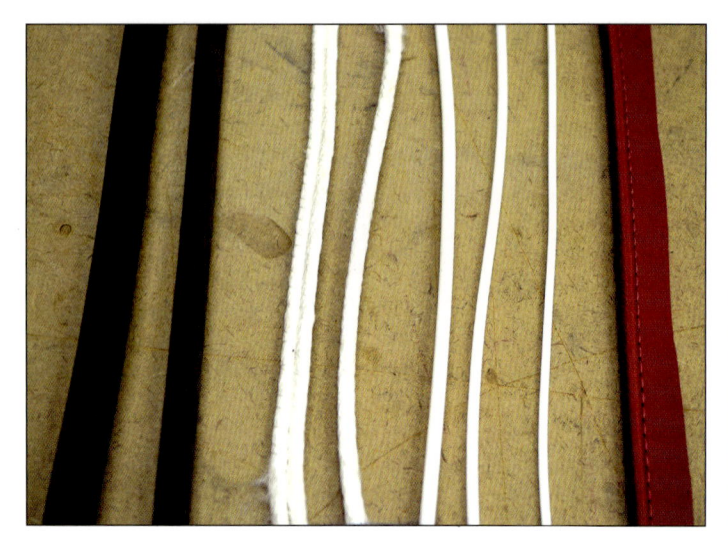

A variety of welt cord core material is use in auto restoration. The larger rubber cord range in size and they are used in windlace. Interior welt uses the fiber and foam welt core. The size and type of welt used depends on the application.

Welt cord is wrapped in fabric or vinyl and it is sewn over the core with a special foot attached to the sewing machine. The welt feet vary in size depending on the material that is used. Sometimes a zipper foot is used to sew the welting.

to prepare it before attaching it to the insert panel. Reinforced panels have a felt underliner bonded to the material to strengthen it from passengers kicking the seat while sitting in the rear seat. Sew the apron panel in place along the rear edge of the insert panel.

Welt Cord

Welt is the decorative bead that helps conceal the seam of a seat cover. The British refer to welt as "piping." Regardless of what you call it, you are referring to the same corded material. Because many different types of welt are available, choosing the correct product for your project is a matter of detail.

What you have is essentially a core covered in a material that complements the project.

This core material can be made from cotton, paper, jute, foam, rubber, and extruded plastic. Welt cord can range in size from 2/32 inch up to 2 inches. The most popular size of welt used for upholstery is 5/32 inch. Auto interiors also use smaller-size welt to accent the insert of the seat. Cutting the cover material strips for welt cord is best done on the bias. This helps prevent wrinkling around curves. The width of the cut material is determined by the amount of selvedge needed.

Cut the cover material for 5/32-inch welt into 1½-inch-wide strips; sew around the core with a special welting or zipper foot.

Listings

The last group of seat cover pieces to be cut is the listings. Wider denim pieces are called stretchers. Generally, a listing holds a wire that is hog ringed to the seat frame, securing the seat cover in place. The listing is sewn to the outside edges of the seat cover. Interior listings are called blind listings because they cannot be seen. The listings are typically made from upholstery denim.

New listings are made from upholstery denim. Listings are sewn to the edges of the seat cover. This strong and durable material encases a wire that is hog ringed to the frame of the seat, holding the seat cover in place.

AUTOMOTIVE UPHOLSTERY AND INTERIOR RESTORATION

SEAT RESTORATION

To make a listing, measure the width and length of the material and transfer these measurements onto the new denim with a pencil. Then, cut the material and fold it in preparation for sewing. After the listings are cut, you can begin the process of sewing the seat cover.

Seat Cover

The seat panels are assembled in a logical order, and understanding the proper order of assembly is basic. Individual pieces are sewn together using a compound walking-foot sewing machine to make a subassembly. The subassemblies are then joined together to make the complete seat cover.

Sewing

Each stitch begins and ends with a tack stitch to lock the thread in place; use a forward and then backward stitch. Work in a logical order to avoid mixing the panels by concentrating on the "A" pieces of the front seat bottom cover before working on the "B," "C," and "D" sections.

Assemble the individual panels face to face by lining up the witness marks and sewing them together to form a larger subcomponent. With the panels aligned at the start point and placed under the presser foot of the sewing machine, begin sewing with a tack stitch to lock the thread in place and continue sewing 1/2 inch from the edge of the panel while keeping a straight and even stitch to the end. Back-tack the stitch to lock the thread before removing the piece from the sewing machine. Trim the thread ends close to the material for a clean appearance.

Seams

Some seams have a welt cord between them and others are finished with a French seam. The factory used a double-needle machine to create the French seams. A French seam can be created equally well with a single-needle sewing machine, although it takes a little more time and effort. To make the French seam, the selvedge of the seam is splayed out and a twill tape or bias backer tape is used to help support the stitching and give the seam additional strength.

With the backer tape in place, you sew along the face of the material on both sides of the existing seam. To keep the stitching even, use the edge of the presser foot as a guide along the seam. Sew along both sides of the seam, keeping the stitches even and parallel with each other.

Sew a welt cord across the leading edge of the rolled front bolster panel and then add the insert panel. Sew a blind listing to the seam on the inside of the seat bottom cover to complete this subassembly. The boxing surrounds the insert assembly. Sew the boxing in place and observe the witness marks for alignment. Then create a French seam to finish the panel. To finish the seat cover and make it ready for installation, sew listings in place around the outside edges of the cover. The listings hold a wire that is inserted into them, giving the hog rings something solid to hold the seat cover to the seat frame. Repeat this process for the rest of the seat covers. Watch your index marks and keep true to your pattern.

Sewing a Seat Cover

1 *Tight, even stitches are essential to sewing. The thread tensions cannot be too tight or too loose or the seam will fail. A locking, or tack, stitch at the beginning and end of a seam is also important. This prevents the seam from unraveling.*

2 Decorative seams are often used to strengthen or enhance a panel. A French seam is used when a welt is in the way. The French seam does not rise above the surface of a panel. It lies flat and makes an otherwise plain seam look nice.

3 Because the seam is exposed, twill tape is applied to the backside of a French seam to help support the stitching and strengthen the seam. The twill backer tape is held in place by a row of stitches that run parallel on each side of the seam.

4 When the seat cover was originally made at the factory, the French seams were sewn with a special double-needle sewing machine. The same results can be achieved with a standard single-needle machine with two passes instead of one.

5 The bottom seat cover insert is sewn to the rolled bolster panel with a welt cord between the two panels. A blind listing is added to the seam on the inside of the seat cover so that the seat cover can be anchored to the lower spring unit.

6 Listings are added to the outer edges of the seat cover to provide a way for the seat cover to be attached to the seat frame. A large listing with a stretcher panel is sewn to the bottom edge of the front seat backrest.

SEAT RESTORATION

Seat Cushion

To finish off the bottom seat springs a new piece of burlap is needed to cover the springs. Cut a piece of burlap about 4 inches longer than the spring unit. The burlap actually does two things: The first is to evenly tension the springs and the second is to provide a barrier to keep the cotton batting from settling into the springs.

Burlap Attachment

Fold the edge of the burlap back on itself and hog ring the double thickness of burlap to the edge wire on one end of the spring unit. Pull the burlap taut and hog ring the burlap to the other end of the spring unit. Continue to roll the burlap over the edge wire and add hog rings about every 3 inches all around the spring unit. The edges of the spring unit need to be covered to keep it from cutting into the padding and seat cover. To soften the edge wire of the seat bottom, 2-inch-wide strips of jute carpet pad are cut and then hog ringed to the outside perimeter edge wire over the burlap-covered springs.

The bolster anchor wire that runs across the top of the springs is located under the burlap cover. It should be highlighted with a marker so that it is easy to locate visually when it is time to secure the seat cover.

Seat Padding

Apply a half-layer of cotton batting to the top of the burlap to even out the surface of the springs. The cotton now provides a smooth and even surface for the high-resilient (HR) medium-firm foam seat cushion.

Seat Foam

Fit a piece of 1-inch-thick by 24-inches-wide HR foam to the top of the seat springs. Trim the foam cushion to the seat base and allow it to overhang the ends of the spring unit by 1½ inches. Hog ringing the foam cushion to the springs will hold it in place. Cut muslin fabric into 4-inch-wide strips and glue them to the outside edge of the foam cushion to provide a foundation for anchoring the foam. Without the muslin it is difficult for the hog rings to hold the foam in place because the rings cut through the foam and create a mess. To prepare the foam for the seat cover, you must cut a slot in the foam to access the bolster anchor wire. You do this because the foam is too thick; you cannot hog ring through it. Locate the end points of the anchor wire, and with the aid of a straightedge, draw a line on the foam. Use scissors to cut through the foam to access the anchor wire. Do not cut into the burlap.

Cotton Batting

To soften the transition from the seat cover to the foam, a full layer of cotton batting is added to the top of the foam cushion. Clear the cotton from the anchor wire slot and apply a piece of cheesecloth to cover the cotton. The cheesecloth prevents the cotton from bunching up when the new seat cover is installed.

Assembling a Seat Cushion

1 *Burlap is stretched over the bottom seat springs and fastened to the edge wire with hog rings. Adding the burlap helps tension the lower seat springs, helps them work together, and provides a barrier for the seat padding.*

AUTOMOTIVE UPHOLSTERY AND INTERIOR RESTORATION

CHAPTER 2

2 The steel edge wire can eventually wear through the padding and cause damage to the seat cover. To prevent this, strips of jute carpet padding are hog ringed to the edge wire of the spring unit to help soften the edge of the springs.

3 A foundation layer of cotton is added over the burlap base of the springs on the front seat bottom cushion. The cotton levels the springs and provides a smoother surface for the sheet of 1-inch high-resilient medium-firm foam.

4 Another layer of cotton batting is applied to the top of the foam cushion. The additional cotton acts as a buffer between the seat cover and the foam and provides additional support. To keep the cotton from matting it is covered with a piece of cheesecloth.

SEAT RESTORATION

Seat Cover Installation

Before you fit the seat cover to the frame you must prepare it by inserting corrugated listing wire or paper-covered wire stake into the listings along the bottom edges of the front bottom seat cover. With the seat cover turned inside out, position the seat cover over the cotton padding. Starting at the center point of the blind bolster listing, hog ring across the top of the seat to secure the cover to the anchor wire beneath the burlap.

With the bolster listing secured, work the front corners of the seat cover to the edge of the cushion and turn the corners down and over the frame to encapsulate the cotton, foam, and springs. Secure the cover through the listing with hog rings. Pull down evenly across the front edge of the seat cover and hog ring the listing to the underside seat frame. The hog rings should cut through the listing fabric and hold the listing wire to the metal seat frame. Work out any wrinkles as you go so that the tension on the seat cover fabric is smooth between the hog rings. You do not want the fabric to look scalloped or puckered. Hog ring evenly around the front corners to the rear corner of the seat, adjusting the padding as you go.

Working along the rear of the insert panel, lift the rear apron cover forward to expose the rear listing. Attach the rear edge listing of the seat cover to the spring frame with even tension. Pull the rear apron cover over the back of the seat frame and turn the seat cushion over. Work the larger stretcher listing along the bottom of the springs. Keep the material taut and smooth. Turn the seat bottom upright and make any padding adjustments necessary to correct any wrinkles that may remain. Give the seat cover a quick steam to make the seat cover look and feel smooth.

Assemble the front seatbacks in much the same way as the bottom section except that you do not use HR foam padding. Instead, build up four layers of cotton batting and wrap that in a cheesecloth cover to keep the cotton from lumping up and shifting when you apply the seat cover over the padding. Then, secure the encapsulated cotton cushion to the burlap-covered springs with hog rings.

Turn the seat cover inside out and begin to fit it over the cotton padding by rolling the seat cover around the back and securing it with hog rings through the listings. Pull the bottom corners of the seat cover over the bottom edge of the seatback and hog ring it to the bottom edge wire of the seatback frame. Attach nylon tufting twine to the button and with a tufting needle, pierce the cover, and pull the needle through the seat and out the backside.

Adorn the upper bolster of the seatback with a button Anchor the button by tying it off on the back. Use a small wad of cotton as a backer for the knot. Tie the button with moderate tension. You do not want the button too loose or too tight. You know it is correct when you rub your hand over the button without feeling it.

To finish the seat cover installation, apply glue to the bottom edge of the seat frame and secure the loose end of the listing into the glue. Work out any wrinkles that may form in the listing.

Installing a Seat Cover

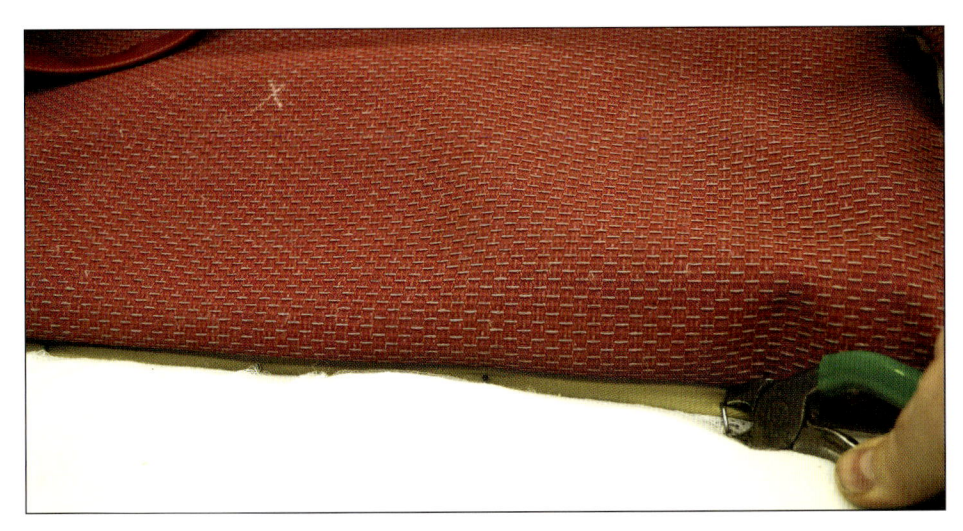

1 Listing wire has been inserted into the seat cover listings to prepare the seat cover for installation. The inverted seat cover is positioned over the seat cushion and the blind listing of the bolster is secured to the anchor wire with hog rings.

CHAPTER 2

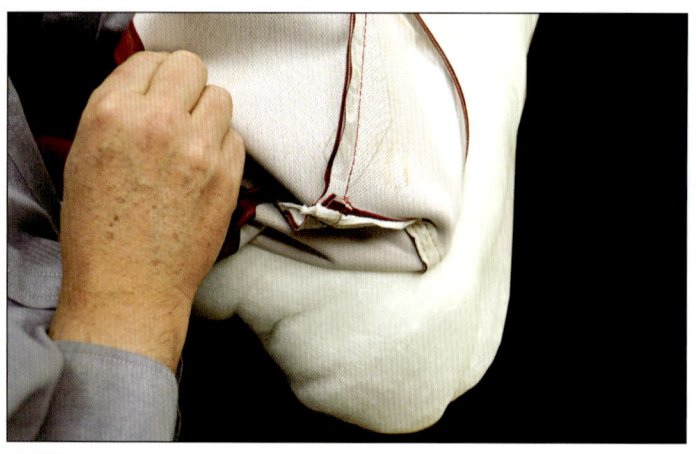

2 *Fitting the seat cover is done by stretching the front corner over the seat padding and attaching the listing wire to the front underside edge of the seat frame with hog rings. Additional cotton padding may be needed to make the corner smooth.*

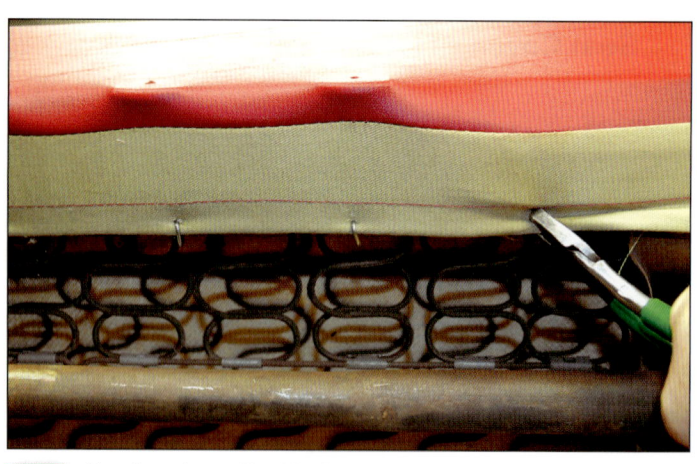

3 *To give the rolled bolster a firm and taut appearance, the cover has been pulled with even tension while the listing across the front of the seat is secured with hog rings. Large areas like this are best worked from the center outward.*

4 *Attaching the rear seat cover panels to the seat frame completes the lower seat cover. The listing is tensioned evenly and secured to the seat frame with hog rings. The bottom seat cushion is turned over and adjustments are made to correct any wrinkles in the seat cover.*

5 *The seat backrest is padded with layers of cotton that are built up and wrapped with cheesecloth to keep the cotton from wadding up. The seat cover is applied over the cotton padding and secured to the seat frame with hog rings.*

6 *A button is prepared with tufting twine. The purpose of the button is primarily ornamental, but it also helps tension the cotton padding and holds it in place. A large tufting needle is used to pierce the seat cover to set the button.*

52 AUTOMOTIVE UPHOLSTERY AND INTERIOR RESTORATION

SEAT RESTORATION

7 *The button must be set at the right tension to look right and not get snagged when entering or exiting the seat. The button twine is knotted over a wad of cotton batting and pulled until the button is just under the surface of the seat cover.*

8 *A little glue helps hold the lower edge of the bottom seat listing in place. The listing is made long on purpose so that it covers the bottom of the backrest. The outer seatback shell covers the glued edge of the listing.*

Outside Backs

To reinstall the outside seatback shell, place the front seatback face down on the workbench. Position the outside seatback shell onto the seat frame. With a regulator, locate the anchor screw holes in the frame. Insert the pan-head screws through the mounting tabs and tighten them to secure the outside shell to the seat frame.

To finish mounting the robe cord to the outside back of the seat shell, use a regulator to locate the robe-cord mounting hole through the fabric so that the escutcheon can be fitted. Attach the robe-cord trim escutcheon to the outside of the seatback shell with its screw. Be sure that the hook end of the robe cord is correctly positioned so that it catches and can be secured by the escutcheon screw. The escutcheon is not only decorative, but it hides the hook end and hog ring at the end of the robe cord.

Final Assembly

Make a new center stop underliner panel board and then wrap it with new seat material. Position the panel in the frame before the seat's backstop bumpers are secured. Remove the old rubber bumpers from the backstop and give a fresh coat of paint to the metal base. Fit new rubber pads to the backstop base. The bumpers provide a cushion for the seatback arms to rest against when in the upright position. Position the rubber bumper backstop in its original location and secure it to the seat frame with a screw. If the outside backs of the seatbacks do not rest evenly, you can rotate the rubber bumper backstop either left or right to adjust the seatbacks up or down.

Fiber Washer

Before you slide the seat backrest into position, place a fiber washer over the pivot post. The washer keeps the metal from cutting into the seat cover. Now, set the seat backrest outer arm over the post and secure it in place with a keeper washer and spring clip. Tap the spring clip into place with a deep well socket.

Pivot Bolt and Washer

Line up the inside pivot points of the seatbacks with the center pivot mount and insert the pivot bolt and washers to hold the seatbacks in place. Secure the bolt with a washer and locknut. Check the movement of the seatbacks to ensure that they move freely and are not binding on the hardware. Also observe that the upholstery is not rubbing, as this causes chaffing marks in the fabric and eventually leads to holes in the fabric.

The side skirt that is mounted along the lower edge of the seat frame conceals the pivot arm hardware. The skirt hangs over a vertical bar; secure it with countersunk washer trim screws in the front. Use a regulator to locate the mounting

CHAPTER 2

holes and align the skirt into position. Insert the trim screws into the skirt and tighten.

The rear corner of this Cadillac seat has an extra-upholstered panel that finishes off the backside of the skirt. Trim screws hold the panel in place. Attach the corner panel in the same manner as the skirt by aligning it with a regulator and trim screws. A machine screw and rubber seatback bumper secure the top of the panel. Attach the front apron panels to the lower edge of the seat frame with countersunk washer trim screws. These small skirts hide the hydraulic seat actuator and the floor-mounted heater fan.

Because of the weight and size of this seat, I recommend assembling the seatbacks and skirts after the seat is installed in the car. This saves your back a lot of stress and makes it much easier to install the seat without damaging anything. You can now return the seat to the car and bolt it into place. This completes the front seat upholstery.

Assembling a Seatback Shell and Bottom Seat Cushion

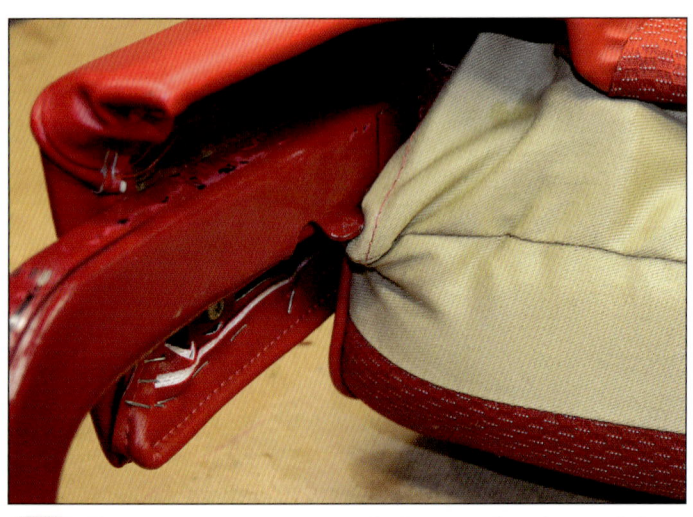

1 *The exposed seat cover listings and springs of the backrest are covered with the seatback shell. The seatback shell is set in place on the backrest and secured to the backrest frame with small pan-head screws.*

2 *The hook end of the robe cord is anchored on the back of the seat shell by a machine screw that also holds the decorative escutcheon to the seatback. The escutcheon covers the hog ring on the raw end of the robe cord.*

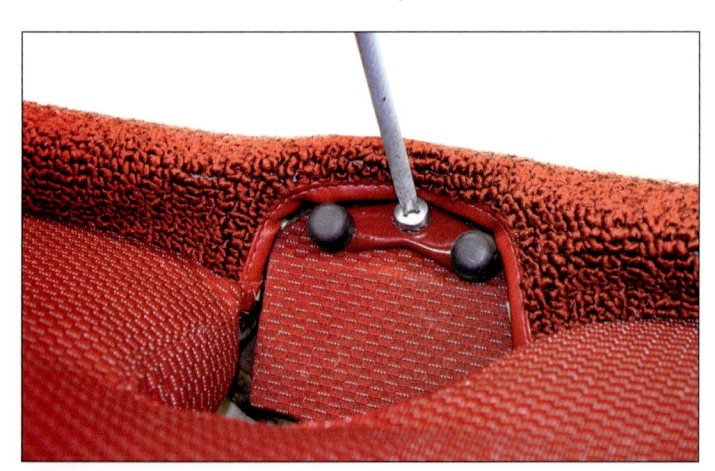

3 *The metal base of the backstop has been repainted and new rubber bumpers have been installed. A single machine screw holds the backstop assembly in place. The backstop assembly also allows adjustment of the backrests.*

4 *A fiber washer is placed over the mounting post of the seat bottom to keep the metal backrest arm from damaging the material of the seat cover. The pivot arm is held in place on the pivot post with a retainer washer and a spring clip.*

54   AUTOMOTIVE UPHOLSTERY AND INTERIOR RESTORATION

SEAT RESTORATION

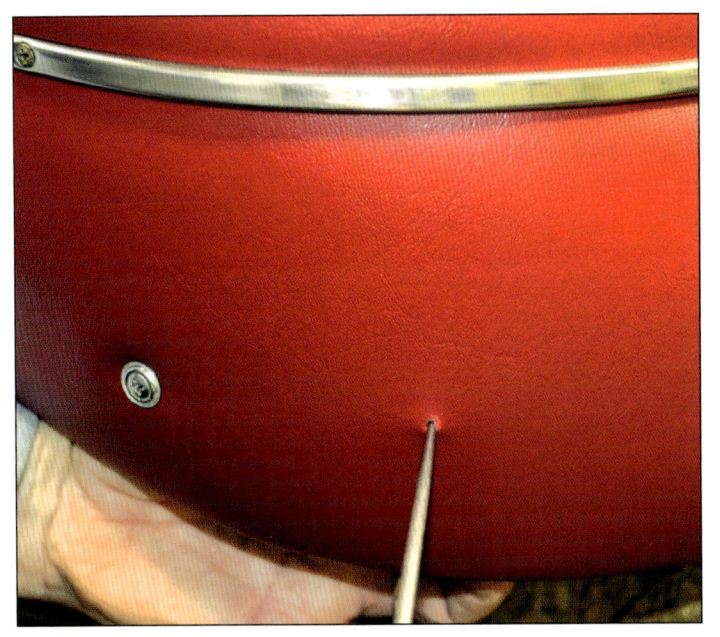

5 *The decorative side skirt is attached to the lower outside end of the seat frame with trim screws. The skirt serves as a cover to conceal the pivot arm hardware and the seat cover listings. The skirt also holds the switch for the power seat.*

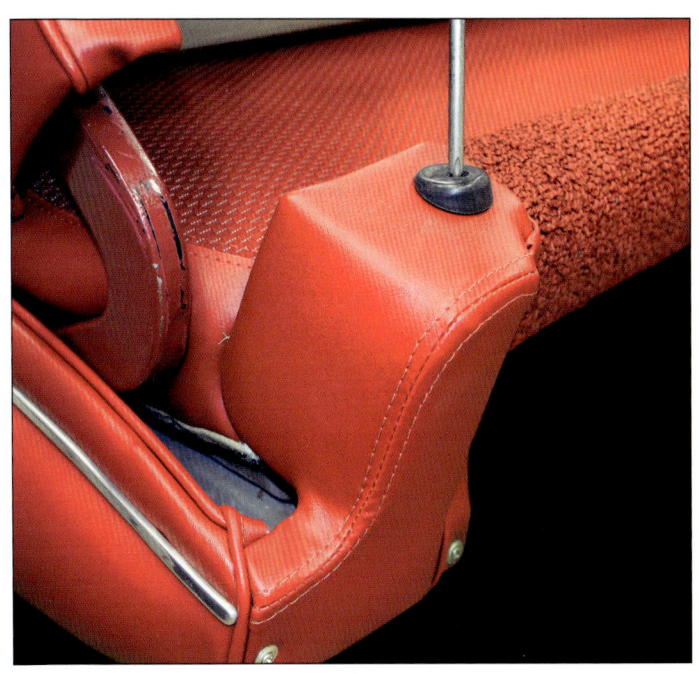

6 *An additional decorative trim panel covers the rear corner of the front seat. The panel is also attached to the seat frame with trim screws. A rubber seat bumper is fitted to the top of the trim panel with a machine screw.*

7 *The new seat cover has been steamed and inspected. It looks just like the original did when it was new. With the front accessory aprons screwed in place, the front seat is complete and ready to be installed in the car.*

Seat Cover Build Without a Pattern

Now that you have seen the process of making a seat cover with a pattern you are ready to create a seat cover without a pattern. When a project comes into my shop that is a bare, spring-only frame and has no seat cover at all to use for a pattern, I rely on my experience of basic seat construction to design and make the new seat cover.

All the processes of restoring a seat remain the same except that there is nothing to tear down. Start by working on the frame. Clean and repair any broken or missing springs as you did in the previous project.

AUTOMOTIVE UPHOLSTERY AND INTERIOR RESTORATION

After the springs are serviced, build up the seat bottom with new burlap, cotton batting, and a foam seat pad. When you reach this point in the restoration, you start to lay out the new panels for the seat cover.

Making a pattern requires a lot of chalking, alterations, and some trial and error. For these reasons I like to use seconds as a low-cost material to mock up the seat cover. This way, I do not waste a lot of expensive materials in the creation stage.

To acquire bargain material or seconds, ask your supplier if any flawed or unsalable material is available at a low cost. I'm sure that they have plenty that they would love to get rid of. The material may not be good enough for the project, but it works great for making a pattern that ends up being thrown away.

Begin by working with oversize pieces of material (vinyl or fabric). The extra allows for chalking and cutting. Do not worry about the nap or stretch at this stage, but be aware of it when you cut your final cover panels. To simplify the patterning process even further, finishing the seams with welt or French seams is not necessary. The seam finish is determined for the final seat cover when the pattern is finished.

Pattern Creation

To get an idea of the overall seat pattern, draw guidelines directly on the cheesecloth along the crowned edge of the seat padding with a marker. This helps you visualize the size and shape of the seat panels. The lines eventually become the seams between the separate panels of the seat cover.

Use this same technique of drawing on the cotton cover to mock up the backrests and rear-seat cushions.

Starting with the bottom seat cover, measure the width and add 4 inches; then measure the depth of the seat bottom cushion and add 2 inches for the rough insert dimensions. Do the same for the rolled bolster and boxing panels. Cut the oversize panels from the patterning material and label the panels on the underside so that they can be easily identified for their location.

Lay the insert panel in place on top of the seat cushion and chalk the perimeter of the insert at the crowned edge of the padding. The new chalk line should follow close to the predrawn line on the seat cushion. Continue the process by chalking the other panels. Add witness marks to indicate intersect points that help with the alignment of the panel for sewing.

The chalk lines become the seam line for the new panel. Before the panel can be cut out it must have a seam allowance added to the edges of the panel. Use a ruler to add 1/2 inch to the outside of the seam line for the seam allowance and then trim the panel material back to the outside line. Add seam allowances and witness marks to all of the other panels; trim them as well. Generally, a witness mark should be placed about every 3 inches outward from a central point on the panel seam.

Each end of the insert and rolled bolster should be the same. To ensure that the panels are identical, it is best to fold the panel in half and trim the profile of the panel to match. Transfer the witness marks and alignment points from one panel to the other.

Blind Listing

A blind listing runs across the leading edge of the insert that holds the rolled bolster and the insert to the seat springs. To determine the size of the listing the thickness of the padding must be measured. The under-pad, foam, and top cotton padding comes to about 2 inches. Allowing for compression of the padding materials, the listing should be made to a finished size of 1½ inches. The bottom edge of the listing, which holds the listing wire, requires an additional 1 inch of material, and the top of the listing is sewn to the insert with a 1/2-inch seam allowance. This adds an additional 1½ inches to the raw size of the blind listing. Measure the width of the leading edge of the insert and deduct 1 inch from both ends. This gives you the length for the listing. Cut the blind listing from upholstery denim, fold the bottom edge of the listing at 1 inch, and sew the listing-wire pocket.

Sew the leading edge of the insert panel to the rear edge of the rolled bolster panel to create the insert subassembly. Measure in 1 inch on each end of the bolster seam and sew on the blind listing. This now completes the insert subassembly.

Boxing Fitment

Position the insert subassembly onto the seat padding and lay the material out smoothly over the cotton padding. The blind listing should be inline with the anchor wire. Attaching the blind listing with hog rings at this time is not necessary; you can hog ring the cover in place later on when the real cover is made and installed. Roll the bolster material over the front of the seat cushion and smooth out any wrinkles.

Set the side boxing material in place and chalk out the desired shape of the panel. Transfer the witness marks from the insert assembly onto the boxing before removing the panel. With the boxing panel flat on the workbench, add a 1/2-inch seam allowance to the panel and cut out the boxing.

With the insert panel still in place, feel for the edges of the center pivot arm access and chalk out the perimeter of the opening. An interior boxing is sewn to the opening that covers the padding and finishes the area. Add a 1/2-inch seam allowance to the inside of the opening and cut away the unneeded interior material. Make a center mark on the leading edge of the opening and measure the distance from the center point to the rear of the insert. Take that measurement, add 1/2 inch to the front for a seam, and cut two strips of material 4 inches wide by the distance you just measured. This becomes the boxing for the pivot access.

Sew the two boxing pieces together to make the inner pivot access boxing. Sew the boxing to the insert panel, making sure that the seam in the boxing aligns with the chalked center point of the pivot access.

Rear Apron Panel

Fold the rear apron material in half to find the center point and notch it with your scissors. Lay the panel out flat on the workbench and mark 1/2 inch from the leading edge. This is the seam allowance that is sewn to the rear edge of the insert panel. Add another 1½ inches for the rise in the seat frame and chalk a line across the panel. This is the reference mark you work from.

Place the apron panel over the rear section of the seat frame and center the panel with the reference line on the leading edge of the metal riser. Feel for the center bumper opening in the metal and chalk the perimeter of the opening onto the apron. Cut out the inner material in the apron to allow the pivot arms of the seatbacks to contact the rubber stops. Sewing on a vinyl binding will eventually finish the raw edge of the opening.

Fold the upper ends of the apron forward and chalk them to indicate a sew line. Remove the apron from the seat frame and then flatten it on the workbench. Add a 1/2-inch seam allowance to the seam line and cut the material. Next, sew the apron to create a wraparound cap on each end of the apron. Refit the apron to the seat frame, pull the leading edge of the apron cap forward, and fold it back on an angle. Chalk this line and remove the apron.

Sew the turned edge of the apron cap to lock it in place. Sew a binding to the raw edge of the bumper access opening. You can now sew the apron to the rear edge of the insert panel. With the apron on top of the insert panel, align the edge of the bumper opening binding to the seam of the pivot access and sew the apron onto the insert. The apron should end about 1 inch from the end of the insert. Repeat this for the other half of the apron.

Seat Boxing Assembly

Sew the seat boxing to the insert subassembly panel by lining up the witness marks and sewing from the bottom of the boxing panel to the rear of the insert subassembly. Set the seat cover in place over the cotton padding and check the fit of the cover. If the boxing does not look right or if it has some puckering, it must be altered to make it fit better.

You can remove puckers by carefully cutting the seam apart at the point of the puckers. This relaxes the material and allows it to flow out smoothly. Rechalk the seam to indicate where the boxing should be adjusted and remove the cover to resew the seam. Fine-tuning the seat cover takes a little time but the results are worth the effort. I like to use fabric because you can take it apart and make adjustments without it falling apart like vinyl would.

Listings

After the seat cover is tailored and fits the seat cushion properly, you can begin to trim the cover material for the listings, which secure the seat cover in place. The listing encases an anchor wire that tensions the seat cover to the frame with hog rings. Pull the bottom edge of the material down so that there is some tension on the material. Do not pull too hard; you want the cover snug and not tight. Chalk along the edge of the metal frame to indicate the new length of the panel. Keep in mind that when you mark for the listings you need to know how big to make the listing to achieve the tensioned appearance you desire for the seat cover.

For example: If the cut length of the tensioned panel just reaches the anchor point where the panel is hog ringed, you should use a 1-inch listing. You would cut the denim 2 inches wide and then fold it in half to create a 1-inch listing. When the listing is sewn to the cut edge of the panel it will have a 1/2-inch seam allowance; this leaves 1/2 inch of listing for insertion of the listing wire and then hog ringing to the seat frame. This equals the cut length of the tensioned panel and the seat cover fits correctly.

An edge listing is typically 1 to 1½ inches wide. A longer listing is called a stretcher. The listings are attached to the outer edge of the seat cover. Similar to the blind listing for the rolled bolster there is also a 1-inch-wide hidden listing that runs across the rear of the insert panel to hold the back edge of the seat cover taut.

An under-seat stretcher holds the rear edge of the apron panel in place. Sew a 4-inch-wide denim listing to the edge of the apron and then attach it to the springs with hog rings. The panel is finished at 4 inches but has 1/2 inch added for the seam allowance and an extra inch to encase the listing wire.

Backrest Layout

The left and right backrests are symmetrical to each other; therefore, only one backrest cover pattern needs to be created. The patterning procedure is the same for making the backrest panels. Take rough measurements to create the oversized panels needed for chalking and cutting the finished panel. Sew the insert panel and upper bolster panel with a blind listing to create a subpanel.

Chalk the insert subpanel and cut it to size. Make the bottom of the insert panel 1½ inches longer, ensuring that it wraps under the bottom edge of the seatback cushion. Always remember to add the seam allowance to the panel seam line or you end up short when it's time to sew the panels together.

Chalk the top and outside boxing panels to fit with the insert subpanel. The seam line between the two boxing panels is most likely joined with a French seam and the seam line should meet at the upper corner of the outside edge of the insert bolster. Use a welt to separate the outside boxing from the insert panel along the top edge and down the outside.

Add the witness marks and blind listing point, as well as the start and end points to the boxing panel before you remove it from the seat. Allow a 1/2-inch seam allowance to the pattern before the panel is cut out. Sew the outside boxing subassembly to the insert subpanel and check the fit. Make alterations as necessary so that the cover lies smoothly over the cotton padding. Mark the inside edge of the boxing for a 1-inch listing. Now trim the fabric to size.

After you sew the cover and it fits well, chalk up the material for the upper rear outside panel. This panel also receives a welt applied from the top inside edge to outside of the panel. Cut the panel and sew it in place.

Inside Boxing

The inside boxing panel is the last panel you sew to the backrest subassembly. You add it after the other panels are in place. A variation must be made to the inside boxing panel on a split-back seat. Divide the inside boxing panel at the insert bolster line; join the upper and lower sections with a French seam. If the insert and bolster materials are different on the top and bottom, then the inside boxing should also be made that way to match. Usually, no welt is applied to the inside boxing seam of a split-back bench seat. This creates the illusion that the seat is continuous even though it is composed of two separate backrests.

Bottom Stretcher

A stretcher must be fitted to the bottom of the backrest insert to secure the seat cover. The insert is 1½ inches short of the attachment point; the lower brace on the backrest needs 3 inches of material to be covered. To make the compound listing, simply take the measurements and add the correct amount of material to the finished size. The first section is 1½ inches plus 3. Therefore, you need 1 inch of material for the listing wire and 1/2 inch for the seam allowance to give a total depth of 6 inches of upholstery denim plus the width of the insert. Fold the material at the 3½-inch mark and sew the 1/2-inch listing pocket first. The remainder of the fabric comes to a flap of 3 inches and a flap of 2 inches. Sew the 2-inch flap to the bottom of the insert.

Mark a 3/4-inch inset from the end of the insert, angle the end of the listing outward, and begin to sew the 2-inch flap to the bottom of the insert with a 1/2-inch seam allowance. Before you get to the end of the listing, angle the other end of the listing outward and complete the sewing, allowing 3/4 inch from the end. When the listing is hog ringed to the seat frame, the angle allows the material to wrap around the pivot arms of the backrest and cover the remaining lower frame.

Outside Back Panel

The cover material for the outside back panel has a French seam along the crest of the curve. Use a straightedge to mark the seam line on the felt underliner that is glued to the back shell. Measure and cut panels as before and then sew the pieces together with a French seam. Fit the cover material to the shell with glue and staples.

Create a decorative 5/32-inch welt cord to trim the outside edge of the seatback. Cut the welt material with an extra 1½ inches of material so that the selvage can be glued and stapled to the shell.

SEAT RESTORATION

Fabricating a Seat Cover

1 I view this seat frame as a gem. It had all the hardware still clipped to it. Although it is typical of the condition of a car seat that I get in my shop, cores like this are getting almost impossible to find. After a good wire brushing the seat frame will be like new.

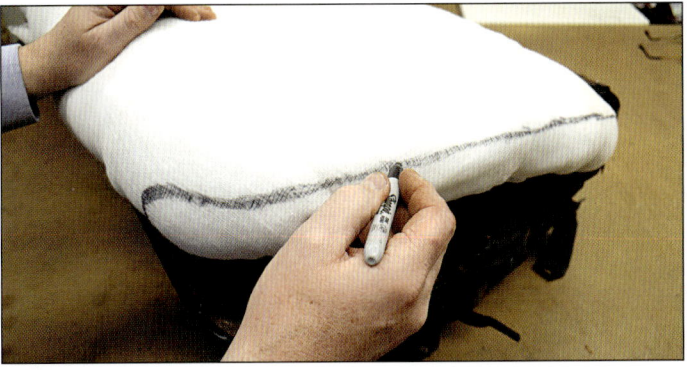

2 The seat frame has been cleaned and painted. The padding has been restored to original condition with all new burlap, cotton, and foam cushion. A new covering of cheesecloth protects the cotton and means it is ready to be marked up for a new seat cover.

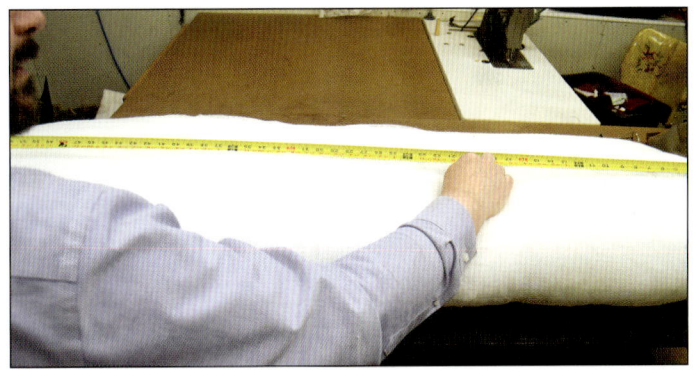

3 After a seat cover design has been established, it is marked onto the cheesecloth. The design helps determine the measurements needed for the new seat panels. The seat material is cut into oversize pieces to allow for trimming during the patterning process.

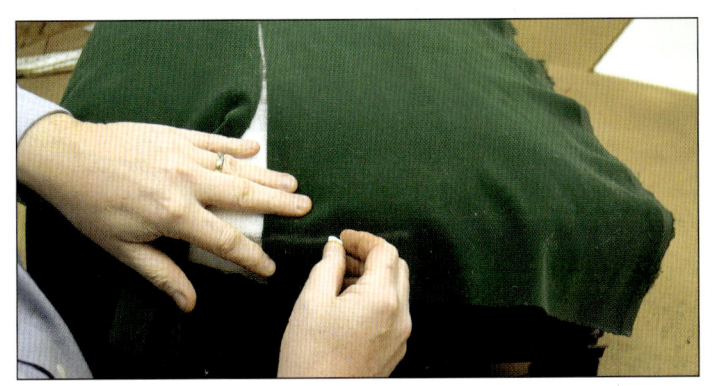

4 Patterning a seat cover is a free-form process. The panel design is defined in chalk on the large panels by marking the seat cushion profile onto the fabric. Chalk is used to make the pattern lines because it can be changed easily by brushing it away.

5 Each panel is given a 1/2-inch seam allowance. The seam allowance is measured carefully and marked on the panel before it can be cut out of the fabric. Witness marks are also added to the panel to help with the alignment of the panel when it is sewn.

AUTOMOTIVE UPHOLSTERY AND INTERIOR RESTORATION

CHAPTER 2

6 The overall appearance of the seat cover relies on the symmetry of the design. Fold the panels in half and trim the material to the same profile to get the look you desire. The sewing and alignment points can also be replicated.

7 Almost every seat cover is attached to the seat frame with a bolster listing. Lightweight upholstery denim is used for the listing due to its strength. A pocket for a listing wire is sewn into upholstery denim before it is sewn to the seat cover.

8 The seam of the rolled bolster is secured to the seat frame with a blind listing. The insert panel and rolled bolster panel are sewn together to create the insert subassembly. The blind listing is then sewn in place before laying out the next panel.

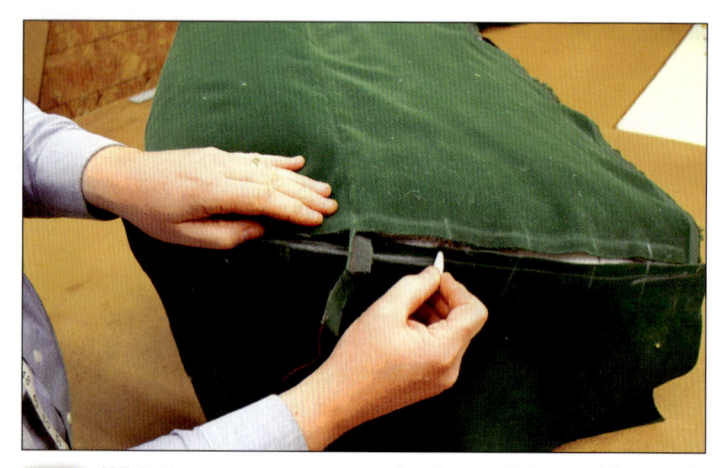

9 With the insert subassembly in position on the seat padding, the end boxing panel is chalked up. Witness marks are transferred from the insert panel to the boxing to ensure correct positioning when the panels are sewn together.

10 An opening for the backrest support arms has been chalked onto the insert panel. A seam allowance has been added for an internal boxing that will be added next. The boxing finishes the opening and allows access to the pivot point on the seat rail below.

SEAT RESTORATION

11 An apron panel covers the rear riser on the seat frame. Access to the seatback bumpers is marked on the apron. This area is cut out of the apron and the raw edge of the material is finished with a vinyl binding.

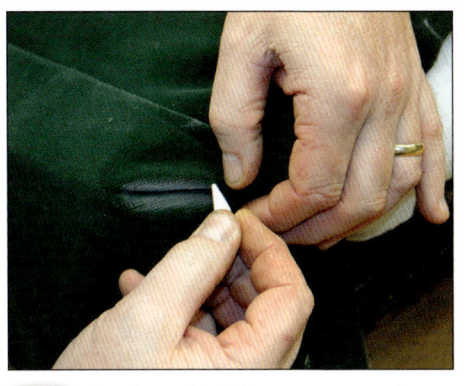

12 Each end of the rear apron is capped to conceal the metal riser of the seat frame. The apron material is fit to the frame by folding and chalking the material. After the apron ends are sewn, the panel is sewn to the rear edge of the insert panel.

13 The boxing panel is being sewn to the insert subassembly. The witness marks are aligned and the panels are sewn together with a 1/2-inch seam. The seat cover is test fit on the padded frame and alterations are made to the seam until the panel fits perfectly.

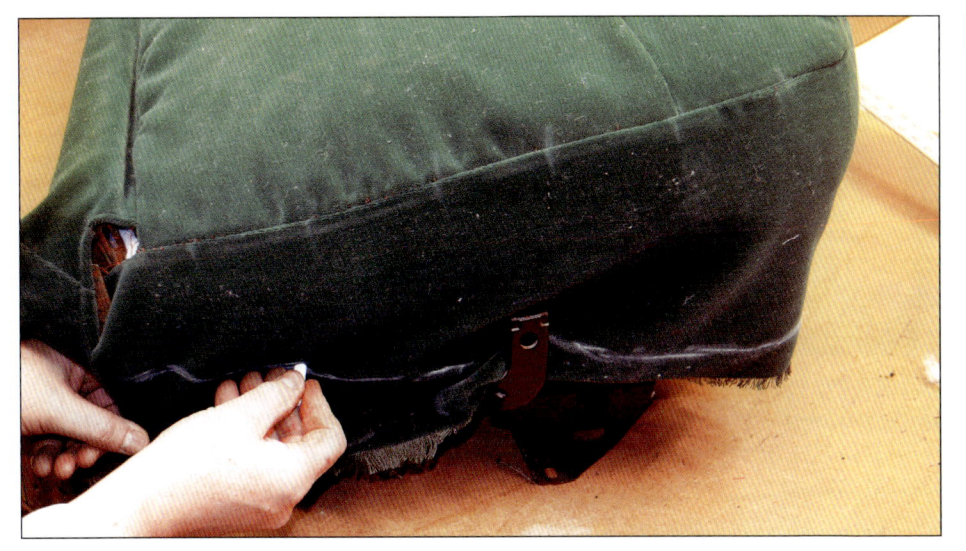

14 The seat cover has been fitted to the seat and the lower edges of the seat cover are marked so that the listings can be sewn in place. The listing holds a wire that tensions the seat cover to the seat frame. Hog rings are used to anchor the listing.

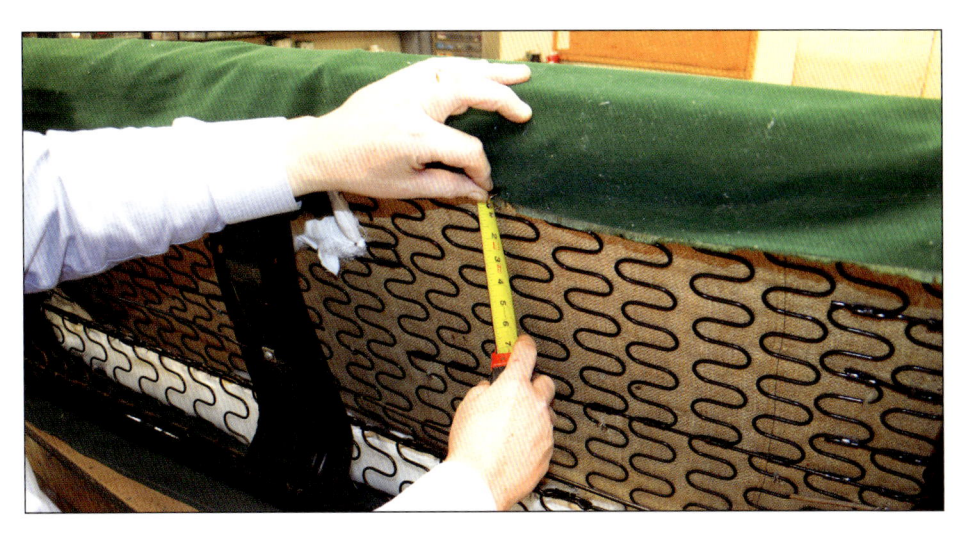

15 Measurements are taken for the denim stretcher that is added to the lower edge of the rear apron panel. The stretcher holds the apron in place because it spans the seat frame bracing. The leading edge of the stretcher holds a listing wire that is hog ringed to the seat springs.

AUTOMOTIVE UPHOLSTERY AND INTERIOR RESTORATION

CHAPTER 2

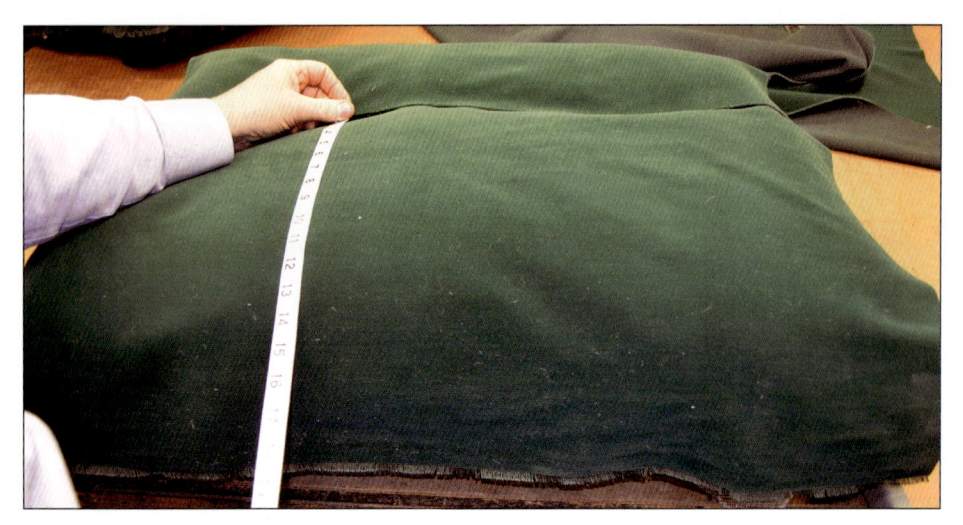

16 Oversize panels have been measured and cut for the creation of the backrest seat cover. The panels are patterned, sized, sewn, and fitted to the backrest. Because the backrests are a mirror of each other, only one backrest needs to be patterned.

17 The size of the backrest panels is defined by chalking along the crowned edge of the padded cushion. Additional material is left on the bottom edge of the insert panel so that the listing seam does not show along the bottom edge of the seat cover.

18 The backrest has boxing panels along the top and sides of the seat cover. The top and outside panels are sewn together and form the seam boxing on the seat. These panels usually have a welted seam that runs across the top and down the outside of the insert.

19 A smaller panel is chalked up and fit to the outside back of the backrest cover. This panel covers the upper backside of the backrest. A welt also runs across the top and down the outside. The backrest shell covers the lower edge of the panel.

20 The inside boxing of the backrest has been seam matched. This is done to disguise the separation of the seatbacks. The omission of welt cord along the inside seam and continuation of the seat pattern give the illusion that the seatback is one piece.

62   AUTOMOTIVE UPHOLSTERY AND INTERIOR RESTORATION

SEAT RESTORATION

21 The bottom of the backrest is fitted with a compound stretcher. The single piece of fabric has two purposes. The front half works as a listing that anchors the bottom of the seat cover in place and the second half covers over the exposed seat frame.

22 With the stretcher installed, you can see how nice the bottom panel looks. No bulk from extra fasteners or material will interfere with the operation of the folding seat. This is a very clean appearance from a simple design.

23 A French seam detail is used on the cover material for the outside back shell cover. The French seam does not add bulk to the seam the way a welt cord does. After the cover material is applied to the back shell a decorative welt is added to adorn the outside edge.

AUTOMOTIVE UPHOLSTERY AND INTERIOR RESTORATION

Pleated Seat Cover Alignment

When working with a sewn pleated insert, the pleats need to be aligned or it looks wrong. Just measuring the panel and sewing it together does not ensure that the pleats line up correctly when the seat cover is installed. I have found that the best way to make pleats align is to pattern the backrest covers after I have installed the lower seat cover. This method allows me to adjust the pleated insert before it is sewn into the backrest. This process requires that you have the backrest insert panels sewn but not trimmed to size.

Sew the bottom seat cover and install it as normal. Now, attach the padded seat backrest frame to the bottom frame. Mark the location of the bottom seat cover pleats onto the backrest cotton padding using a marker. The backrest frames can now be removed and the patterning process can proceed as normal.

Take the oversize presewn pleated insert panel and align it to the index marks on the cotton pad. Next, chalk up the sew lines the same way as in the last sequence. Sew on the upper bolster, boxing, and listings to create the backrest cover as you did previously.

Install the seat cover and check that the sewn pleat lines are all in the proper alignment with the index marks on the cotton padding. Finish the seat cover install by hog ringing the listings on the cover to the seat backrest frame.

Check the alignment of the pleats and make any adjustments necessary to ensure that they line up. At this time you might need to give the seat cover a light steam to remove any small wrinkles that may have appeared during assembly. You can now return the seat to the car and bolt it into place.

Aligning a Pleated Seat Cover

1 *The front seat has been assembled on the workbench and the pleats of the bottom seat cover are transferred to the padding of the seat backrest. The backrests are removed so the new seatback cover can be patterned for perfect alignment.*

2 *A pre-sewn insert panel is lined up with the index marks and sized for the new seat cover. After sewing, the finished seat cover is repositioned on the padded backrest frame with the pleats lining up with the index marks. Hog rings are used to keep the seat cover in place as the seat cover is installed.*

3 *After the seat is assembled you can see that the pleated inserts all align perfectly. Others will never truly appreciate the amount of effort it takes to build a seat cover from scratch, but the real satisfaction comes from knowing that you did it.*

CHAPTER 3

DOOR PANELS

The British refer to them as a door card, but in America they are called door panels. The door panel serves two functions. The first is to pad and add sound deadening to the cab of the vehicle. The second is to add beauty to the interior by covering up the internal door components.

Early door panels were made from cardboard and upholstered with leather, fabric, or vinyl to complement the car's interior. Present day cars employ modern manufacturing techniques and use plastic injection molding and vacuum forming equipment to create panels that are nearly impossible to re-create by hand.

Automakers attached door panels to the inside of the door in many different ways. Early wood-framed cars had interior panels attached with brad nails. Later-model cars with metal frames used spiral nails, screws, and spring clips to hold the door panel in place. Before the door panels were attached, a moisture barrier of tarpaper or a plastic film was installed between the door panel and the doorframe to protect the door panel from water damage. After the door panel was attached, an armrest was installed with screws that secured it directly into the door. The armrest served two practical purposes: comfort for the driver/passenger and a convenient way for the door to be pulled closed.

Recreating a Door Panel

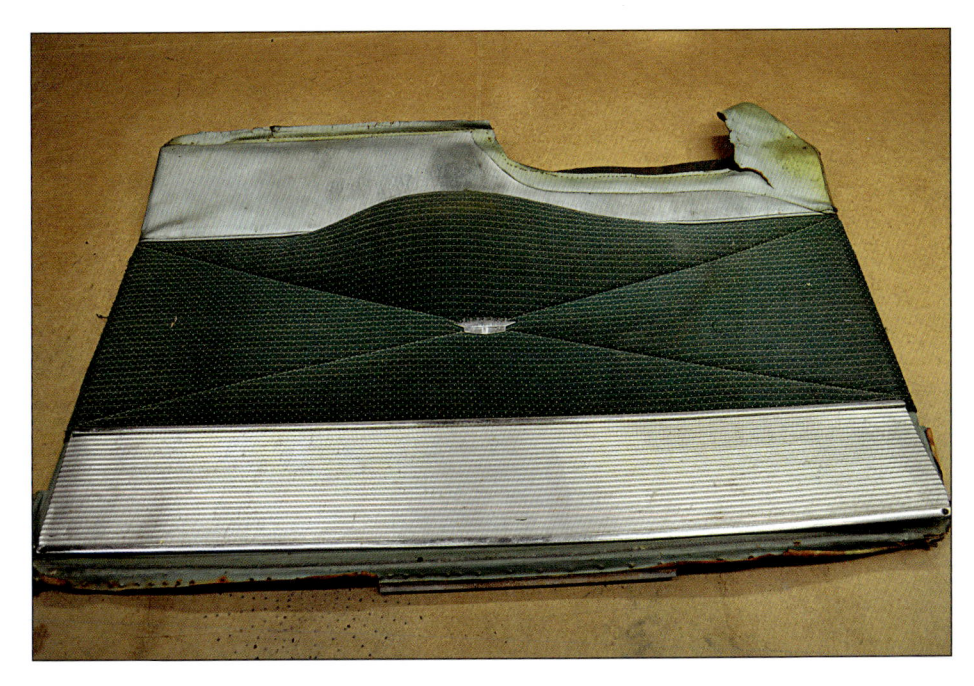

1 *The owner changed the paint color of this 1952 Cadillac Coupe de Ville from green to red. I will create a new door panel in red to the exact detail of the original. The trim from the old panel will be reconditioned and applied to the new door panel.*

AUTOMOTIVE UPHOLSTERY AND INTERIOR RESTORATION

CHAPTER 3

2 Removal of the door panel is straightforward. This armrest is built into the door panel. A metal finger cup inside the armrest helps hold the door in place. A single screw is removed and the finger cup is lifted out. Two additional screws underneath the finger cup also must be removed.

3 Removal of the door handle requires the use of a clip removal tool. The tool is placed under the base of the handle to release the spring clip that retains the handle to the regulator stud. With the spring clip removed, the handle is easily removed from the door.

4 This door panel is attached to the edges of the door with panel nail fasteners. A panel clip tool is used to lift the nails out of the receivers in the door. The nails in the fasteners become weak as they age and are prone to breaking off. This is not a concern; they will be replaced with new fasteners.

The first thing is to visually inspect the door panel to determine how to remove the panel from the door. On top of the door panel is a metal cap, or garnish molding, that holds the upper edge of the door panel to the door. This molding is held on the door by oval-head sheet-metal screws. Before the door cap can be removed, unscrew the door lock button from the lock rod. If the door has a remote mirror control lever this must be removed too. Loosen the setscrew with the correct size Allen wrench. Remove the door cap trim screws and the door cap can now be removed from the door.

Armrests can be attached in different ways. An applied armrest is secured to the door by two #14 sheet-metal screws. Using a #3 Phillips head screwdriver, remove the screws and armrest from the door. On a door panel with a built-in armrest the finger cup must be removed. It is held in with small trim screws that secure the armrest to a cleat that is screwed to the door.

Window cranks and door release handles are held by screws or spring clips. Removal of the window cranks and door release handles is done with special tools designed to unclip the spring retainer hidden underneath the base of the crank. The spring clip is displaced, and that releases the crank from the splined regulator post on the door. Use of the correct removal tool makes removal much easier. To release the window crank spring clip a clip tool is slid under the window crank and the spring clip is pushed out. From 1932 until 1948, Ford Motor Company attached its window and door cranks to a square regulator shaft with a 1/8-inch-diameter pin. This required a special fork-like tool to make the pin removal and installation easier.

Using a door panel tool, pry the nail panel fasteners from the doorframe by sliding the panel tool directly under the fastener and pry the door panel away from the door. The nail fasteners used on this door panel are fragile and most of them are usually broken before I ever get to them. Do not worry about breaking them during the removal process. New panel nails are used to fasten the new door panel to the door. Spring clip fasteners hold on some door panels. These wire clips were inserted into a small hole in the door and held the door panel in place. General Motors also used a metal cleat along the bottom of the door panel to hold the panel to the door. In later years, trim screws were used along the bottom edge of the door panel.

Check for and remove any additional screws that may be in the lower corners of the door panel and remove the door panel from the car and place it on the workbench.

Material Choices

Door panels can be made from a lot of different materials. Some are better suited than others for interior restoration. The recommended thickness of the base panel is to be no more than 1/8 inch thick. If the

Door panels may be constructed from wood or plastic. There really is no right or wrong material; it just depends on the application. I prefer the traditional waterproof automotive panel board.

base panel is any thicker there will be problems with the normal opening and closing of the door after it has been upholstered.

Your original door panel was most likely made from paper. Early models had door panels made from heavy paper that was coated in oil or wax for water resistance. It was common for these door panels to delaminate over time. A lot of street rod builders use Luan plywood. This is thin material that is easy to work with, but it is prone to warping and it can crack if bent. Another material that is often used for making door panels is Masonite. Ford Motor Company built a lot of its interior panels with a Masonite base panel. Masonite is also easy to work with but because of its dense and solid nature, it does not take staples well. Masonite is also prone to cracking, swelling, and warping due to water retention.

Lexan, ABS, and other plastics are waterproof and do not warp. They are popular material choices for the modern restorer, but they tend to crack from staples and are difficult to glue materials to.

My recommendation and go-to solution is to use the waterproof panel board designed for automotive use. This special paper board is well suited for all applications since it is easy to cut, staple, and glue to. The waterproof panel board sheets come in two sizes and can be purchased individually or by the carton of 25 sheets.

Deconstruction

Door panels are symmetrical and it is only necessary to disassemble one door panel for patterning. Leave one untouched; you will use it for reference. Place the door panel face down on the workbench to gain access to the fasteners on the backside of the panel. If the panel has any stainless trim, carefully lift the bent-over retaining tabs and pins without breaking them and remove the trim piece from the panel. Try not to bend or damage the trim when removing them. The stainless pieces will be reconditioned to like-new and reinstalled on the new door panel.

After removal of a trim piece, it is best to make a notation on the backside of the part as to the orientation of the trim panel so that it can be reinstalled correctly. You can mark smaller parts by applying a piece of tape with location details. It is also a good practice to clean and polish the trim as it is removed from the panel. Repairs to any broken or missing mounting pins can be made now so that the trim can be installed later.

Peel back the cover material from the edges of the door panel and turn the panel face side up.

Cut away anything that is holding the cover material in place and continue to lift the material from the panel until the panel is down to the padding and underlining.

If the door panel has a metal banding on the edges, it most likely has door panel retainer nails welded to it. These nails fasten the door panel to the door. Because of the age of the door panel the nails are usually bent over or missing. The position of the fastening nails needs to be transferred to the panel prior to removing the metal retainer. To locate the position of the missing nails, look on the metal retainer for the spot-weld mark. Another indicator of the missing nail is that the cover material has a relief cut where the nail was. The old metal banding will not be reused on the new door panel but leave it attached for the patterning process.

Along the bottom edge of the door panel you find a metal retainer cleat. This strip of flared metal slips inside a slot on the door and holds the bottom edge of the door panel tightly to the door without additional fasteners. The cleat on this door panel shows signs of severe corrosion and a large portion has rusted away. This is a part that is no longer available and is currently not being reproduced. A new cleat must be made before the door panel can be assembled.

CHAPTER 3

Disassembling the Old Panel

1 Removal of the stainless trim pieces requires that the retainer pins holding them onto the panel be lifted. The pins are carefully pried up without breaking any of them off. This trim will be reconditioned and installed on the newly made door panel.

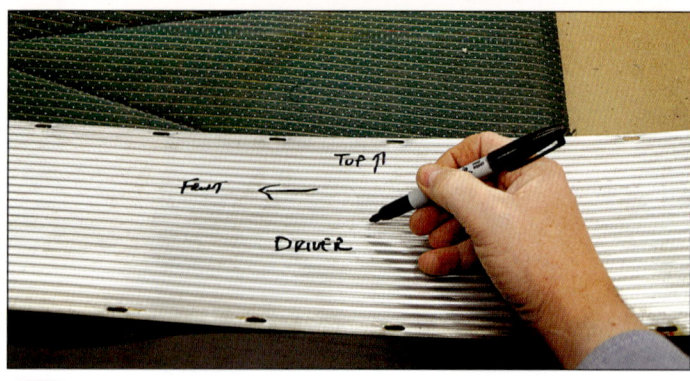

2 This trim panel is marked on the backside to ensure the correct positioning when it is reinstalled. It is important to keep track of the trim pieces that are removed; it is almost impossible to locate replacement pieces for these parts if they are lost or damaged.

3 Cutting away the stitching frees the old upholstery from the panel without causing much damage to the old parts. Cutting the stitches carefully helps preserve the pieces so that they can be referenced and reproduced accurately later on.

4 Index marks are made on the old door panel indicating the location of the retainer nails. A missing nail position can be found by looking for the spot weld on the metal edging. Another clue to their location is the relief cut mark in the wrapped material.

5 Some door panels have blind fasteners that hold the door panel in place. These are often rusted or damaged from age and neglect. Reproductions of these parts are not available for purchase, which means they have to be made by hand.

AUTOMOTIVE UPHOLSTERY AND INTERIOR RESTORATION

Door Panel Cleat Fabrication

Measure what is remaining of the old metal cleat to determine the width of the metal needed to make a new part. The new cleat is made from a piece of 22-gauge sheet metal. Always be careful when working with sheet metal. The edges of the metal are sharp and you can hurt yourself.

The new cleat is formed with the help of a metal shear and press break. The metal is cut into a workable strip and bent to the dimensions of the original cleat. Continue to work the metal until the desired shape is achieved.

A hand seamer tool is used to flare the outside edge of the cleat, gradually bent to the correct radius. You can also use other basic metal shaping tools to form and straighten the metal. I prefer working the metal in small increments because it allows me more control of the piece. Power tools are nice, but they are not always necessary.

Form the bottom edge of the cleat by fitting it to a scrap piece of panel board. This is the part that wraps around and attaches the cleat to the bottom of the door panel. This sizing process ensures that the cleat has a good fit to the panel. Do not over-hammer the metal and stretch it too much. This causes the piece to warp and creates more work straightening the metal.

Dress the edge of the metal with a file to clear away any burs that are on the cleat and then clean the surface of the metal. I use lacquer thinner to clean almost everything. Because the lacquer thinner evaporates fast, it degreases the surface without leaving a residue behind. Later you will be gluing vinyl over the edge of the cleat and the glue will not work if the metal is dirty or oily.

When the cleat sections are completed, they will be set aside until it is time for them to be installed on the bottom of the door panel.

Creating a Door Panel Cleat

1 A small metal shear and press break is used to help form the new cleat. This tool can handle metal up to 12 inches wide, so you need to make the new cleat in sections. The metal can also be worked with hand tools.

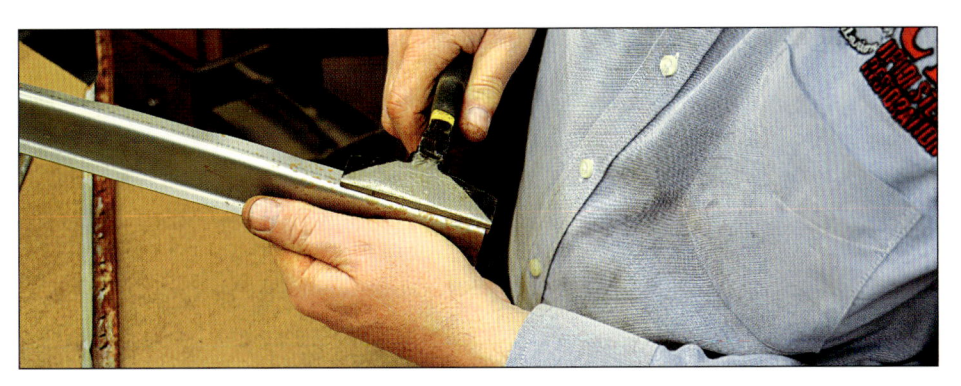

2 To make the flare on the cleat, a hand seamer is used to bend and shape the metal. Power tools are great for some jobs, but limited shop space allows for only some tools. Hand tools are usually adequate; it just might take a little longer to get the same result.

CHAPTER 3

3 *A piece of scrap panel board is used to size the bottom edge of the cleat. The metal is hammered over the edge of the panel board and then sized for a secure fit. It is easy to overwork the metal on small flanges like this, which causes the piece to warp.*

4 *The cleat has reached its desired form and it is deburred with a file. The surface is also cleaned and degreased with lacquer thinner so that it can accept a coat of glue later in the assembly of the door panel.*

Creating a New Door Panel

Now that the old door panel has been stripped down to the base board, you can start to pattern the pieces for the new door panel. You need to make a left and right panel. To make the opposite door, simply turn the pattern over and repeat the process of tracing, cutting, and punching. Clearly mark the opposite door panel pieces with an "X" so that the pieces can easily be identified when they are assembled.

Place the old door panel on top of a new sheet of waterproof panel board. It may help to use some weights or even temporarily staple through the panels to keep them in place while tracing around the perimeter of the old door panel. I recommend that you use a very sharp pencil to get the best pattern. Without moving or lifting the old panel board, trace the inside openings for window crank, door handle, and any trim mounting holes. Also mark the position of the material transition design lines and the door mounting nails.

Panel Fastener Positioning

Before the panel is cut out, it is important to get the position of the panel mounting nails correct; otherwise you will have trouble fitting the new door panel to the car door. From the panel nail reference mark, measure in from the edge of the door panel line 5/16 inch and mark this on the door panel. This is the position that the panel nail must be in when the door panel is assembled.

The original panels were die-cut at the factory in one step. It takes time and patience to re-create the same panel by hand. Sharp blades and punches make short work of this task. To get the best fit for the new door panel, the new panel blank is rough cut from the sheet of panel board and then trimmed to the exact size. Using a straightedge and a utility knife with a new blade installed, carefully cut no more than 1/4 inch on the outside of the traced line of the new panel to remove it from the sheet of panel board. Doing this reduces the bulk of the panel board material. Finish trimming the new door panel base to the inside of the traced line with scissors.

Cut in the trim mounting holes with the correct size hole punch.

DOOR PANELS

Also cut out any other areas such as the armrest bracket on the panel blank. These access areas are required for the assembly of the door panel. Accuracy here ensures that the panel and trim fit properly.

Fitting Fasteners

The dimensions for the panel fasteners are based on the Au-ve-co part number 12671 nail-on door panel repair clips. To make a slot for the panel fasteners, locate the marked positions of the door panel mounting nails along the outside edges of the door panel blank. Measure an additional 1/4 inch from the reference mark and make a vertical line 1⅛ inches long or 9/16 above and below the mark. This is where a slot is made allowing the new panel nail fastener to be inserted into the door panel.

To create the slot for the nail fastener clip, cut along both sides of the vertical line with a utility knife to make an opening in the panel just big enough for the metal panel fastener to be inserted. The nail should now line up perfectly with the reference mark made earlier.

Vinyl Orientation

The vinyl for the door panel is laid out with the stretch going up and down on the pieces. You do not want any extra stretch from side to side because this causes wrinkles in the finished door panel. Pulling the vinyl around the edges of the panel blank keeps the vinyl taut, and this helps the vinyl look better. Use the old door panel pieces as a guide and cut the vinyl pieces 2 inches oversize to allow enough material to be wrapped around the edges of the panel blank.

Disassemble the center armrest section by removing the fabric from the armrest form. Peel up the fabric and cut the stitching to reveal the cotton padding below. Discard the cotton padding and clean the surface of the metal armrest form. The rubber armrest pad was found to be in excellent condition on this project and does not need to be replaced. If your pad needs to be replaced, make a new one from a high-density poly foam and carve it to shape.

Turn the center panel unit over and straighten the legs of the industrial staples that are holding the armrest core to the panel. Remove and discard the staples to separate the armrest form from the panel. The top of the armrest has a vinyl panel that has been sewn to the fabric. Mark the start and end points of the vinyl and add some witness marks along the seam before you cut the pieces apart. Make the same marking to the inner finger cup piece before it is cut apart. With the center panel section torn apart the rebuilding process can begin.

Rebuilding the Center Panel

The center panel section is built up from five separated pieces of panel board. Separate the panels by sliding a broad blade putty knife under the upper sections to free them. Try not to damage the panel pieces as you separate them. The panels are used as a pattern for the new pieces.

You also need two sets of these panels to build both door panels. Again, during this process mark the opposite door panel set of materials with an "X." The base panel is traced along with all the cutouts and alignment marks. The top panels are also traced and marked for position placement. The pieces are then cut from the panel board and access holes are punched as necessary.

Reproducing a Door Panel

1 *The old door panel is used as a template by tracing its profile to a new sheet of waterproof panel board. All the reference marks you made during deconstruction must be transferred to the new panel. A sharp pencil gives you the most accurate results.*

AUTOMOTIVE UPHOLSTERY AND INTERIOR RESTORATION

CHAPTER 3

2 *Accurate measurements are made to ensure the correct position of the door panel mounting nails. The panel nail must rest 5/16 inch from the edge of the door panel. Take the time to get this right or the panel will be difficult to fit.*

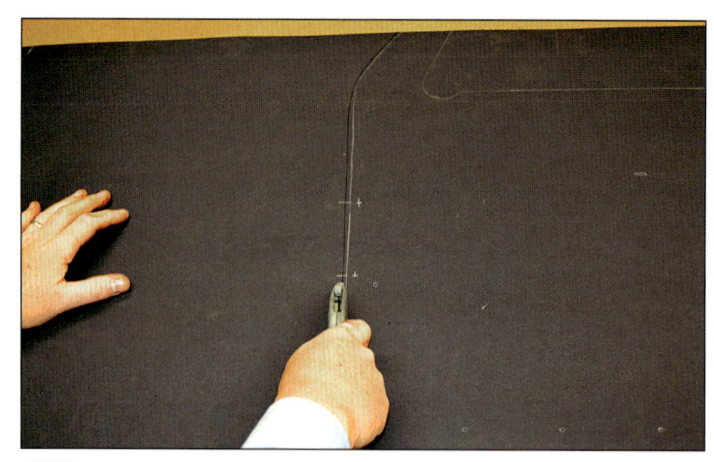

3 *The traced panel board blank is first rough cut from the sheet of waterproof panel board and then trimmed to the exact size. It may take a little longer to work this way, but the result is a better cut edge and a panel that fits perfectly.*

4 *A punch is used to open the access points for the stainless trim pins and other mounting holes. These holes are necessary to allow the fragile pins of the trim to pass through the heavy panel board. Prepunching the holes makes assembly go faster.*

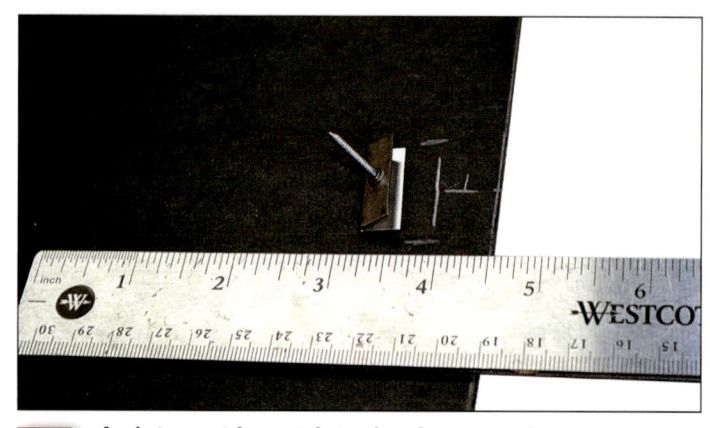

5 *A slot must be cut into the door panel to accommodate the new panel fasteners. A new vertical line is made 1/2 inch from the reference mark that was made during the layout. This new line becomes the new opening for the nail fastener.*

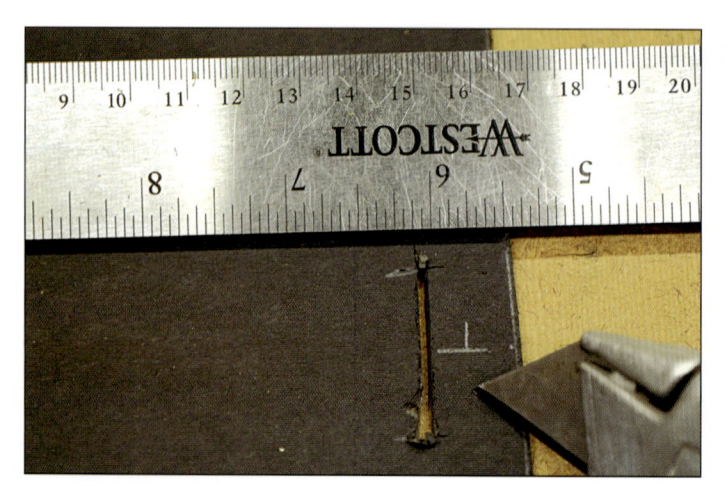

6 *By cutting along both sides of the vertical line, a slot is made in the door panel base. When the metal base of the panel fastener is inserted into the slot, the nail of the fastener is in the exact position it must be so that it mates with the receiver on the door.*

72 AUTOMOTIVE UPHOLSTERY AND INTERIOR RESTORATION

DOOR PANELS

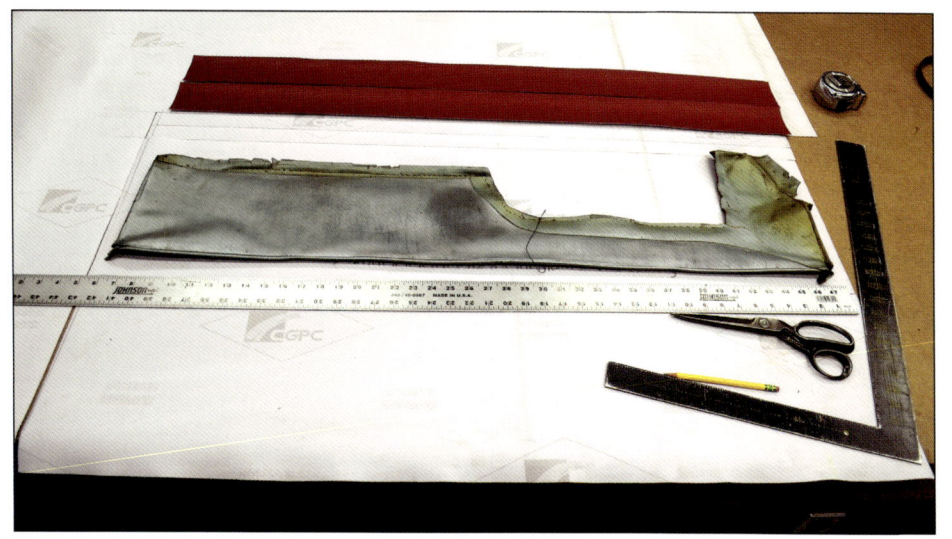

7 The old panels are measured for size and new vinyl pieces are cut to cover the door panel. It is important to watch the orientation, or direction, that the stretch of the vinyl flows. These panels require the stretch to move up and down.

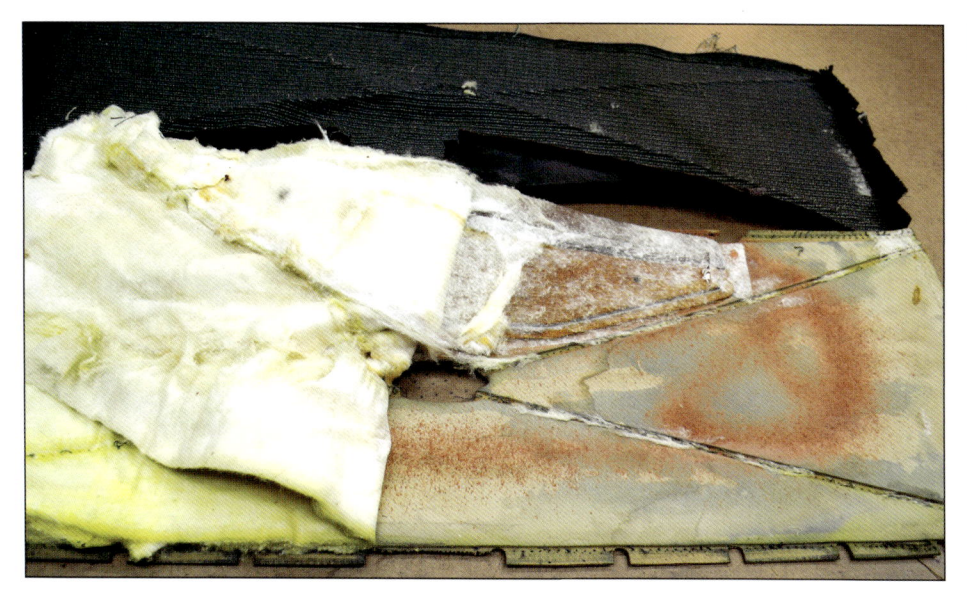

8 The armrest is built into the center section of this door panel. The material is sewn in place to help it contour to the armrest form. Cut the thread to remove the fabric and cotton padding, giving you access to the base panel material.

9 The metal armrest form is attached to the base panel with industrial staples. The staples must be removed from the armrest to free it from the base panel. The legs of the staples are straightened with pliers and then removed.

AUTOMOTIVE UPHOLSTERY AND INTERIOR RESTORATION

CHAPTER 3

10 *Before the cover material is cut apart for use as a pattern, the sewn panels are marked with reference points to aid in the reassembly process. A razor blade is used to carefully cut the stitching that holds the armrest panels together.*

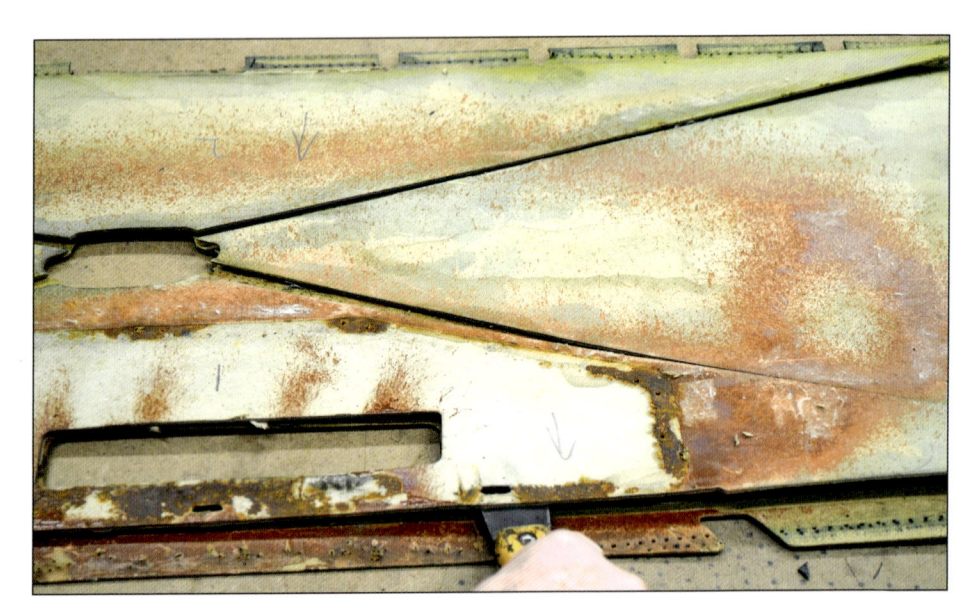

11 *Removal of the center panel section requires the use of a stiff-blade putty knife. The locations of the panel pieces are marked before they are separated from the base panel. Each piece will be used as a pattern to make the new door panel.*

12 *The center-section panels have been laid out and traced onto a piece of waterproof panel board. A utility knife is used to cut the pieces apart. Additional reference holes and alignment marks are cut into the individual panels.*

AUTOMOTIVE UPHOLSTERY AND INTERIOR RESTORATION

Door Panel Assembly

Glue is sprayed onto the panels and they are aligned into position on the base piece of the center panel. The channel between the pieces allows the thread to be drawn into the panel, making a stronger definition in the fabric. The center of the panel is cut out to allow the Cadillac emblem to be recessed.

The armrest form is attached to the panel with 1/8-inch pop rivets. Set the metal armrest form in place on the center panel. Locate the staple holes in the flange of the metal armrest form and predrill a 1/8-inch hole through the metal flange and into the panel board. Rivet the metal armrest form in place. Use a hammer and dolly to flatten the pop rivet.

Install Foam Underliner

The center of the door panel was originally padded with cotton. Working with cotton is messy and it almost never turns out as smooth and even as it should be. The alternative is to pad the panel with foam-backed headliner material. This gives the same appearance as the cotton, but it is much easier to work with and it yields a perfect result every time.

The headliner material is lightly glued in place and smoothed into position over the metal armrest form and panel board. Glue a second layer of headliner material over the first and trim it to fit.

Make a Cover

Flatten the old armrest top and fabric pieces by steaming them. Now they can be used as a pattern for the new armrest cover. Pattern the top of the armrest in vinyl by tracing the old piece and transferring the witness marks on new vinyl. Add a 1/2-inch seam allowance to the pattern for sewing. Chalk out the fabric piece the same way as the vinyl and cut the pieces out.

To make the new armrest cover, the witness marks are aligned and a regular stitch is used to join the pieces of the armrest. The finger cup section of the new cover is given a cap stitch to help it lie smoothly along the inside of the finger cup area of the armrest. Care is taken to trim the selvedge close to the cap stitches without cutting the thread. This keeps the bulk of material out of the finger cup area, making more room for the insertion of the metal finger cup upon installation of the door panel.

Create a French seam in the vinyl and fabric connection. Back the seam with a piece of upholstery denim or bias-facing tape. Trim the selvedge close to the stitching, but do not cut the thread.

Apply a light coat of glue to the backside of the newly sewn cover and apply the cover to the armrest form. Align the edge so the French seam flows evenly along the outside ridge of the armrest. Brush some glue into the finger grip area and secure the inside finger grip vinyl in place. Brush glue along the top edge of the center panel and secure the top edge of the armrest material. Keep the vinyl tight and smooth over the top of the armrest pad as it is pressed into the glue. Work the material from the center outward until the top is sealed. Glue a small piece of vinyl to the backside of the finger grip area to finish off the top of the armrest.

Chalk the sew lines onto the fabric following the channel in the panel board as a guide. The stitching should be in the channel of the panel board. Place the center panel section under the presser foot of the sewing machine and from the center of the emblem area sew outward with a wide stitch. Repeat this for all four lines.

Now begin finishing the center section by turning the fabric at the bottom edge of the center panel over. Glue the material to the backside of the panel board. Keep the fabric taut and smooth it out evenly working from the center of the panel outward to reduce wrinkles as it is pressed into the glue. Set this section aside and work on the base section.

Make a mark 1/2 inch above the sew line on the bottom of the base panel. Align the vinyl to the index line and sew the vinyl to the bottom and sides of the base panel with a wide stitch. About 1½ inches of vinyl should extend past the edge of the base panel. Later on, the trim panel will hide the sewn edge of the vinyl.

Attach the Cover

Apply the door panel cleat to the bottom edge of the door panel base and secure it in place by cinching the lower edge onto the panel board with pliers to lock it in place.

Cut a strip of felt underliner and glue it to the surface of the panel board. The felt underliner should span the area of the stitching and be trimmed flush with the edge of the door panel.

Brush glue along the bottom edge and lower sides of the door panel and onto the exposed vinyl. Pull the vinyl taut, wrap it around the panel, and press it into the glue. Work the corners keeping the vinyl flat to the backside of the panel; use 3/32-inch staples to secure the vinyl in place while the glue dries. The vinyl along the bottom edge of the panel is secured with glue and it is tucked up and lies flat into the cleat.

Now take the center panel section and set it in place on the base panel. Turn the door panel face down on the workbench and align the armrest bracket hole and metal armrest form pins to the corresponding holes in the base panel. Bend the metal pins downward and hammer them flat. This secures the armrest form to the base panel.

Brush glue along the outside edges of the door panel, wrap the fabric around, and press it into the glue. Check that the fabric is smooth and tight along the panel and make any adjustments necessary.

The upper vinyl panel is prepped for installation by sewing a 4/32-inch welt cord and a paper tacking strip to the lower edge of the material. The welt conceals the transition of the armrest to the upper panel while the tack strip creates a sharp transitional line.

With the door panel facing up, center the upper vinyl panel in place along the top edge of the center panel. To secure this panel it is stapled along the edge with 9/16-inch wire staples. The panel must be moved to the edge of the workbench to prevent the staples from going into the surface of the workbench. The staples are bent over on the backside of the panel to lock the assembly in place.

Place the welt cord as close to the top of the armrest as possible, and from the center point outward staple it in place along with the tack strip. Keep the welt cord straight and apply a little tension to the welt as you work your way to the edge of the panel. After the stapling is complete, turn the door panel over and bend the legs of the staples over with the tack hammer. Cover the staples with a piece of Gorilla Tape.

Pad the Upper Panel Section

Instead of cotton, additional pieces of foam-backed headliner material are used as padding on the upper panel section. The vinyl cover material is pulled over the top of the headliner material and then sewn along the top edge with a wide stitch to hold it in place. Glue is now applied to the outside edges on the backside of the panel board base. The edges of the vinyl panel can now be turned and pressed into the glue.

Apply Emblems and Trim

The center of the door panel is adorned with a chromed Cadillac emblem. The mounting holes for the Cadillac emblem are located with a regulator and enlarged to accommodate the mounting studs of the emblem. The emblem is applied to the door panel with the mounting studs of the emblem pushed through the fabric and exposed on the backside of the panel. Push nuts are used to hold the emblem in place. A block of wood is placed under the emblem and the push nuts are gently tapped in place with a small socket and hammer. Do not hammer too hard or you can cause damage to the emblem.

The lower trim panel protects the door from scuffs and abrasions when the passengers step out of the car. Use the regulator to locate the through-holes for the trim mounting pins. Align the panel in place and then apply the upper and lower moldings by pushing the pins through the panel. With the door panel facing down, support the trim as you gently bend the pins over with a tack hammer. Be careful as you secure the stainless trim to the door that you do not break the pins.

The door panel in now complete and other than the color change it looks just like the factory original. Be sure to clean any chalk marks off the surface and give it a quick steam to ease any stress marks from assembly.

Assembling a Door Panel

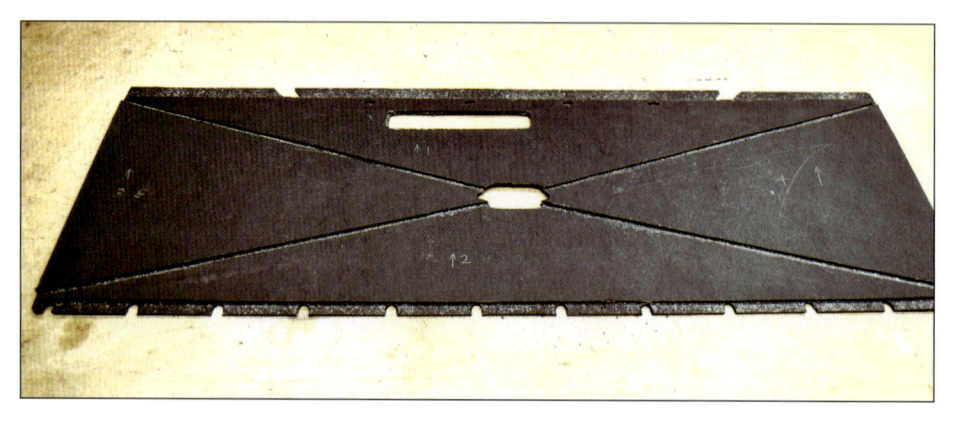

1 *Four center panel pieces are carefully aligned onto the base panel. The panel pieces are then glued to the base panel to create a composite panel with relief channels that allow for the sewing of the new cover material.*

DOOR PANELS

2 The 1/8-inch holes are drilled into the flange of the metal armrest form after it has been set in place on the composite panel. Aluminum pop rivets are used to secure the metal armrest form to the panel board permanently.

3 The center panel is now ready for the padding material. Two layers of foam-backed headliner material are glued lightly to the metal armrest form and trimmed to fit the panel. This provides the same appearance and feel to the panel that the cotton did.

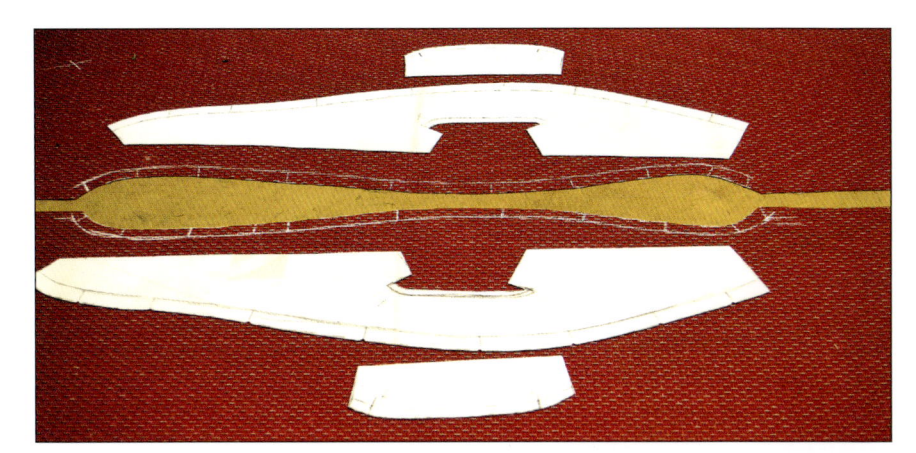

4 The pattern to make the new armrest panels comes from steaming the old panels flat. New armrest panels are then created by transferring the design and witness marks of the old panel pieces onto the new vinyl and fabric.

5 The armrest panels are sewn together by aligning the witness marks and sewing along the seam lines. A cap stitch is used to define the finger cup area of the armrest. Excess material is trimmed from the selvedge of the seam to reduce bulk when the new armrest cover is installed.

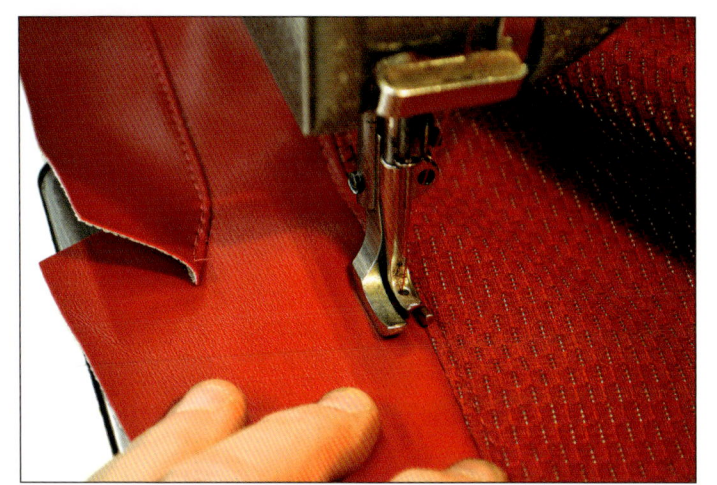

6 The outside edge of the armrest is given a decorative French seam. The French seam is made with a thin, bias backing tape, which gives the seam extra strength and also eliminates bulk, allowing the armrest cover to wrap around the armrest form smoothly.

AUTOMOTIVE UPHOLSTERY AND INTERIOR RESTORATION

CHAPTER 3

7 The armrest cover is given decorative stitches to help the cover material contour with the built-in armrest. Guidelines are chalked onto the fabric to aid the sewing process. Wide, even stitches are used to prevent tear out of the panel board below.

8 The lower edge of the center panel is finished by turning the fabric under and securing the material to the backside of the panel board with glue. The material is worked from the center outward to eliminate wrinkles. The upper edge of the armrest is finished in the same manner.

9 Oversize strips of vinyl are sewn in place along the bottom and then the sides of the door panel blank. These strips eventually wrap the bottom edges of the door panel. The sewn edges of the vinyl are covered with the stainless trim.

10 The metal cleat is fitted to the bottom of the door panel and cinched in place by crimping the lower edge with pliers. A felt underliner is placed under the vinyl and trimmed flush to the edge of the panel board before the vinyl is pulled over the edge and secured with glue and staples.

11 The center panel section has been aligned into position and the mounting tabs of the metal armrest form are extended through the base panel. The metal tabs are bent over with the aid of a tack hammer to secure the armrest to the base panel.

AUTOMOTIVE UPHOLSTERY AND INTERIOR RESTORATION

12 The vinyl that is applied to the upper portion of the door panel needs a welt cord and a tacking strip sewn in to finish the lower edge of the vinyl panel. This gives the seam a tight, finished appearance when the panel is assembled.

13 Staples are used along the inside edge to attach the upper vinyl panel to the door panel. A tack strip helps keep the welt cord straight because it creates a nice, sharp transitional line at the seam between the armrest and upper panel.

14 A layer of foam padding is placed under the upper vinyl panel before it is pulled and sewn to the top edge of the door panel base. Turning the vinyl over the edge of the panel and securing it with glue finishes the sides of the panel.

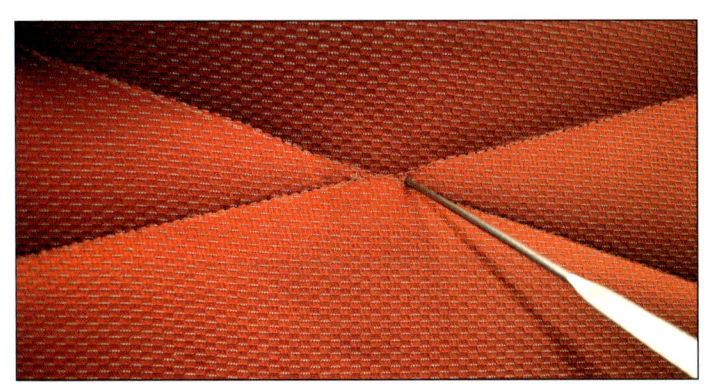

15 Locate the mounting holes for the center medallion by piercing the fabric with a regulator. The holes in the fabric are enlarged to allow the mounting studs of the medallion to pass through and emerge on the backside of the door panel.

16 The medallion is secured on the backside of the door panel with push nuts. A small socket is used to help seat the push nut onto the exposed stud of the medallion. Gentle blows with a tack hammer set the push nut firmly in place.

AUTOMOTIVE UPHOLSTERY AND INTERIOR RESTORATION

CHAPTER 3

17 Holes have been pierced in the material to allow the mounting pins of the stainless trim to reach the backside of the panel board. A tack hammer is used to gently bend the pins flat against the panel board, locking them in place.

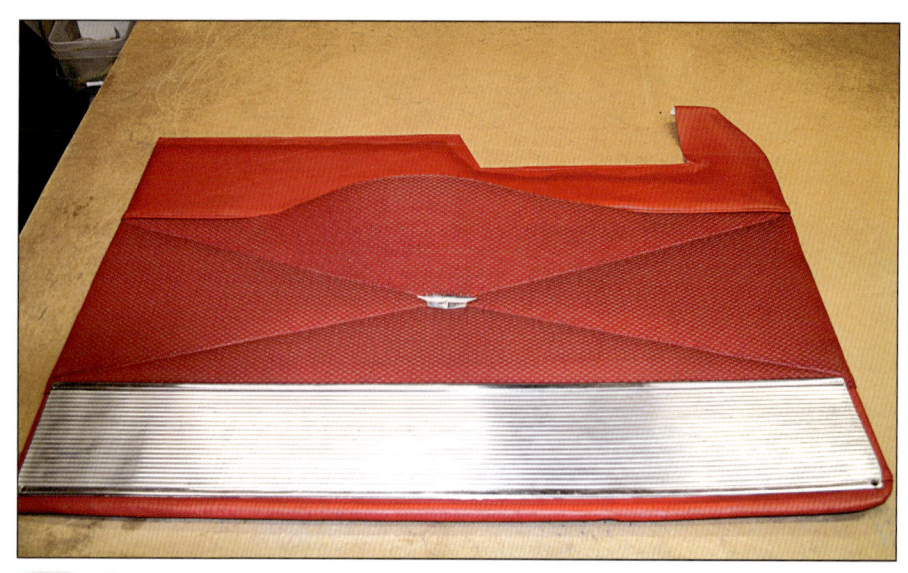

18 The new door panel assembly is complete. This reproduction has all the detail of the original and it looks as if it could have rolled out of Detroit in 1952. The red color fits right in with the new paint job.

Door Panel Installation

Each manufacturer used different methods and fasteners to attach the door panels to the car door. The early wood-framed cars attached the door panels with brad nails. The nail was driven through the surface material covering the panel and into the wood of the doorframe to hold the cardboard panel in place. The material that covered the panel was then "popped" over the small head of the nail to conceal it.

When all-metal-bodied cars were produced, Ford and Chrysler used a wire-style spring clip along the outside edge of the door panel. The spring fastener was clipped to the door panel and the taper end of the fastener was then inserted into a hole in the door. The clip expanded and held the panel in place.

A small ring shaft nail welded to a metal edge band was commonplace for cars made by General Motors. These fasteners were small and unobtrusive; they often failed by rusting or just breaking off due to their frail nature. By the mid-1960s General Motors had adopted the use of a spring clip fastener.

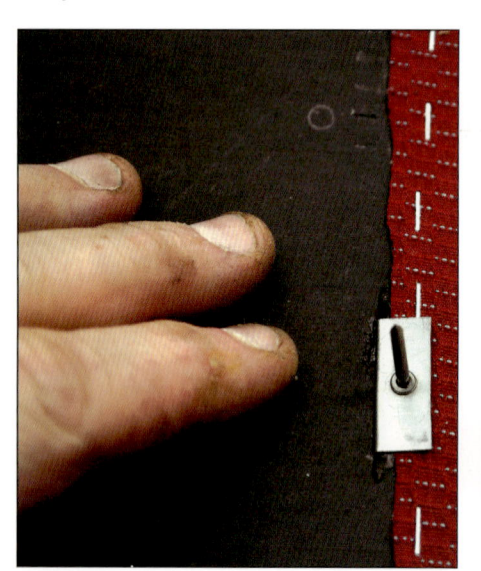

Before the door panel can be installed, the panel fastener nails need to be installed. They simply slide into the slot at the edge of the panel and crimped in place. Be careful when handling the door panel because the nails are sharp and can cause damage.

The door panel is fit into position on the car. The nails should all line up with the receivers on the door. Working from the bottom upward, a soft rubber mallet is used to tap the nails into the receivers until the door panel rests flush against the door.

80 AUTOMOTIVE UPHOLSTERY AND INTERIOR RESTORATION

Manufacturers also used small trim screws along the bottom edge of the door to help keep the panel from being kicked loose. General Motors often used a metal cleat to secure the center of the panel and only used trim screws in the lower corners of the door panel.

You spent a lot of time measuring to get the placement of the panel nails correct and now it is show time. The replacement nail fasteners are slid into the slots at the edges of the door panel. Flatten the metal base of the fastener to conform it to the panel board. This locks it in place. Do not bend the nail when flattening the fastener.

The nails are sharp and cause damage to paint and upholstered surfaces. Care must be taken when handling the door panel after the nail fasteners have been installed.

The door panel is positioned on the door and the cleat is placed over the tab or slot in the door and pushed down to seat the panel. Check the alignment of the door panel along the edges. The door panel should be flush with the sheet metal.

Look at the nail fasteners to see that they are in the correct position to go into the receiver on the door. Start at the bottom of the door panel; align the point of the nail in the receiver and gently tap it into place with a rubber mallet. Continue up both sides of the door until all the fasteners are fully seated.

Install the finger cups and secure them with the correct size trim screw. Connect any electrical wires to the power accessories before installing the metal cap molding on the door. Use a regulator to find the screw holes and fasten the cap molding to the door.

Place the escutcheons over the regulator post before installing the door and window crank handles. Make sure that the retainer clip is installed in the crank handle before pushing it onto the regulator post.

Inspect your work and clean up any fingerprints and smudges made during the door panel installation.

Creating a Door Panel Without a Pattern

What if the project you are working on does not have any door panels to copy? This scenario is par for the restoration trade because working from severely damaged components and dealing with missing parts is all too common. This is the reason you have to rely on archived images for reference to guide you to create the new door panels. The process of creating a new door panel from nothing is basic and can be accomplished with a little research and determination.

It is usually necessary to remove all the hardware associated with the door operation before the door panel can be removed. If you do not have a door panel, chances are you may have only a door handle to remove. Check the door for any remnants of screws or panel clips that were left behind and remove them. Once the interior surface of the door is clear the layout process can begin.

This project is to make new original-style door panels for a 1950 Cadillac Coupe de Ville. The problem is that my customer does not have the original door panels for a pattern. This may seem like a difficult task, but by taking measurements and doing a little research you will be able to reproduce an original design. ■

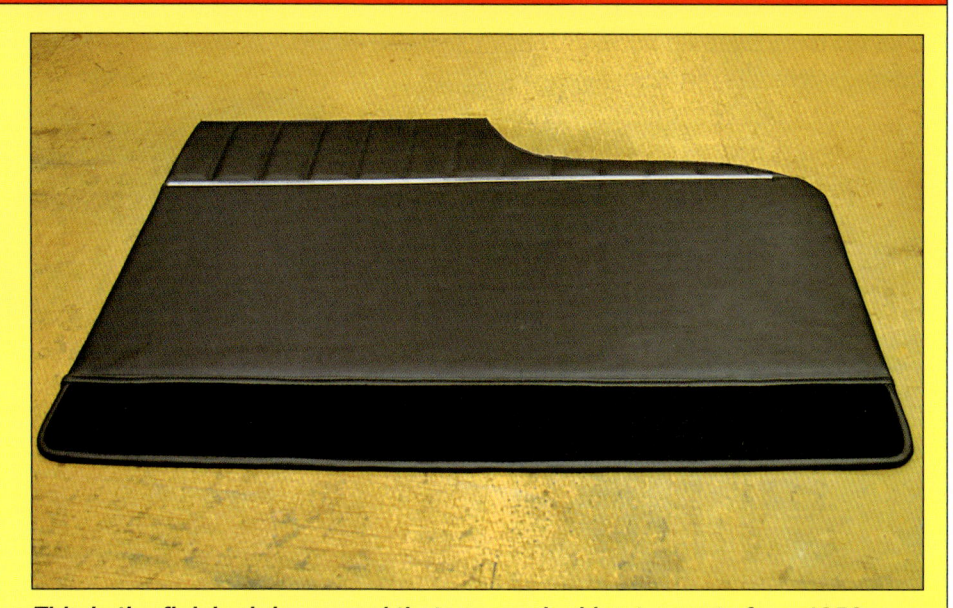

This is the finished door panel that you are looking to create for a 1950 Cadillac Coupe de Ville that had no door panels at all. By referencing archive images, I re-created an original-style door panel from basic modern upholstery materials.

AUTOMOTIVE UPHOLSTERY AND INTERIOR RESTORATION

CHAPTER 3

Creating a Door Panel Without a Pattern CONTINUED

Measuring for Panel Creation

1 *Measure the door in both directions to gather rough measurements of the door. These measurements are then transferred to a new sheet of waterproof panel board. The new panel blank is cut 1 inch oversize, allowing the exact profile of the door to be transferred.*

2 *Through-holes are needed in the panel blank so that it can lie flat against the door. A hammer is used to make an index mark by tapping over the window regulator and door release posts. A hole is then punched into the panel.*

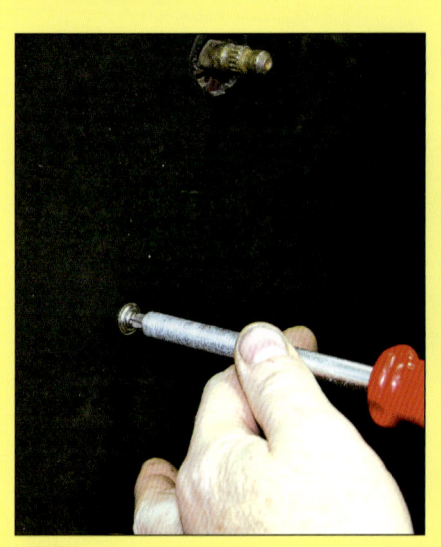

3 *To get an accurate tracing of the door profile the panel blank is attached to the door with two trim screws. The screws hold the panel blank to the door in the correct position so features can be added. This ensures that the door panel has a perfect fit.*

4 *A short pencil is used to carefully trace around the outside profile of the door. The small size of the pencil allows access to tight places that a longer pencil cannot reach. The panel is trimmed along the line that was just traced to reveal the new door panel.*

5 *The top of the door panel is defined by tracing along the bottom profile of the door cap molding. This line provides a reference point of where the top of the panel blank needs to be. An extra 3/4 inch is added above the line before trimming.*

AUTOMOTIVE UPHOLSTERY AND INTERIOR RESTORATION

DOOR PANELS

6 A relief mark is added to the outside edges of the panel. This reduces the size of the panel by 3/16 inch, allowing the cover material to wrap over the edge of the panel board without causing the door to bind when it is opened and closed.

7 The locations of the armrest mounting holes are measured and transferred to the new door panel. Through-holes are cut in the new door panel with a 1/2-inch hole punch. These access holes make the attachment of the armrest hardware easier.

8 Before the door panel can be attached to the door it must be fitted with panel clips. The positioning of the panel clip locations is done quickly with a special template so that each panel clip can be marked accurately without measuring.

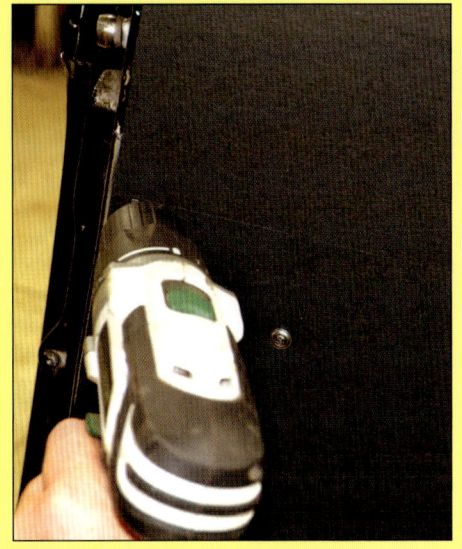

9 The index mark from the template is transferred to the door by drilling through the panel board and into the metal door with a 1/8-inch drill bit. This pilot hole in the door will be enlarged later to 3/8 inch to accommodate the door panel clip.

10 The bottom of the door panel must be fastened in place securely. Trim screws with recessed washers are used along the bottom of the door panel. The corner screw locations are measured equidistant from the lower edges of the door panel.

AUTOMOTIVE UPHOLSTERY AND INTERIOR RESTORATION

Creating a Door Panel Without a Pattern CONTINUED

11 Five trim screws are used along the bottom edge of the door panel. Equal spacing is achieved by dividing the distance between the end screws in half to find the center. The new divisions are divided in half again to create equal distances between the screws.

12 A design line separates the door panel into sections. The upper design line is established by using a straightedge to extend the height of the rear armrest forward. The design line helps determine the position of the new upholstery on the panel.

13 The lower design line originates at the top of the rear seat riser and wraps around the lower portion of the interior. The line is marked onto the bottom of the door panel to establish the height of the carpet that is added to the bottom edge of the door panel.

14 The index holes made along the edges of the door are enlarged to 3/8 inch with a modified drill bit. A wire door panel clip is inserted into the larger holes and holds the door panel tightly in place.

Planning and Layout

After spending a little time on the Internet, I found an archived photo of an original 1950 Cadillac Coupe de Ville door panel, and just from looking at the photo I knew that I could replicate the design and make a new door panel. From past experience I know that the new door panels are constructed from waterproof panel board, vinyl with the period-correct grain pattern, and loop carpet on the bottom kick area of the door panel to finish.

Prep the Panel Board

The base of the door panel is made from waterproof panel board. This is a high-density paper product that is about 1/8 inch thick and designed specifically for automotive panel construction because of its ridged nature and ability to hold up under extreme weather conditions. The raw panel board sheet measures 32 inches by 48 inches. It must be cut down to within 1 inch larger than the door so that it is easier to work with. Start by measuring across the door and from top to bottom to get a rough size to cut the new panel. Transfer these dimensions to the sheet of panel board and cut the new panel with a utility knife.

To get the panel blank ready for tracing, you need to mount it to the door. For a consistent and accurate tracing, the blank needs to lie flat against the door by allowing the window and door handle regulator studs through the panel. To index the location for the through-holes the panel blank is held in place over the door with an even margin around the edges. A hammer is used to tap on the panel blank directly over the posts to leave an index mark. Remove the panel blank and take it to the workbench. Here you use a 1-inch hole punch to make the through-holes for the posts.

Trace and Drill

Now the panel blank can be secured flat to the door for tracing. To do this the panel blank is attached to the door with two trim screws. You predrill a 1/8-inch hole through the panel blank near the centerline and about 4 inches in from the left and right edges. Before you start drilling, the window should be in the up position to prevent accidental damage to the glass from the drill bit. Position the panel blank over the window and door regulator posts; locate a solid place to drill. Carefully drill the first hole and then use a 1/2-inch trim screw to secure the panel blank to the door. Do the same for the other side of the panel.

With the panel blank securely in place the tracing of the door profile can begin. I like to use a short, stubby pencil for this task. A long pencil will not be able to get into the tight places along the front of the door. Sharpen the pencil to a nice point and run it around the outside edge of the door as close to the metal as you can get. After you have finished tracing the profile of the door, remove the trim screws, get the panel blank up on the bench, and cut along the trace line to free the new panel from the blank.

Check the Fit

Re-fit the panel to the door and secure it with the two trim screws. Check for size and make any adjustments necessary to fine-tune the fit. Install the metal door cap molding to the top of the door and trace the profile along the bottom of the molding onto the panel. Remove the cap molding, trim screws, and the new panel; trim the top of the new panel to within 3/4 inch of the door cap line. Reinstall the new panel and metal door cap and check the fit. Make any adjustments necessary so that there is no binding or puckering under the door cap when you are finalizing the rough patterning of the new door panel.

Remove the door cap, trim screws, and the new panel from the door; set the new panel up on the bench. After all the fitting and trimming of the new door panel it still must be relieved before the new covering material can be applied. It is necessary to cut back the side and bottom edges of the new panel by 3/16 inch to accommodate the new upholstery material. If you do not do the relief cut, the panel becomes oversize when it is covered and this puts the new upholstery in jeopardy of damage from binding with the door latch and body panels.

Prepunch for Armrests

Thinking ahead, you need to mount the armrest on the door. Accessing the armrest bracket mounting holes that are in the door through the finished upholstery is not easy when you have a 1/8-inch panel board to get through. The best way to access the holes is to prepunch through the panel board prior to adding the upholstery. To determine the location for these armrest bracket holes simply measure across the door from one side and up from the bottom, transfer these dimensions to the new panel, and mark them accordingly. Cut the holes in the new panel with a 1/2-inch hole punch and then use the two trim screws to secure the panel to the door.

Install Fasteners

The original panel fasteners used on this vintage of GM cars were

CHAPTER 3

> ### Create a Template
>
> Using this template saves you measuring time when laying out the placement of each panel clip. You can make your own template out of a 2 x 1¾–inch piece of scrap panel board and punching the holes in it at the correct dimensions. The wire panel clip that this template works for has an offset of 1/2 inch from the front of the clip base to the center of the clip hole that is drilled into the door. The clip hole is 3/8 inch and the clip index hole is 1/8 inch. The clip hole is enlarged to 3/8 inch in the door after the layout is complete. I usually make four or five of these templates at a time because they tend to get lost or swept up, as they tend to look just like a scrap piece of panel board. Go figure.
>
> **Panel Clip Template** — 1/2", 1/2", 1", 1 3/4", Panel Edge, 1/8", 3/8"
>
> Make template from scrap piece of panel board. Cut to size and punch holes as indicated.
>
> *The panel clip template saves time and makes layout simple.*

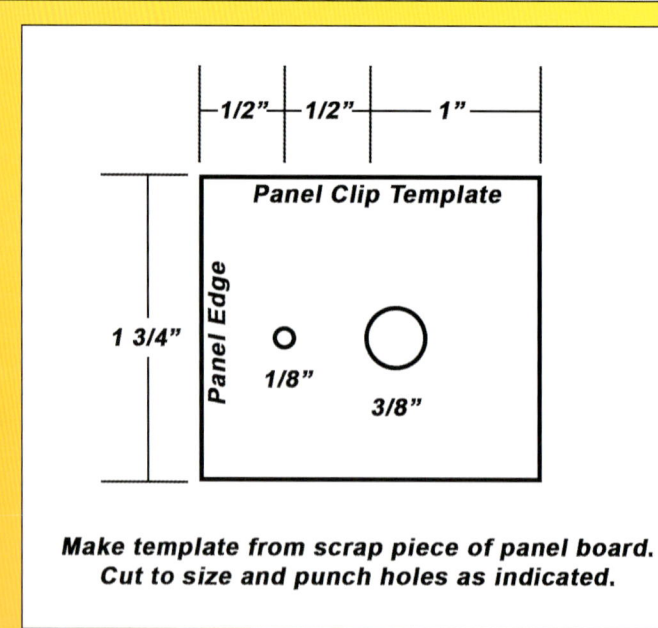

panel nail fasteners that were spot welded to a metal band that edged the door panel. This type of fastener was prone to breaking off due to its size and weak nature. For this project you use the more reliable wire fastener clips to attach the new panel. This requires drilling a hole into the door to accept the fastener. Four or five panel clips are needed on each edge to securely hold the door panel in place. Each fastener is measured and marked before the fastener can be installed. To save time a special template is used to mark the position of the fasteners. This speeds the time it takes to measure each fastener position and it accurately replicates the clip position for the fasteners. During the layout and marking of the clip positions, it is important that the panel clips are clear of the hinges and door latch mechanism.

Drill Index Holes

After the fastener positions have been marked on the new door panel, drill all the 1/8-inch index holes for the panel clips through the new panel and into the metal door below. This index hole in the metal door will later be enlarged to 3/8 inch to be able to receive a wire panel clip.

Secure Panel Bottom

The bottom of the door panel always gets a lot of abuse from being kicked open and the use of panel clips in this location is not advised because they cannot take the rough service. Originally the door panel was held to the bottom of the door with a metal cleat along with a screw in each lower corner. You are not going to attach the door panel this way. Therefore, to secure the door panel at the bottom you use five #8 oval head screws and recess washers.

To accurately establish the panel base screw height, you measure up from the bottom of the door and in from the side 1¼ inches and mark the corner screw position. Do the same for the other corner. With the corner screw positions determined you can now measure for the location of the remainder of the bottom panel screws. To find the center screw position divide the distance between the corner screws in half and make a mark. Now divide the distance between the center and each corner mark in half again and now you should have five symmetrical marks along the bottom of the new panel. Cut these marks into the panel using a 1/8-inch hole punch. Reattach the new panel to the door with the two trim screws and drill through the newly punched bottom panel holes with a 1/8-inch drill bit for the panel anchor screws.

Establish the Design Line

From predetermined points the design lines of the Cadillac flow horizontally around the cab and define the separations in the upholstery. The upper design line is established from the top of the rear armrest and the lower line is extended from the height of the rear seat riser. Close the door, and using a straightedge ruler, extend the upper design line from the top of the rear armrest onto the new door panel. Make sure that the line is continuous and level from the rear panel edge to rear edge on the new panel by using a small spirit level.

Repeat this process with the lower design line by running a line onto the new panel from the upper edge of the rear seat riser. When you make this line on the new panel it may not measure exactly parallel to the upper design line. This is acceptable as long as it visually looks like it does. The center section and lower carpet sections tend to be taller at the front edge of the panel. The shape of the door causes this variation.

You should now have a new base door panel with all the attachment points and design lines marked and punched. Since the car you are working on has two doors, you have to make another panel. The second one is much quicker to produce because it is a mirror image of the first panel.

Make the Other Panel

To get started, remove the two trim screws and the panel from the door, flip it over, align it within the other door, and observe equal margins all around the panel. Drill your two attaching screw holes and attach it to the door with the trim screws. Now check the panel for fit. It should be the same as the other door. If there are any differences in the doors, do not modify the first panel. Use chalk to mark the variations and create a new panel with the changes. Make sure the design lines are added and line up correctly.

When you are satisfied with the fit of the door panel use a 1/8-inch drill bit and drill all the index and lower anchor holes into the door; then remove the door panel.

To get the wire panel fasteners to fit into the door, the 1/8-inch index holes you drilled earlier along the outside edges of the door need to be enlarged to 3/8 inch. To avoid damage to the door skin, a 3/8-inch drill bit is modified with a depth stop. The depth stop can be added by simply wrapping the shaft of the drill bit with duct tape so that the tape is almost 1/2 inch thick in diameter with about 1/2 inch of drill bit exposed. This prevents the drill bit from going too deep and accidentally causing damage to the door skin.

Chuck up the modified drill bit and enlarge the index holes on the edges of the doors. Do not enlarge the five anchor holes at the bottom of the doors.

Trace a copy of the first panel to make the second door panel. Mark all the locations of the holes and any changes needed onto a new piece of panel board. Cut the panel out and punch the holes for the door panel fasteners. Marking the index holes is not necessary because they have already been drilled in the door. Clearly mark the backside of this second panel with an "X" to indicate that it is the opposite of the first panel.

Panel Construction

With all the layout and design work completed, work on the upholstery of the new panel can begin. A potential problem is that the multiple layers of material at the seams of the panel sections will cause a bulge at the edge of the door panel. To prevent the bulge from occurring, the panel board is notched and relieved by 3/16 inch at the design line to allow for the excess thickness of the cover material.

Now the 3/8-inch hole for the wire panel fasteners must be punched into the panel board. Using a 3/8-inch hole punch make all of the wire clip holes in the new panel. Do not enlarge the 1/8-inch index holes in the new panel as they were only for making the reference holes in the metal door.

Source the Stainless Trim

Nothing sets off a door panel like a shiny piece of stainless-steel trim. Most door panels made use of the trim to conceal the line separating the upper and lower panel materials. Missing original trim pieces can be hard to locate and cost a small ransom. Parts yards and swap meets are a great place to find trim if you know what you're looking for. Searching for stainless on the Internet is also an option. You just have to take your chances that the seller is honest and you get what you pay for. New generic trim pieces are also available from some hot rod shops, and they can also make you custom pieces, but that can get expensive, too. It is always good to plan ahead and pick up what you can for the project you are working on.

Fix the Trim

Age takes a toll on stainless steel trim. It becomes dull and the mounting pins used to hold the trim onto the panels generally break off or rust away. Using a flat-jaw pliers carefully straighten the pins on the backside of the stainless trim. Broken or missing pins can be replaced by fabricating new pins from 22-gauge sheet metal. The new pins can be bonded to the backside of the stainless trim piece with an epoxy adhesive.

The stainless should lie flat when it is applied to the upholstered panel. If it has been kinked or dented you may need to take it to a professional polishing shop for repair to get it back to its original condition. Deep scratches can also be removed by the polishing shop, but do your research and find one that is reputable and can get your parts done without damaging or losing them. Stainless trim that is in good condition can be brightened up using #0000 steel wool to give it a fresh shine.

The pins on the stainless trim can be damaged quite easily while trying to install the trim on the door panel. To make the installation of the stainless trim less stressful it is recommended to prepunch the mounting holes in the door panel base. To do this just lay the stainless trim on the panel in the place that it will be applied and mark the panel where the attachment pins will go through the panel board. Cut through-holes in the new panel with an appropriately sized hole punch and test fit the stainless trim. Do not bend the pins over at this time.

Install Felt Underliner

Our door panel design is transferred to a felt underliner that has been cut to 1 inch larger than the panel base. By drawing directly on the felt underliner you know precisely where the components are going to line up. This panel is covered in black vinyl and divided into three sections. The upper part of the panel is made of 2½-inch sewn vertical pleats and the middle section is solid with no design. Loop carpet is applied to the lower kick section of the new panel.

Cut the upper panel vinyl with 2 inches of extra material at the top and the sides with a 1/2-inch seam allowance on the bottom. This section is pleated using 1/4-inch sew foam as a filler to make the pleats stand out. The foam is glued to the felt underliner at the design line. With the 1/2-inch seam allowance below the design line, the vinyl is lightly glued to the top of the foam to help hold it in place. Sew lines are chalked onto the vinyl every 2⅜ inches. The extra 1/8 inch is taken up by the thickness of the foam, making a finished pleat of 2½ inches.

Cut the middle section vinyl to size allowing 2 inches of extra material at each end with a 1/2-inch seam allowance along the top and bottom of the panel. Align the vinyl panel face to face with the pleated upper section and sew the two sections together at the design line above the 1/2-inch seam allowance. This line should be sewn perfectly straight to avoid detection under the stainless trim that will eventually cover it. Glue the felt underliner to the door panel base with the sew line directly over the design line on the door panel.

With the felt underliner properly aligned and secured to the panel base, lift back the middle section vinyl material to expose the felt underliner and lightly glue 1/4-inch sew foam directly below the seam allowance; then trim the bottom of the sew foam to the lower design line. To avoid accidentally getting glue on the face of the sew foam, carefully brush contact cement onto the bottom section of the panel base, below the foam. Cover the sew foam with the middle section of vinyl and press it into the exposed glue to secure it in place.

Install Panel Carpeting

The bottom section of the door panel is covered with the period-correct loop carpet. To get a perfect fit for the carpet I start with a piece of carpet that is oversize and I trim the top edge straight to get a tight fit against the middle section of the panel. The carpet is then temporarily stapled in position flush with the lower design line. Carefully turn the door panel over on its face and trim the carpet back to the edge of the panel base. Turn the panel face up and remove the staples. Be very careful when you remove the staples because they are sharp.

The newly cut carpet section must be bound to hide its raw edge. This gives the carpet a finished look. Using the same vinyl that you used on the upper sections of the panel, cut a 2-inch strip long enough to reach around the outside edge of the carpet and then sew it face down on the top of the outside edge of the carpet with a seam allowance of 3/8 inch. Cut another 2-inch strip of vinyl long enough to bind the top edge of the carpet in the same way as the outside edge.

Before the carpet can be attached to the bottom of the door panel the raw edge at the top of the carpet must be finished. Roll the vinyl binding over the top edge of the carpet to create a smooth band across the top of the carpet and secure it by blind stitching, or sewing "in the ditch." Sew as close to the vinyl as possible without the thread showing. The top binding must be clear of any visible stitching at this point. Glue the bound carpet to the new panel bottom taking care to line up the outside edges. The top binding should be flush with the lower design line and fit flush to the bottom of the middle section foam.

You finish attaching the carpet by sewing the upper bound edge of the carpet directly to the door panel base. Place the door panel under the sewing machine and use a wide stitch along the top edge of the upper binding with a reveal of 1/8 inch. This decorative stitch holds the top of the carpet to the door panel.

Finish the Panel

Turn the door panel face down on the bench and trim back the felt underliner to the outside edges of the panel base. Finish the top of the door panel by sewing across the edge to secure the material to the panel board. With the door panel face down under the sewing machine, give the material a slight pull as you sew across the top edge. Keep the stitching within 1/8 inch from the top edge of the panel. Check that the pleated cover material is lying flat and not bunching up as it is sewn. Trim the overhanging material flush with the edge of the panel. Apply glue to the vertical edges of the panel base and the vinyl. Evenly fold the vinyl over the edge and press it into the glue. Use short staples if necessary to hold the material in place until the glue sets. The carpet binding is also glued to the backside of the panel the same way as the door panel edges. This finishes the raw carpet edge and holds the carpet to the door panel.

After the edges are turned and fastened you can turn your attention to applying the stainless trim to the door panel. The holes for the trim pins must be opened and the regulator is the perfect tool for indexing the trim mounting holes. From the backside of the door panel, carefully pierce a hole through the door panel cover. Opening the trim holes helps you install the stainless trim without losing any pins.

Apply the Trim

Flip the door panel over, and working from the front, locate the through-holes for the stainless trim molding by poking a regulator through the trim-mounting hole from the front side of the panel to enlarge the hole. Take the time to line up the pins with the through-holes and then push them into the door panel. If you have trouble getting a pin through the cover material, use the regulator to clear a path for the pin. Do not force the trim into a hole as it will surely break.

With the stainless trim inserted into the door panel it can be carefully flipped over and placed face down on the bench with the stainless trim solidly resting on the surface of the bench. The stainless trim pins can now be bent over with the aid of a tack hammer. Use a gentle touch when tapping on the pins so they do not break off.

Install Wire Panel Clips

Our door panel is almost complete. The last things that you need to install on the door panel are the wire panel clips. The clips are inserted into the clip holes and slid forward to lock in place. The panel clips are sharp and can scratch paint and cause other damage to whatever they may come in contact with so be advised and be careful once the panel clips are installed in the door panel. I also recommend the door panels stay face to face before they are installed. This protects them from unforeseen damage.

Constructing a Panel

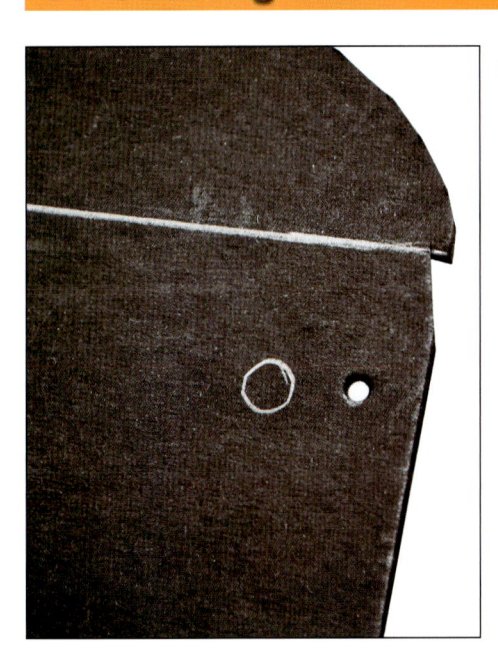

1 Before the cover material can be applied to the door panel base, small relief cuts are made at the design line to prevent an excessive bulge from the cover material seam when material is wrapped over the edge of the panel board.

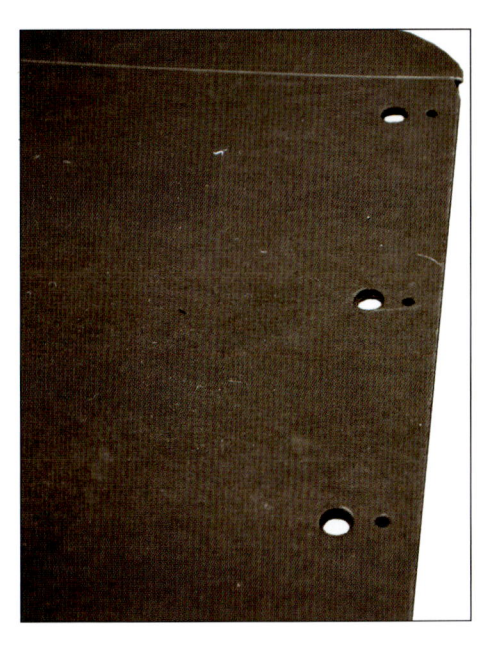

2 Holes have been made in the door panel with a 3/8-inch punch at the corresponding marks made by the panel clip template so the wire panel clips can be fastened to the door panel. The hole you used for indexing the door does not get enlarged.

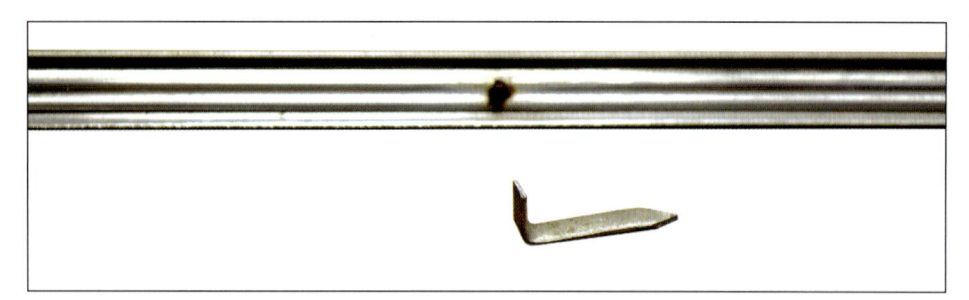

3 It is not uncommon to find stainless in disrepair. The mounting pin on this piece of stainless has rusted away and must be repaired. With some epoxy adhesive and a new pin cut from sheet metal the stainless is like new again.

4 Giving the stainless trim a quick polish with #0000 steel wool helps make it shine and look like new. If your stainless trim has been kinked, dented, or scratched deeply, you might want to take it to a professional polishing shop for repair.

5 The stainless trim is marked and test fitted before covering the panel. The installation of the stainless trim is easier if the holes for the mounting pins are prepunched in the panel board prior to the panel being upholstered.

6 The pattern of the door panel is marked onto an oversize piece of felt underlining. This helps with the sizing of the panel pieces and provides reference lines for the panel pieces as they are sewn onto the underliner.

DOOR PANELS

7 The upper panel has been cut to proper size and a pleated design is chalked onto the vinyl material as a reference for sewing. This panel is then placed over a thin layer of 1/4-inch sew foam that is glued lightly to the felt underlining to prepare it for sewing.

8 The door panel skin is assembled by aligning the precut middle section to the pleated upper section along the upper design line. A 1/2-inch seam allowance is used to sew the panels together. Precision sewing is the key to making the door panel look good.

9 The subassembly was glued to the panel board and foam has been cut to fit the middle section and glued lightly onto the felt underliner. The middle vinyl section is pulled over the foam and glued to the bottom of the door panel.

10 To get a perfect fit an oversize piece of carpet has been stapled in place temporarily at the bottom of the door panel. The carpet is trimmed to the exact size of the panel board. After trimming, the carpet is removed for binding.

AUTOMOTIVE UPHOLSTERY AND INTERIOR RESTORATION

CHAPTER 3

11 A 2-inch strip of vinyl is sewn along the outside raw edge of the carpet panel to give it a finished appearance. The binding seals the lower edge of the door panel. The top edge of the carpet also receives a band of vinyl to finish it.

12 The top edge of the carpet is finished by folding the vinyl binding over the top edge and blind stitching across the face of the carpet as close to the vinyl as possible without any stitches showing. Glue the carpet to the bottom of the panel by aligning the top of the binding to the foam edge of the middle panel.

13 The top edge of the carpet is secured to the door panel by sewing across the top carpet binding with a nice reveal stitch about 1/8 inch from the top edge of the binding. The top stitch not only looks good, it also holds the carpet in place.

14 The binding makes the panel look nice and fastens the carpet to the door panel. Glue has been sprayed along the back edge of the new panel and the binding is folded over into the glue. Short staples are used to help secure the binding in place.

15 The best way to apply the stainless trim to cover the seam line is to first pierce the door panel's cover with a regulator from the backside of the new panel. This allows the fragile pins to get through the thick panel without them breaking off.

92 AUTOMOTIVE UPHOLSTERY AND INTERIOR RESTORATION

DOOR PANELS

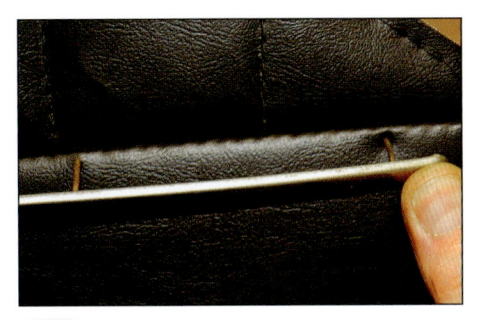

16 *The mounting pins of the stainless trim molding are aligned with the through-holes that were made with the regulator and inserted carefully through the panel. It may be necessary to use the regulator again to open the hole up for easier insertion of the trim pins.*

17 *The door panel has been turned over with the stainless trim supported on the workbench. The pins on the stainless trim are gently bent over by tapping them with a tack hammer. Always be gentle when securing the pins because they are prone to snapping off.*

18 *The wire panel clip has been inserted into the 3/8-inch hole and slid all the way forward to position it for installation. After the panel clips are installed, the new door panel is ready to be installed in the car.*

19 *The new door panel has been installed on the door along with the door cap and handle. A new armrest has been mounted in place. The finished door panel is now ready for service.*

Installation

Position the new panel on the door and align the panel clips into their respective holes. Using a soft rubber mallet, tap the fastener into the door to secure the panel.

Locate the five prepunched holes along the bottom of the door panel and secure them with 3/4-inch #8 oval-head trim screws with recessed washers.

Connect the power window wire connector to the switches and set the door cap in place. Secure the door cap with the correct trim screws. Reinstall the lock button by screwing it onto the lock rod.

Using your finger, feel for the access holes in the panel board that reveal the armrest mounting holes. With the regulator tool, pierce the door panel outer covering and locate the screw hole. Mount the armrest bracket to the door with two #14 pan-head sheet-metal screws. Attach the armrest to the bracket and secure it to the bracket with two 1/2-inch #8 oval-head sheet-metal screws.

Place the door handle escutcheon over the door release actuator post. Insert the spring clip into the door release handle and press the handle onto the release actuator post until it clicks and locks into place. Do the same for the vent window crank.

With the newly created interior panels installed, the interior is looking much like it did when it rolled out of the factory. This is the result of a little research and a lot of effort to create something from nothing.

AUTOMOTIVE UPHOLSTERY AND INTERIOR RESTORATION

CHAPTER 4

ARMRESTS

The earliest car models were limited on accessories and were very utilitarian. Most of the early cars did not have doors or fixed roofs. When doors were added to the body, they were made of wood and steel and did not have much in the way of upholstery. It wasn't until people demanded an enclosed cab to keep them dry that creature comforts were added to the car.

When armrests were added to the door panel they provided additional comfort for the driver and passenger. These simple devices also served as a handgrip to close the door. Prior to the fitted armrest, the door was pulled closed by a finger pull that was built into the top of the metal door cap molding.

Early-model armrests were constructed of a simple sheet-metal base that was covered in fabric with a thick rubber pad laid on top of the steel. The armrest was applied to the inside of the door over the top of the door panel and held in place by screws. As armrests evolved the bases were made of injection molded contoured plastic with a vinyl-covered molded rubber pad screwed on top. By the late 1950s styling had reached a new level and some car builders incorporated the armrests directly into the door panels.

Armrest Replacement

Most armrests show signs of wear; more often the driver-side armrest understandably has much more damage than the passenger's side. Use, age, and neglect wear down armrests. The rubber pad deteriorates from temperature and air exposure, while the cover material breaks down because body oils and sunlight change the chemical composition of the vinyl. The solution is to remove the armrest from the car and replace the worn-out pieces.

With the armrest on the workbench, remove the screws that hold the armrest base plate and pad in place. Remove what is left of the cover material and set it aside for reference. Under the armrest covering is the rubber pad. The pad is glued to a metal base plate. The rubber is replaced with modern high-density open-cell foam. Recondition the metal base plate by cleaning and painting it to prevent future rust.

Inspect the molded plastic base of the armrest for cracks and damage.

The armrests from this 1950 Ford are in bad shape. The cover material has already been removed to reveal the dried-out and shrunken rubber pad. This is the typical condition of an armrest that is more than 60 years old.

Repair any flaws and feather in the repair so that it cannot be detected. Clean the surface of the plastic and then spray with SEM Sand Free and a light coat of SEM Color Coat spray dye to match the interior of the car. After the base coat flashes, apply three more light color coats to the reconditioned armrest base and allow it to dry.

Foam Pad

Use 1/4-inch-thick high-density foam to make the new armrest pad. Glue the foam to the metal base plate and keep adding layers of foam until you have built up the foam to the correct height. Five layers are needed to reach the proper thickness for the new armrest pad.

The built-up foam pad can now be trimmed to the basic shape of the pad with a foam-cutting saw. The saw is run around the outside edge of the metal base plate and it quickly removes the excess foam. Along the perimeter of the metal base is a 1/4-inch margin of foam that is left behind for contouring.

The rough shape of the armrest needs to be defined. Begin rounding the edges of the pad with a 2-inch sanding disc. The small size of the abrasive pad allows better control for fine shaping. Care must be taken that not too much material is removed or the armrest pad will be ruined and need to be built up again. Contour the profile of the armrest to fit the plastic armrest base.

Cover

The armrest pad is covered in a vinyl that matches the interior of the car. Place the armrest pad face down on the vinyl and cut the vinyl with an additional 2 inches of material all around. To make the covering process easier, the stretch of the vinyl should be from side to side. This way the vinyl conforms to the shape of the metal base plate and contours to the foam pad.

Contact cement is used to fasten the vinyl to the metal base plate. Center the foam armrest pad facing down on the vinyl and spray glue around the outside edges of the metal base plate and onto the backside of the exposed vinyl. Do not get glue on the foam armrest pad. You want the vinyl to be able to move over the foam.

Vinyl

The key to covering an armrest like this is to allow the glue to get tacky before you stretch the vinyl and press it into place. When you can touch the glue without it sticking to your finger, the glue is ready. Pull the vinyl from side to side and fold it over the ends of the metal base plate. Press the vinyl into the glue on the metal base plate and hold it there for a few seconds to ensure a good bond. It may also help to warm the vinyl with a heat gun to allow it to stretch easier. Be very careful that you do not overheat the vinyl. If you overheat the vinyl and then pull on it, the vinyl develops creases that are undesirable. In addition, overheating the vinyl causes the grain in the vinyl to disappear.

With the ends secured, warm the vinyl some more and pull it snugly across the front and then the rear of the armrest. The action of the four-point stretch helps define the shape of the armrest pad. Reposition the vinyl to relieve any puckering or wrinkling if necessary.

Trying to wrap the armrest all at once will lead to disastrous results. Work the vinyl in quarters to get the finish that you hoped for. Heat the vinyl and work half of the front edge of the vinyl; pull it evenly across the outside edge of the armrest and wrap the vinyl over the metal base pan, securing it into the glue. The vinyl should smoothly conform to the metal base and the new foam pad.

Turn the armrest pad over and trim away some of the excess vinyl after it has been set in the glue. Removal of the bulk vinyl will help later if the vinyl needs to be repositioned to relieve any wrinkles.

Repeat the process with the other end of the vinyl to finish off the front edge of the armrest pad. The vinyl can be repositioned if necessary to help it lie tight and smooth over the armrest pad. Do not overstretch the vinyl as this creates excessive tension on the foam and waves in the vinyl cover.

Now work the rear corners of the armrest. Warm the vinyl and then pull it smoothly over the foam and secure it to the metal base. Reapply glue if needed after the vinyl has been lifted and reset.

Trim the remaining excess vinyl from the bottom of the base. The bottom surface should be smooth and bulk free so that it can lie flat on the plastic armrest base. Visually inspect the cover material for any flaws that may need addressing.

Assembly

A dry fit ensures that the new armrest pad is now ready to be mounted to the plastic armrest base. Verify that you have the correct hardware to secure the armrest pad to the plastic base.

It takes two 1/2-inch #8 pan-head sheet-metal screws to secure the armrest pad to the plastic base. Do not

CHAPTER 4

overtighten the screws. The base metal is thin and it doesn't take much torque to strip out the screw hole. Snug is good enough to hold the pad in place.

Two additional 3/8-inch #6 pan-head sheet-metal screws hold the pad in place. These screws are hidden inside the ends of the plastic base and are as vital as the larger base screws.

The finished armrests are now ready to be installed into the car. The armrest unit is attached to the door panel with two #14 pan-head screws that are 1½ inches long.

Re-Covering an Armrest

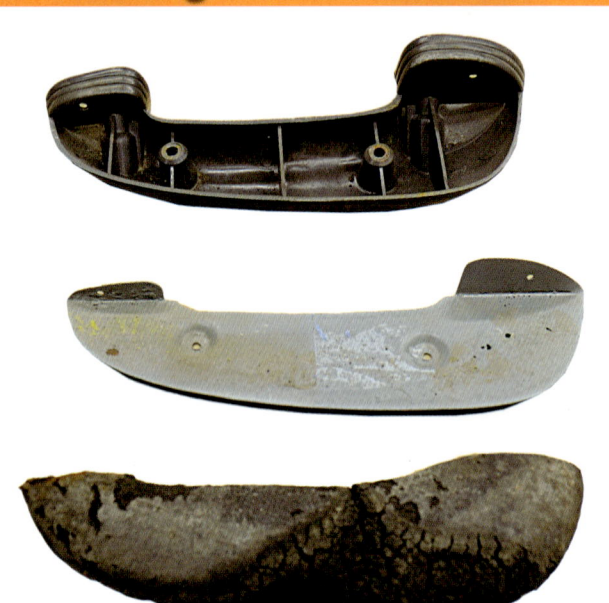

1 The basic components of this armrest are a plastic base, a metal anchor plate, and a rubber pad. The pan-head sheet-metal screws that hold the armrest together have been lost. Since the screws are common hardware, they are easily replaced.

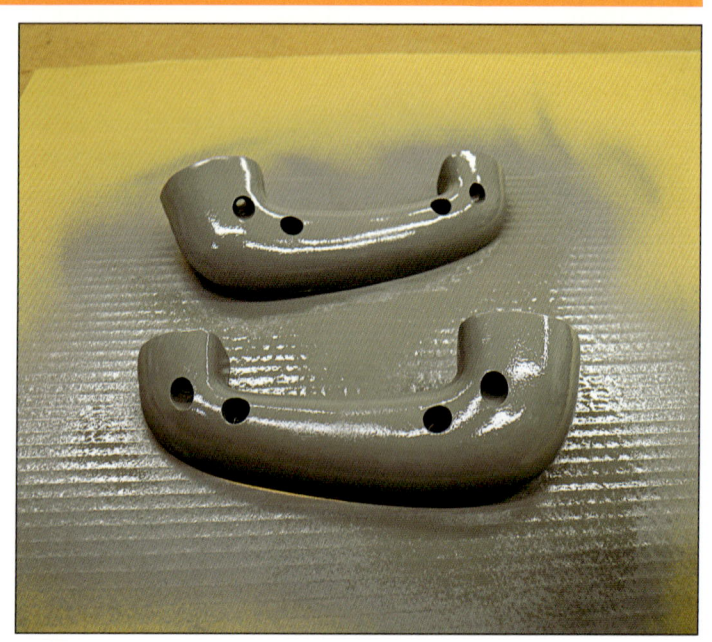

2 The plastic base has been cleaned and repaired. The surface of the plastic has been reconditioned with a fresh coat of SEM Color Coat. The color has been matched to blend with the interior of the car. The new finish looks great and will last for many years.

3 High-density foam is used to replace the rubber pad of the armrest. Layers of foam are built up and bonded to the metal anchor plate until the proper thickness is achieved. Modern foam performs exactly the same as a rubber pad.

4 To get the armrest pad to a workable size for shaping, a foam-cutting saw is used to remove the unwanted material and reveal the basic shape of the armrest pad. Just enough material has been left behind for the fine shaping of the armrest pad.

AUTOMOTIVE UPHOLSTERY AND INTERIOR RESTORATION

ARMRESTS

5 A 2-inch sanding disc is used to sculpt the foam. The foam pad must be rounded and tapered to fit the original armrest base. Care must be taken with the sanding disc to reach the desired shape. The small-diameter disc makes the tool easier to control.

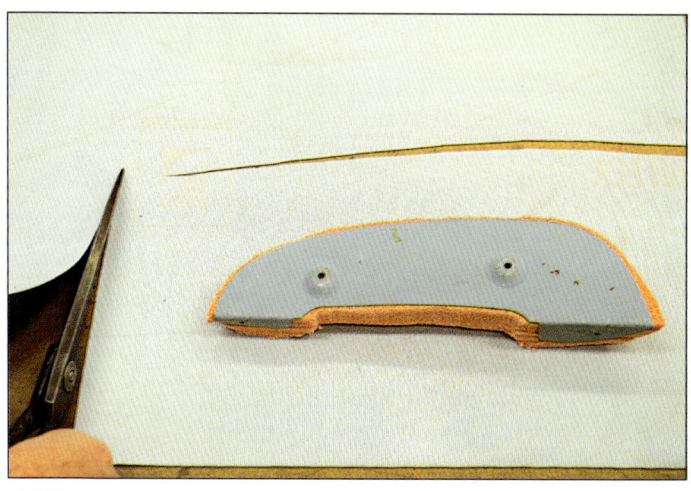

6 The durability of vinyl makes it an excellent choice of cover material for this high-use area. The new vinyl material is cut 2 inches larger than the foam pad to ensure that it will wrap the foam pad completely.

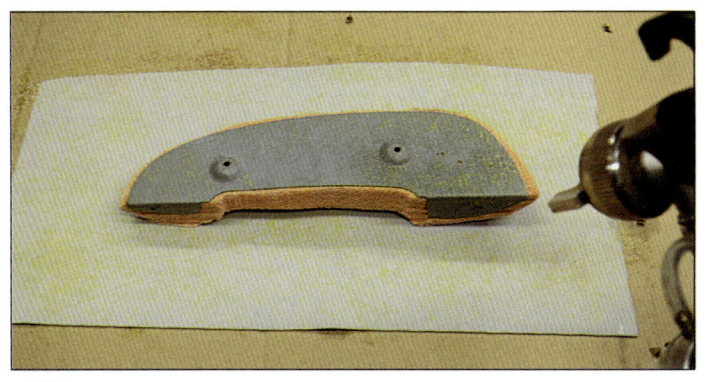

7 No mechanical fasteners are used to secure the vinyl to the metal base plate of the armrest pad. Contact cement is used to fasten the vinyl cover material. The glue is sprayed onto the metal base plate and the backside of the vinyl.

8 Once the glue has become tacky, the vinyl cover material can be warmed with a heat gun to help it stretch better. The ends of the vinyl are pulled over the ends of the metal base plate and they are held in place by the glue.

9 The front and rear edges of the vinyl are warmed by the heat gun, pulled over the foam pad snugly, and then secured in place by pressing the vinyl into the glue. The shape of the foam pad should now define the vinyl.

AUTOMOTIVE UPHOLSTERY AND INTERIOR RESTORATION

CHAPTER 4

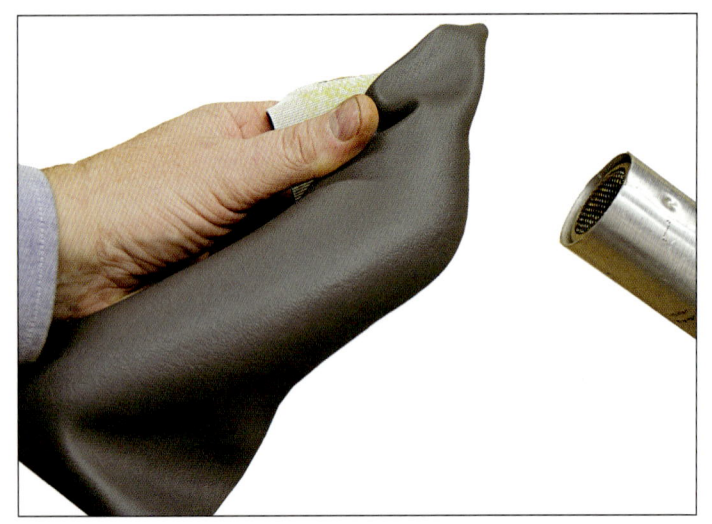

10 The vinyl is worked from the center outward along the front edge of the armrest. A little heat is applied to the vinyl as it is stretched and smoothed into position. This quarter of the armrest is taking shape.

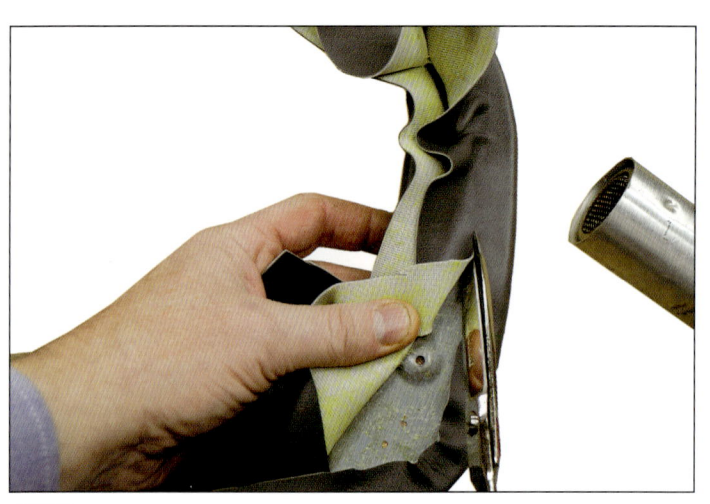

11 Attention to the bottom side of the armrest pad is also necessary. This area must be as flat and smooth as possible so that it fits properly on the plastic armrest base. Excess material is trimmed away to allow the wrapping of the armrest to progress.

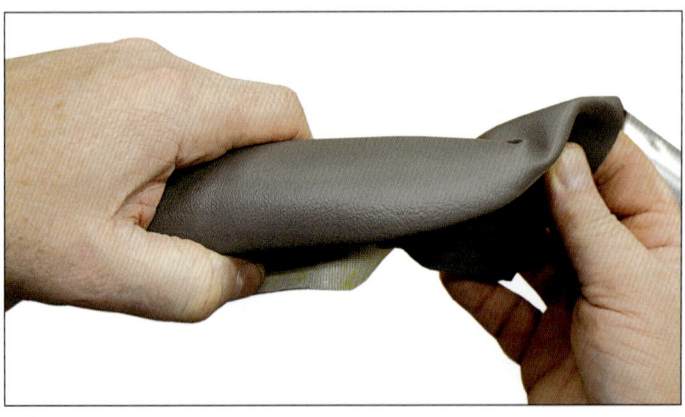

12 More heat has been applied to the vinyl on the opposite end of the armrest pad. The vinyl has been stretched to the end of the metal retainer plate and folded over the edge. Secure the vinyl in place by pressing it into the glue.

13 More trimming is done to the underside of the armrest pad. Additional adjustments can now be made to help the cover material lie smoother over the foam pad. Glue is brushed in as needed to keep the cover material tight and in place.

14 With the final wrapping of the cover material, the balance of bulky material has been trimmed away from the bottom of the armrest pad. The finished armrest is inspected for any issues that may keep it from resting squarely on the plastic base.

98   AUTOMOTIVE UPHOLSTERY AND INTERIOR RESTORATION

ARMRESTS

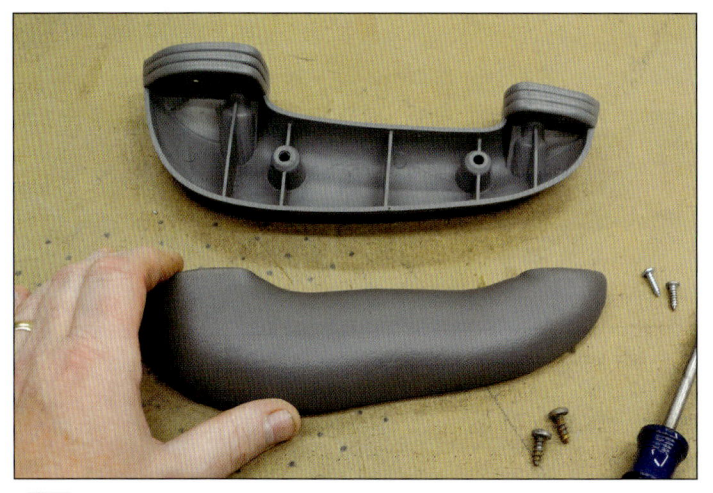

15 All the reconditioned components have been gathered and they are awaiting the assembly of the armrest. The armrest pad can now be dry fit to the plastic base. A regulator can be used to align the base to the holes in the metal base plate.

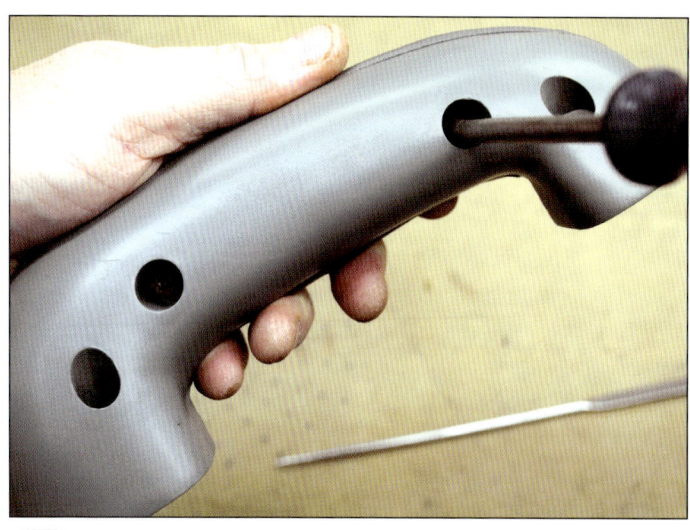

16 The correct pan-head screws are inserted into the mounting holes and secured with a screwdriver. The screws draw the pad and metal retainer tight to the plastic base, making a tight seal on the wrapped vinyl cover.

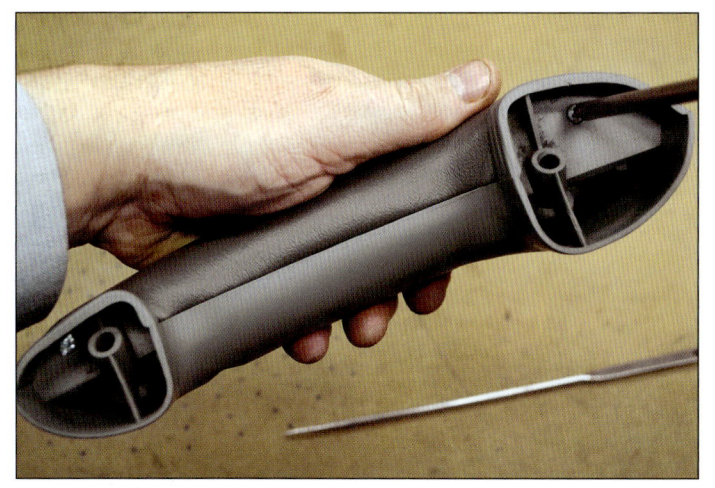

17 Smaller pan-head screws are used to draw the ends of the armrest pad into the base. These additional screws help keep the armrest pad in place without the pad shifting, no matter how many times the door is pulled closed.

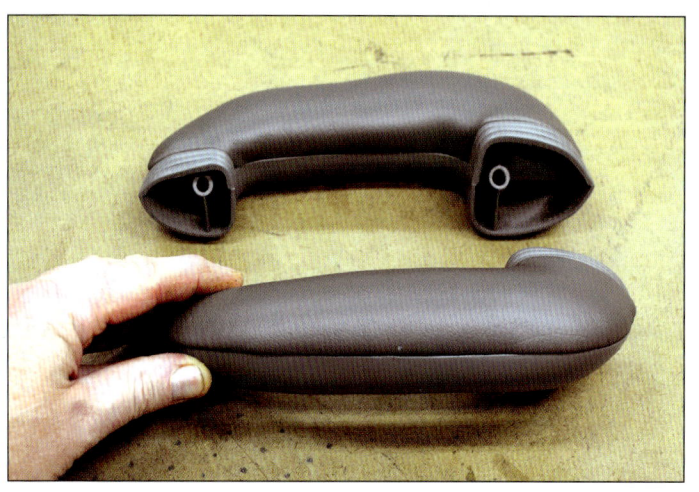

18 It took some effort to bring these armrests back into serviceable condition and it was worth it. The reconditioned armrests are complete and waiting to be installed.

Console Restoration

It was during the late 1950s when automakers started to offer bucket seats as an option to bench seating. It was about then that the center console became a part of the auto interior. The void between the driver's seat and the passenger's seat needed to be filled with something other than a shifter.

Center consoles started out very basic with nothing more than a place for the shifter and a compartment for gloves. Manufacturers added courtesy lights, cigarette lighters, and ashtrays. The sport models included gauge sets and tachometers. Modern cars now have multiple cup holders and USB ports. Consoles have come a long way in a short time.

This project is the center console for a 1964 Impala SS. My customer thought it was in great shape, but at first glance I saw that parts were missing and the overall condition was poor, but I've worked with a lot less.

The process of restoring this console begins by taking the console completely apart and giving the components a thorough inspection to evaluate the condition of the parts

AUTOMOTIVE UPHOLSTERY AND INTERIOR RESTORATION

to determine what is missing and what needs to be done to make it whole again.

At first glance I can see that the lid to the storage compartment has a padded insert with an SS emblem. The padding has deteriorated under the vinyl cover and the paint on the emblem is chipped and dirty. The finish on the sides of the case has been rubbed off along with the embossed grain in the plastic.

We are also missing the console shift indicator and compartment lock. Overall the chrome on the pot metal is good, and a good cleaning does wonders to the machine-turned center insert.

The liner inside the storage compartment is made from loop carpet. The carpet is dirty and in a state of dry rot. Carpet will also be added to the list of items that must be replaced.

On a good note, the switch for the compartment light is intact and functional.

Disassembly

The plan now is to disassemble the whole console and thoroughly clean everything. The process of cleaning the parts allows you to inspect them much closer and inventory what parts are to be replaced or repaired and what needs to be ordered.

Begin by removing screws from the trim and around the shifter cover. Keep track of the screws and where they came from. Be careful that you do not cause additional damage to the parts as you remove them from the console.

After the base of the console has been disassembled, give it a good cleaning. This case has no other issues and can now be prepped for a new coat of color.

Before I spray any parts I wipe the surface down with a clean rag and lacquer thinner. The lacquer thinner evaporates quickly and removes all the grease and oil on the surface of the plastic or metal. Be careful when using lacquer thinner as it can damage some plastics and lift old paint. This process requires that you work in a well-ventilated area and wear protective gear, including a respirator.

Painting

The product of choice to bring the color back on this project is SEM Color Coat. When applied properly the results are excellent. The finish matches the interior vinyl and it can be applied to hard or soft surfaces equally well.

The key to successful SEM Color Coat application is all in the preparation of the surface. After the surface has been cleaned and tacked for dust, a coat of SEM Sand Free is applied. While the Sand Free coat is still wet, a light dusting of the Color Coat is applied. This coat is allowed to dry and the Sand Free actually pulls the Color Coat to the surface. Three additional Color Coats are applied to even out the finish.

Allow the freshly coated parts plenty of time to cure. At least 24 hours is recommended before handling them. This allows the new surface to become harder and reduces the possibility of the finish being marred by fingerprints.

The next problem area to address is the armrest pad on the storage compartment cover. Remove the screws that hold the armrest pad and SS medallion in place. Mark the screws for location and store them in a plastic bag to keep them from getting lost.

If the compartment cover is chipped it must be repainted. Clean and degrease the surface of the compartment cover before proceeding with any painting. Fine-grit sandpaper is used to smooth out any chips in the paint. Feather the edges of the old paint before the chromed areas are mask off.

Tack the surface for dust and prime and paint the metal surface with a high-quality satin finish of acrylic enamel. Allow the finish to cure before removing the tape.

Medallion Reconditioning

The SS medallion on the armrest has faded and chipped paint. The chrome surface is not pitted so this medallion can be restored. New medallions are available, but it will save money if you restore this one.

The surface of the medallion is cleaned and then polished with #0000 steel wool. Tack the surface for dust and use gloss enamel and a fine artist brush to flow the paint onto the medallion by allowing just the tip of the brush to contact the surface of the medallion. Try to avoid brushing the surface as this leaves marks in the paint. Stay inside the raised areas and wipe away any paint that gets onto the chrome.

This process takes a little time and a steady hand, but the results are satisfying.

Console Armrest Pad

Restoring the console armrest pad starts by removing the old vinyl. Peel off the vinyl from the metal base and throw it away. Use a scraper to remove the remaining foam from the surface of the metal base. Wash the metal base with lacquer thinner to remove any adhesive and foam remnants.

A new piece of high-density foam is cut to size and glued to the metal

ARMRESTS

base. Holes are made in the new foam to allow access for the installation screws of the SS emblem.

A new piece of Seville grain vinyl is cut to cover the new foam on the console armrest. The metal base is positioned on the vinyl and glue is applied to the backside of the materials.

The vinyl is then wrapped around the edges of the metal base and secured in place by the glue. Heat may be applied to help form the vinyl while it is being stretched and pulled into position.

Compartment Liner

With a stiff-blade putty knife, scrape between the carpet and storage compartment tub to loosen the old compartment liner. Remove the carpet lining from the tub and steam it out flat. Notice the direction of the carpet stitches in the old carpet and line up the stitch pattern with a new piece of carpet. Working with the carpet face down on the workbench, use the old carpet as a pattern and trace the profile of the carpet onto the new carpet with a piece of chalk.

Create the openings for the mounting screws and storage compartment light using the correct size hole punches; make the openings in the carpet before it is cut out. Scissors are used to cut along the inside of the chalked line to reveal the new carpet liner.

The carpet liner folds into the storage compartment tub and is held in place with glue. With the liner face down, spray glue along the edges of the carpet only. Fold the liner in half with the glue facing outward and put the liner into the tub. Align the two mounting holes at the bottom and work the liner across the bottom and up the sides of the tub. The upper edges of the carpet liner should be flush with the top edge of the tub.

Work the liner front to back until the liner ends meet at the center point of the storage tub. The edges must meet flush and form an invisible seam. Check the positioning of the light opening and adjust as necessary. The carpet liner should not obstruct the mounting holes or the light opening.

Final Assembly

With all the painted parts dried and ready to be assembled, the first subassembly to go together is the storage compartment lid. Place the armrest pad and SS medallion into the correct position on the compartment lid and fasten them securely in place with the correct screws.

Continue to assemble the cover to the storage compartment on the back end of the console. Tighten the screws until they are snug and be careful of pinching the courtesy light wires when assembling the unit. Screw the stainless trim to the top of the storage compartment tub.

The new replacement lid latch button is set into position and is held in place by two machine screws. Elongated holes in the casting allow the latch to be adjusted. The latch needs a final adjustment after the shifter section is mounted to the console base.

The shifter indicator is attached to the underside of the center shifter casting with custom retainer brackets. The special brackets were made from sheet metal to hold the indicator in place and are snugged up with small lock nuts.

Fit the center shifter assembly into the console and finish attaching it with the correct hardware. Now the lid lock button can be properly adjusted and tightened.

Recheck all the screws and wipe down the console to remove any smudges leftover from the assemble process. The console is now completely restored and can be fit to the car.

Restoring a Center Console

1 *This original center console is from a 1964 Impala Super Sport. After years of neglect and abuse it shows signs of wear, and it is missing some important parts. Overall, this is an excellent candidate for a restoration.*

AUTOMOTIVE UPHOLSTERY AND INTERIOR RESTORATION 101

CHAPTER 4

2 *The armrest pad on top of the storage compartment cover has deteriorated and must be repaired. A lot of paint work must be touched up as well; a missing compartment lock button and shift indicator panel must be addressed.*

3 *Time has not been good to the carpet liner inside the storage compartment. Heat has caused the carpet to dry rot and you need to replace the worn and dirty liner with fresh nylon-loop carpet. The light switch is intact and it seems to be in working condition.*

4 *During the disassembly phase of the project a list can be made of parts that should be ordered and those that can be restored. The chrome has no pits, so that is good, and no cracks were found in the plastic base of the console.*

5 *Years of dirt and grime have been washed off the console base to reveal a worn but solid console case. Lacquer thinner is used to clean and degrease the surface of the console, which prepares it for a fresh coat of satin black.*

6 *SEM Color Coat is used to refinish the surface of the console. The product is designed for use on plastic surfaces and it will wear well for many years. SEM Sand Free is used to give the color coat a bite into the plastic surface.*

102   AUTOMOTIVE UPHOLSTERY AND INTERIOR RESTORATION

ARMRESTS

7 Several light coats of satin black are applied to the surface of the console. Light coats are applied to prevent buildup of the color coat, which allows the product to cure properly. This results in a harder and much more durable surface.

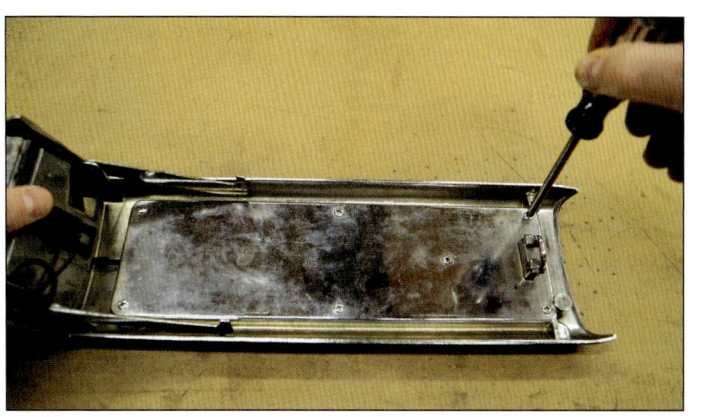

8 Removal of the storage lid armrest pad is done by simply removing a few screws and lifting the pad. The SS medallion is also removed so that it can be restored. All the hardware has been tagged for reassembly and stored properly in little bags.

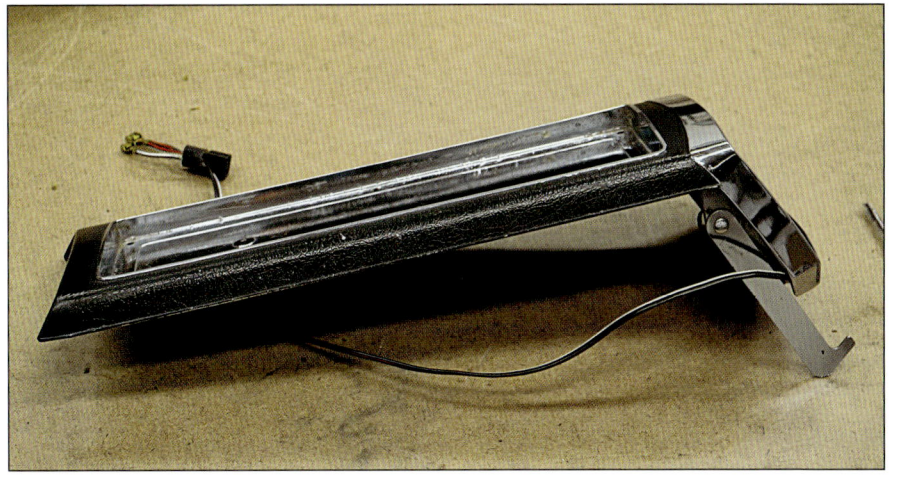

9 The metal on the compartment cover is cleaned and sanded to prep it for painting. The chrome areas are masked off and the cover receives a nice coat of satin black acrylic enamel. After the paint dries the cover will look new again.

10 The chrome was good on this medallion, so I opted to restore it instead of replacing it. After a thorough cleaning the color on the medallion was restored with a fine artist brush, adding a high-gloss paint to the surface a drop at a time.

11 The old vinyl is taken off the armrest pad to reveal rotten foam that must be scraped from the surface of the metal base. A putty knife is used to remove the foam before the base can be cleaned.

AUTOMOTIVE UPHOLSTERY AND INTERIOR RESTORATION

CHAPTER 4

12 The metal armrest base is fitted with a new piece of high-density foam. The foam is glued into place and access holes are cut into the foam to allow the mounting posts of the SS medallion to be inserted through the metal base.

13 The new foam on the armrest is covered with a matching piece of original Seville grain vinyl. Glue is applied to the new vinyl and metal armrest base before the vinyl is wrapped around the metal base to protect the foam pad.

14 The old storage compartment liner has been removed from its tub with a putty knife and a pattern has been made from the old carpet liner. The profile of the old liner is chalked onto a new piece of nylon loop carpet to make the new liner.

15 Access holes for the mounting screws and storage compartment light are punched into the new tub liner before the carpet is cut out. The new carpet liner is cut out along the inside of the chalk marks with heavy scissors.

104   AUTOMOTIVE UPHOLSTERY AND INTERIOR RESTORATION

ARMRESTS

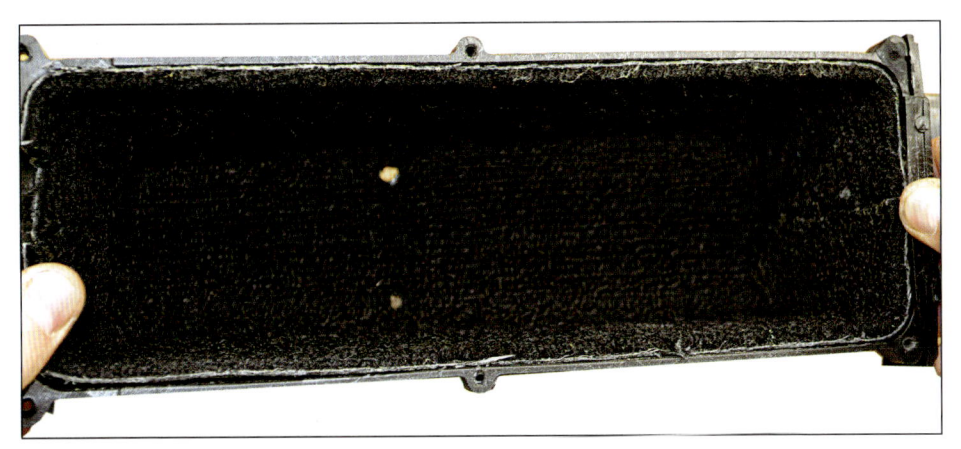

16 Glue is applied to the outside edges of the carpet liner before it is placed inside the storage tub. The mounting holes in the bottom of the tub are used to reference the position of the carpet liner because it flows around the inside of the tub forming a seamless loop.

17 Complete the storage compartment lid assembly by screwing the reconditioned armrest pad and SS medallion in place. The screws are snugged down from underneath the compartment cover with a Phillips-tip screwdriver.

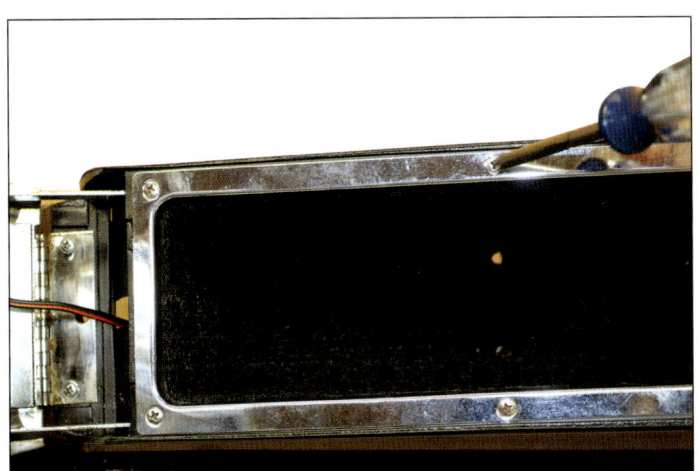

18 The compartment lid is joined with the storage tub and the unit is tightened in place at the hinge along the rear of the console. A stainless band of trim is secured to the storage compartment bin with screws along the top of the bin.

19 The locking lid latch release button is mounted in place on the center shifter casting. Two machine screws and washers keep the button housing in place. The elongated slots in the housing allow for adjustment to the lid after the shifter casting is installed.

CHAPTER 4

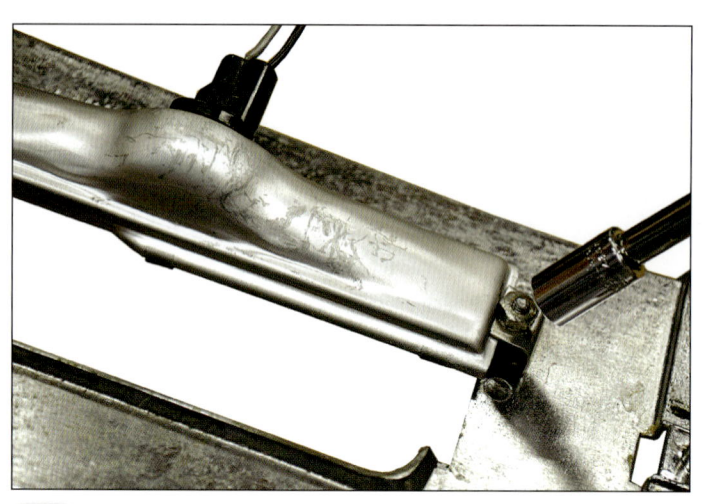

20 *The automatic shift indicator is set in place on the underside of the shifter casting. The indicator housing is secured in position by two small brackets and retainer nuts. A new light bulb is installed before the socket is inserted into the housing.*

21 *The shifter assembly is set into the console, the mounting screws are replaced, and the final adjustment to the storage compartment lock button can be made. The mounting screws are snugged tight when the latch is in position.*

22 *The restored center console looks as good as new. The cost to restore the console is almost half the cost of a replacement console. The difference is that this is still an original part and it will fit the car without additional modifications.*

Fabrication

The reward for working on old cars is that you get a feeling of accomplishment from having a restored project back on the road. The best part is when the owner of the car calls you to say that they just won a trophy for best in show because of the interior of their car. The process of restoring the interior is not only challenging, but it is also very frustrating at times. Many of the interior components are either worn out, broken, or missing and trying to find the correct parts is getting more and more difficult if not sometimes impossible. Fitting a reproduction part into a project or using a part from a different model might get you by, but it just isn't going to look right.

At this point you must make the part you need. So what do you do? Many parts can be made from raw stock such as aluminum, steel, and plastic. If you have access to a machine shop, these materials can be turned on a lathe, welded, or hand shaped with grinders and files to resemble the originals.

Some pot metal pieces may need to be replaced. They can be re-cast and then chrome-plated for an authentic look. Modern casting methods can also be used to create these hard-to-find pieces. For small ornamental pieces such as emblems and knobs, the process of resin and epoxy casting is relatively low cost and can be done at home. Kits are available with step-by-step instructions on how to make the mold, mix the resin, and pour the part. High-stress pieces that need the strength of metal can be produced at a local foundry. Some of these foundries can work with you, but one-off parts can be expensive to produce. If you belong to a car club and other members need the same piece, it is beneficial to have several pieces made to get the cost down.

Interior panels and brackets can be made from sheet metal. Bending and shaping metal is not that hard and with a little practice you can make almost anything. If you are not familiar with metal-shaping tools or procedures a local body shop may be able to fabricate the parts for you.

At first glance the front door armrest of this 1950 Cadillac doesn't look all that bad. The vinyl cover is still intact and has no holes and not much wear. It is not what you see, however, but what you do not see that is a concern.

When the armrest is turned over you see a whole different story. The first is that it has some rust issues that need to be addressed. The other is that the cover material is no longer attached to the metal. The true condition of the base metal can only be determined after the cover material has been removed.

Once the vinyl cover and padding have been removed from the armrest base, you can see that the rubber cushion padding has completely decomposed. It has no useful life left in it. In addition, a great portion of the metal base has rusted beyond repair, so this armrest base must be replaced.

I have both good and bad news. The bad news is it will be very difficult to locate another armrest that is in good enough condition to use on the project. The good news is that there is still enough material left on the old armrest base to gather measurements and show you what the armrest base should look like. This information will help when you make a pattern for a new armrest.

Making a Pattern

To create a pattern of the armrest base you need tracing paper and a pencil. The piece of tracing paper is placed over the rusted armrest base and shaped to fit the contours of the old part.

Each section of the armrest is scribed onto the tracing paper. A pencil is used to mark the outline of the old armrest. Mark as close to the edges as possible and make allowances to bridge the gaps for the material that has been rusted away. The same procedure is done for the top panel and inside pieces of the armrest.

After all the pieces of the armrest have been traced, they can be cut out of the paper. Take each new pattern piece and lay it out flat onto a piece of 22-gauge sheet metal and trace around the pattern.

Since I only have the driver-side armrest for this car and I need another for the passenger's side, I need to make two armrest bases. The passenger's armrest base is exactly opposite the driver's side so the same pattern can be flipped over to make the passenger-side parts.

Because you are making both a left and right armrest at the same time, you want to avoid any confusion during assembly about the orientation of the parts. Clearly label the top or outside of each part with a "T." To distinguish left from right mark all the left parts with an "X."

Cut out the sheet-metal pieces with sheet-metal snips and file off any burs or rough edges left over from cutting.

Shaping the Armrest

Begin the basic shaping process of the armrest by using standard metal-shaping tools. A sand bag and mallet get you started. Stretch the metal as best you can and refine the piece with a hammer and dolly. A French wheel would be great for this project but it is not necessary. Do not be afraid of working the metal; it takes time to gain metal-working skills.

Continue to stretch and fold the metal until the panels reach their desired contour. File the edges of the metal to remove any burs before you test-fit the pieces. Periodically compare the new part with the paper pattern. It may be necessary to trim a little off the panel until you have it shaped to match the original.

Tack weld the top pieces together first. This allows the lower section to curve around the top better. Make any adjustments necessary before moving on with the front section. Use a stitch-weld technique to reduce warping of the metal pieces. Let the metal cool and straighten up the armrest as you work. Continue to weld the individual sections together to form the new armrest base.

Carefully measure and mark the position for the placement of the internal mounting bracket. Tack weld the bracket in place and check that it is correct before it is securely welded to the inside of the armrest.

After all the welding has been completed, the armrest is ready to be metal finished. Be sure to degrease the metal before proceeding because glue does not adhere to dirty metal.

Making an Armrest Pad

The armrest pad is made from high-density foam that does not bottom out when pressure is applied. To make the pad, the armrest base is placed upside-down on the foam and the profile is then traced onto the foam with a marker. Cut the foam

CHAPTER 4

to size and then glue it into position on the metal base. Build up the foam and contour it to the proper shape.

The outside of the armrest can now be padded with a felt underliner. The underliner adds softness to the armrest, and it also smooths any small imperfections in the metal. Glue is applied to the felt underliner and to the metal surface of the armrest. The felt is then wrapped and shaped to the contour of the armrest base. Excess material is trimmed flush with the edges of the armrest base.

Vinyl is patterned for the top, face, and finger cup area of the armrest. The pieces are sewn together and a cap stitch is used on the face edge of the top seam to define the shape of the armrest cover. The selvedge is trimmed close to the stitching to remove bulk in the vinyl cover. Doing this helps the material lie flat and smooth when it is installed.

The vinyl cover is prepped for installation by applying glue to the backside of the vinyl cover and along the inside edge of the armrest base. With a little stretching the cover is smoothed across the ridgeline of the armrest pad and pressed into the glue on the backside. Stretching helps remove any wrinkles and gives the armrest a sleek appearance.

More glue is applied to the finger cup area of the armrest and the vinyl is smoothed into place, finishing the armrest.

Reproducing and Refabricating Armrest Parts

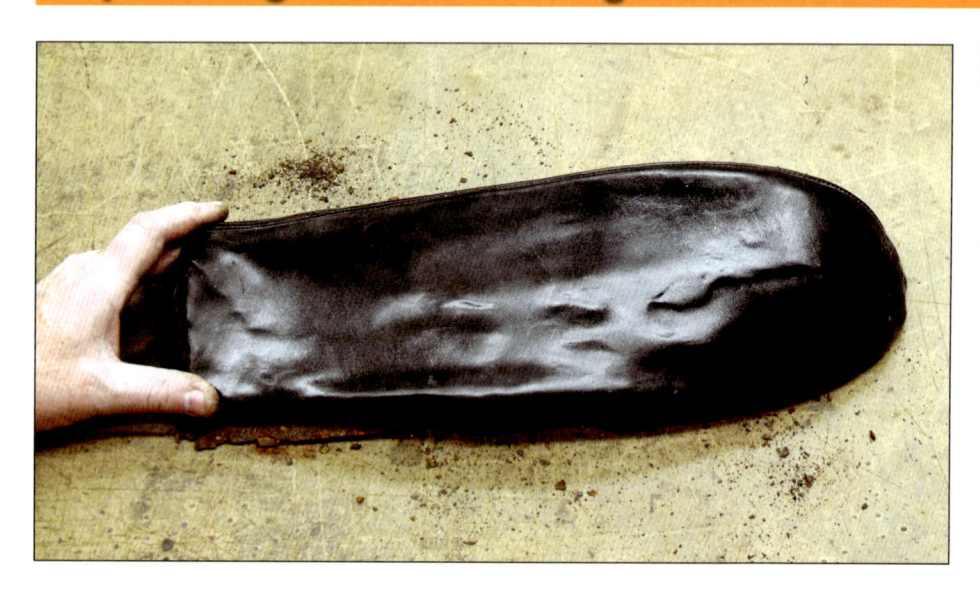

1 *This gem of an armrest appears to be just another part that needs to be re-covered. All too often this is the scenario in the auto upholstery world. It is what lies beneath the surface of the upholstery that you must look at.*

2 *The backside of the armrest reveals a lot more of what you can expect to find when the vinyl cover is removed. The cover is no longer attached to the metal and there seems to be a lot of rust that must be addressed.*

108   AUTOMOTIVE UPHOLSTERY AND INTERIOR RESTORATION

3 With the cover and padding removed you can clearly see that the base metal of the armrest form is beyond saving. Welding a patch to the metal is not an option and covering over the problem is just wrong. Fabricating a new armrest is the solution.

4 Make a pattern of the armrest by forming tracing paper over the surface of the metal. The thin tracing paper conforms easily to the surface of the armrest. This allows you to scribe an accurate profile of the armrest for the pattern.

5 A pencil is used to mark along the edge of the armrest to transfer its profile onto the tracing paper. Each piece of the armrest must be patterned. Any voids in the metal base can be spanned to make the profile complete.

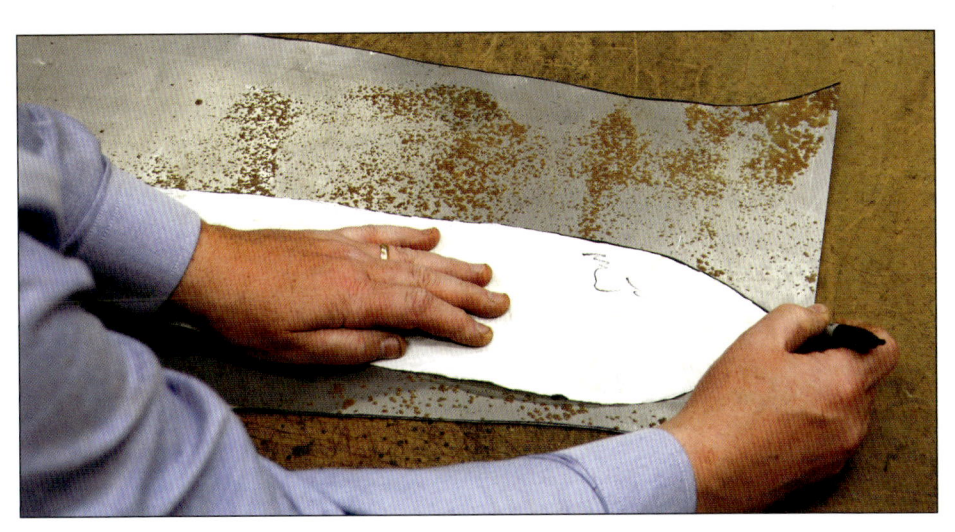

6 The traced pattern pieces are cut out of the paper and the profiles are then transferred onto 22-gauge sheet metal. Each armrest piece is carefully marked for orientation and identification before it is cut from the sheet metal.

CHAPTER 4

7 Turn the flat metal into an armrest with a shaping hammer and sand bag. Basic hand tools are all you need to work the metal pieces and give them the shape and contour required. Fine-tune the metal shaping with a hammer and dolly.

8 The hammered and shaped metal pieces have been worked until they look like the original armrest. File off any burrs on the edges of the metal and continue to dry fit the parts until they fit well together. Now the pieces are ready to be welded together.

9 The top of the armrest is assembled with tack welds so that adjustments can be made as it is worked. The thin metal is prone to warping from the heat of welding. Let the piece cool and straighten the metal as you work.

ARMRESTS

10 The bracket inside the armrest holds the bottom of the armrest tight to the door panel. Measure its location carefully before welding the bracket in place. The welds are cleaned up with a disc grinder before the armrest can be upholstered.

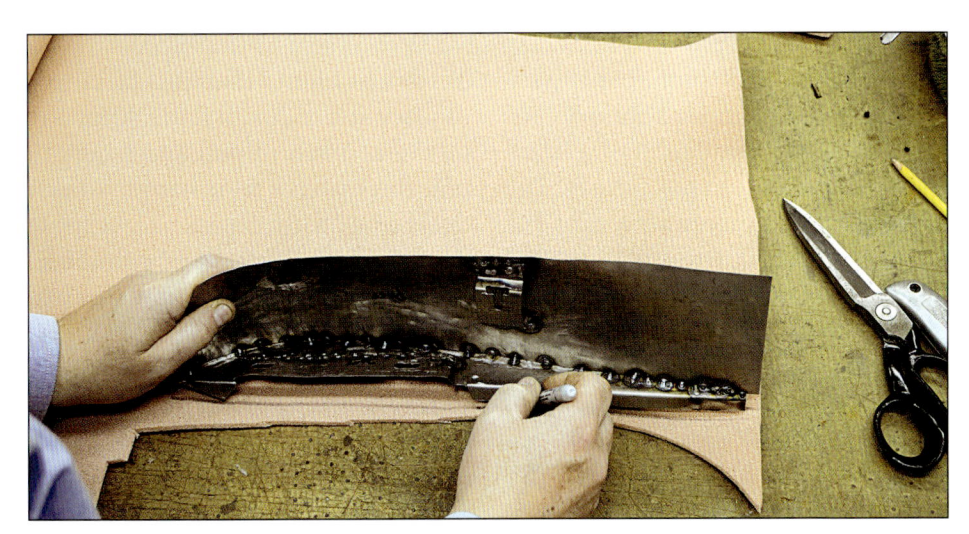

11 A high-density foam pad is cut and shaped to fit the top of the armrest. The metal base is inverted on top of the high-density foam and it is traced to get the general shape of the pad. The foam is cut to size and glued in place on the metal armrest.

12 The cover material for the armrest is made from matching interior vinyl. The pattern is taken from the profile of the armrest and the new cover is sewn and fit to the armrest form. A decorative cap stitch is used on the seam to help define the shape of the armrest.

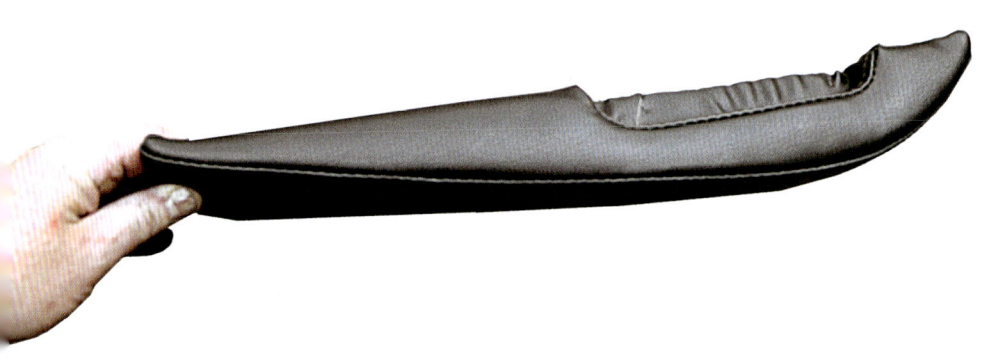

13 The vinyl cover has been applied over the foam pad and glued in place. The finger cup area is finished and smoothed for the comfort of the passenger. The new armrest looks just like the original and will serve the owner for many years.

AUTOMOTIVE UPHOLSTERY AND INTERIOR RESTORATION

CHAPTER 5

HEADLINER

The headliner is the most often overlooked element of the car's interior. It is also considered the second most difficult item to install, following a convertible top. The primary function of a headliner is to conceal a layer of insulation and finish off the interior roof, making the cab more comfortable. Basically, it just hangs there and looks nice.

Headliners come in two basic types. Suspended, or bow-style, headliners are typically found in cars prior to 1974 and solid board headliners are found in later-model cars. The successful installation of a headliner depends on many factors. The first factor is the preparation of the interior roof area. Removal of the old headliner, rust, and animal damage is only a small part of the preparation process. Cleaning and repair to the trim and moldings is also important to make the job look great.

Next is the fit of the new headliner. It takes a lot more finesse to finish a headliner than just tacking it in place and calling it done. Knowing just how much to pull and where to pull the material so it hangs wrinkle free comes with experience. A loose headliner will never look good, and if you overstretch the material it will look puckered.

Finally, the last factor is the finish of the headliner. Working the wrinkles out is half the battle. Replacing the trim moldings, garment hooks, and dome light sets off your work and complements a sharp look if you take the time to detail these pieces and install them with the correct hardware.

A few different procedures are practiced for the installation of a headliner. Some trimmers prefer that the windshield and back glass be removed from the car to make the installation easier. The method that I prefer does not require removing the glass. Removing the glass and reinstalling it not only adds a lot of time to the job but it can be a costly step that involves replacement of the rubber gasket and sometimes risks possible damage to the glass itself.

When the rubber gasket surrounding the windshield has deteriorated and shows signs of damage, or

The headliner project is evaluated to see what condition it is in and if there are any missing components that may cause delays. Although the actual headliner is no longer in the car, all the vital parts needed to complete the project are there.

the glass has cracked or delaminated and must be replaced, then this work should be done prior to installing the new headliner.

Wrapping the headliner material around the rear window opening and then installing the glass and rubber gasket potentially allows for water to wick into the car. This can cause water stains in the new headliner, which also lead to the development of mold and cause the metal to rust. Another reason is that during glass installation, the headliner is prone to damage from the installer while working the new rubber over the headliner fabric. The headliner may become wrinkled, torn, and soiled while working the glass into position and spoil the entire look of the headliner. This is why it makes sense to save money, time, and frustration by having the glasswork done before installing a new headliner.

Inspection

Prior to starting any work, make a visual inspection of the project. You need to look for the current condition of the headliner. For example: Is the headliner complete or are any parts missing? How many bows are in the headliner? Are there sun visors and do they need to be restored? Does the package tray need to be restored?

If the headliner and all its components are intact, work can begin right away. When parts are missing or damaged (e.g., moldings, bows, dome light), replacement parts should be secured before you continue with the headliner installation. If the project starts and then stalls because you end up waiting for parts, you will surely have problems reassembling the headliner due to the time delay.

The remaining dome light socket is removed from the inside roof of the car by straightening the tabs that hold it to the inner bracing structure of the roof. The dome light wires were found to be dry rotted and they are replaced with new wire.

Listing rods or headliner bows have been re-fit to the car to establish their correct position. The bows were removed and numbered to preserve their placement order. The practice of labeling the right end of each bow makes placement of the bows much easier.

When you are searching for missing replacement parts, you should also see if a new ready-made headliner is available for purchase for your project. If not, you may need to make a new headliner from scratch. Do your research, decide what material the new headliner should be made of, and gather all the materials necessary to complete the project.

Pay close attention to the model and style of car you have when ordering a headliner. Sedans and coupes have completely different rooflines and require specific headliners. Also note the number of bows used in your project because some cars have an early- and late-year model change and ordering the correct headliner saves you time and money.

Many times you encounter debris left by mice or insects, which should be removed completely. I recommend that you wear protective equipment consisting of safety goggles, a dust mask, and gloves while removing the old headliner and cleaning the interior roof area because the dust and debris is very toxic and can cause future respiratory problems.

Carefully remove the garnish moldings, dome light, sail panels, visors, headliner, and windlace. Mark and store all the screws and fasteners so that they can be replaced when necessary. Take note of the position each bow is in and make a reference mark on the interior roof rail prior to removal.

Sometimes the bows have already been removed from the car and are not marked. To determine their position the bows need to be fit back into the car. Start by installing each bow and check the fit. Some bows are similar in shape and others only fit in one location. The bow should fit the contour of the inside roof line and connect with the roof rail on each side. Do not reshape the bow to fit; instead try moving it to another location. After you have the bows sorted in order they need to be numbered.

Number the headliner bows from front to rear with a piece of tape. Some bows fit the car in only one direction, so always place the tape on the right end of the bow. This serves as an easy reference on bow orientation when the bows are inserted into the new headliner listings.

Some car models use a metal retainer to secure the headliner over the door. The headliner is tucked under this retainer; triangle fingers extending from the retainer hold it in. Underneath the retainer you find a tack strip that the windlace is attached to. Remove the screws or clips that hold the retainer to the roof rail and carefully remove the retainer.

Reset the triangle fingers on the retainer pieces to about a 45-degree upward angle with flat-nosed pliers and then set the retainer aside.

Now remove the old windlace material and all the staples and tacks that held it in. Discard the old headliner insulation material and clean the inside roof of the car. Remember to vacuum around the edges to remove any hidden dust and debris.

It is always a good practice to thoroughly clean all surfaces and recondition the parts that you removed from the car before installing any new upholstery. Wire brush, wash, and paint any rusty parts to prevent staining of the new headliner.

Clean and polish any chrome and stainless trim pieces with #0000 steel wool and use chrome polish to protect the surface from future corrosion.

If the car you are working on has a dome light, now is the time to inspect the wiring and repair any frayed wires and damaged connectors. Always disconnect the battery or pull the dome light fuse prior to working on the dome light. It is best to secure the wire along the roof support rail so that it does not hang down and cause unsightly bumps in your new headliner.

Take the time to remove all the staples or tacks remaining from the tack strip. Replace any missing or damaged tack strip from around the door opening. The windlace is attached to this tack strip and it must be strong enough to hold a staple and support the new windlace.

This metal headliner retainer has been bent and is now being straightened to fit the car. The retainer holds the headliner in place over the door with little triangle tabs that grip the headliner material when it is tucked under the retainer.

Reposition the metal triangle fingers of the retainer by carefully flattening them and then bending each finger to a 45-degree angle. The angle allows the headliner fabric to be tucked up and held in position under the retainer without damaging the material.

Create a Headliner

Many of the cars I restore do not have a reproduction headliner available for purchase. On top of not being able to buy a premade headliner, I have to make the headliner without a pattern. It all comes down to taking accurate measurements and sewing straight lines.

You need to get some measurements from the car to make new panels for the headliner. Take your time and measure as accurately as you can so that the new headliner fits without issues.

Install a new bonded Dacron insulation pad to the roof of the car. The Dacron helps with heat and noise as well as helps hold the headliner bows in an upright position, which helps you get accurate measurements for the new headliner.

Bow Measurement

Install the bows in their proper place along the interior roof rail of the car. Each bow should stand straight up and touch the insulation pad. Bows are numbered from the front to the rear. The headliner section between each bow is referred to as a panel. The front of the headliner is called the header. The header panel is labeled "A," the next panel "B," and so on. The back panel that meets the rear window is called the curtain.

Once the bows are set in place, the length of each bow can be measured from rail to rail. This dimension gives you the panel width at the seam. Create a legend card and record the dimensions as you get them. The legend card becomes the source of the headliner pattern. Any notes that you can add that help you create a new headliner should be recorded on the legend card.

Carefully measure the distance between each bow at the centerline and write down that measurement to begin making the pattern.

Now measure each bow from the centerline to the roof rail every 6 inches and record any variation from the center measurement. The panel lines are usually straight until you get to the panels behind the rear quarter windows. These panels tend to taper at the outside edges to compensate for the curvature in the roof.

Once you have all the measurements recorded, add 1/2 inch to the leading and trailing edge of each panel for the seam allowance. Also add an extra 2 inches to the outside edges of the panels for attaching the headliner to the inside of the car.

Headliner Prep

The pattern measurements need to be transferred to the headliner material. Lay the headliner material face down on the workbench and chalk a baseline with a long straightedge to square up the material. Start chalking up the panels on the backside of the headliner material by locating the center of the panel and measuring equal distances in both directions.

Be sure that you make a "witness" mark every 10 inches from the centerline on each panel seam. These witness marks help keep the panels aligned correctly when the headliner panels are sewn together.

Once you have all the panels laid out and numbered they can be carefully cut apart. To prepare the panels for sewing, arrange the panels by carefully stacking them in reverse sequential order from the rear to the front.

Sew the Panels Together

At the sewing machine, start with header panel "A" facing up and placing panel "B" facing down on top. With the edges of the panels even, line up the witness marks and place 1½-inch headliner listing tape underneath the panels with the open end facing out. Using a standard-width stitch, begin to sew the panels together allowing for a 1/2-inch seam allowance. Make sure to keep the material smooth and flat while sewing the seam straight and even.

Do not pull or let the headliner material pucker when you sew the seam. The materials should glide on the listing tape while under the presser foot of the sewing machine. Continue to do the same with each sequential panel by placing it face down on top of the last panel until all the panels are sewn together.

After checking all the seams and listings, the headliner is complete and ready to be prepped for installation in the car.

Windlace

To help conceal the door gap, attach a decorative bead around the edges of the door opening. This bead is called windlace; it is made up of a 1/2-inch rubber core wrapped in fabric, leather, or vinyl that complements the interior of the car. Windlace is available premade or it can be sewn together out of matching material and bulk 1/2-inch extruded rubber core.

To make the windlace, you can purchase a coordinating woven cover material or cut your own from the matching interior material. Strips should be cut on the bias of the material to a width of 3½ to 4 inches by the desired length required for your project. Typically, 10 feet of windlace is required per door, but measure your project to make sure you have enough. You also need high-quality rubber-core filler for the windlace. Different sizes are available from 1/4 to 1/2 inch with 1/2 inch being the standard used in most cars.

Windlace is sewn just like a welt cord with the difference being that the windlace is larger. The sewing foot you use depends upon the application. You can use either the correct size welt foot that works with your core size or a zipper foot attached to the sewing machine.

The rubber core material is placed inside the cover material and sewn close to the core, creating a tight cord with a selvedge tail used for securing the windlace to the tack strip in the car.

On some GM cars, the kick panel retainer holds the front edge of the windlace in place. This requires an additional retaining bead to be sewn into the selvedge. To accomplish this, trim away one layer of the selvedge and fold over the other edge to encapsulate a 3/32-inch cord (typically about 30 inches long).

To sew the cord, I remove the zipper foot from the sewing machine and use just the center needle foot from a double-welt-cord foot set. With the aid of a small flat-blade screwdriver I can hold the cover material in place as I sew the bead tightly in place.

Other variations to the windlace may also be required depending on the model and style of car you are working on, such as sewing additional headliner material to the windlace to cover the "A" pillar on this 1950 Buick.

Headliner Installation

The first item that is installed is the windlace. Most cars have a windlace that surrounds the door opening and helps cover the gap of the doorframe.

Slide the windlace into the retainer sleeve on the kick panel retainer. There should be about 3 inches extra windlace coming out of the bottom of the retainer. This material will be tucked under the sill plate later. Install the retainer into the car and secure the assembly to the car with the proper screws.

Install the new windlace by fitting it with the core as close as possible to the outside metal edge of the door opening by stapling to the tack strip. Keep an even tension on the windlace to prevent wrinkling as you work it around the door opening.

Install the reconditioned metal headliner retainer strips over the doors using the correct fasteners. Be careful that you do not snag the windlace with the teeth of the retainer when it is being reinstalled. The edge of the retainer should be very close to the sewn edge of the windlace when it is installed correctly.

Insert the Bows

At this stage the newly sewn headliner needs to be prepped for installation. On a clean surface, turn the headliner face down and insert the bows into their corresponding listings. Center each bow in the headliner leaving an equal amount of material on the ends. Carefully expose the bow ends by cutting the listing material about 1 inch from the inside end of the bow. Take care when you cut the listing material so that you do not cut into the seam. After all the bows have been inserted into the listing on the headliner it can now be fitted to the car.

If metal spikes hold in the center bow, start hanging the headliner there. Align the center mark on the headliner to the centerline of the roof and begin to pierce the listing fabric with the spikes to give a reference point on where to trim the listing material. Remove the headliner from the car and make some relief cuts to remove that pierced section of the listing so the headliner hangs on the suspender bow without being restricted by the metal spikes.

Carefully cut the listing material away from the spike area. Again, be careful while cutting so that you do not cut into the seam of the headliner. Align the headliner from the centerline and bend back the spikes to secure the bow to the car. If your headliner does not have a bow secured by spikes then start hanging the headliner from the rearmost bow and move forward.

Working forward, insert the bow end into the roof rail at its corresponding mounting point and then fit the other end of the bow into its retainer and tighten the set screw to keep it from moving. Work the headliner side to side, relieving any wrinkles that may have formed. Make sure the bow is set in a vertical position and that the panel section is taut and not tight. Move on to the next bow and do the same as the last bow, lightly pulling forward to snug the headliner as you set the bow vertically. Continue until all the bows are set.

Once the headliner is suspended in the car, adjust it so that it is centered side to side and front to back. Work the seams by giving them a slight tug to help remove any wrinkles in the panels. When the headliner hangs smooth and the seams are even the headliner is ready to be glued in place.

Attach the Headliner

At the top center of the windshield, apply glue to the header tack strip about 3 inches long. With a little pressure, pull the headliner fabric taut and press the headliner material into the glue, lining up the centerline of the headliner with the center point in the windshield tack strip. Do not pull the headliner tight as this causes a puckered appearance. This beginning stretch allows you to work the material from side to side so that it lies smooth.

Continue to apply glue to the tack strip, moving out about 3 to 4 inches at a time on each side of center. Pull gently forward and work the material to the sides smoothing as you go. Continue until you have the headliner attached all across the front of the car.

Now move to the rear curtain panel and do the same as the front half of the headliner. Apply glue to the roofline and pull and smooth from the center outward until you have the material secured all the way across the back of the car. It may be necessary to trim off some of the headliner fabric to relieve the fabric so it is easier to work around the rear window.

Cover the Pillars

Finish off the "A" pillar by brushing glue onto the leading edge of the pillar next to the rubber windshield gasket. Working with the top edge of the "A" pillar material, fold the material over to make a smooth transitional seam where it meets the headliner. Stretch and smooth the material over the pillar and press the material into the glue to hold it in place. Tuck the lower part of the material under the dash panel to hide the raw end of the fabric.

The "B" pillars are next to be trimmed. Begin by stapling a piece of headliner material approximately 4 inches wide face down to the pillar tack strip. The material should be about an inch above the end of the metal retainer strip and extend about 1 inch past the lower edge of the quarter window.

Fit a strip of panel board the width of the pillar on top of the headliner material and push it tightly up to the edge of the windlace seam. Staple the panel board strip securely in place along the leading edge and into the tack strip below.

Fold the top of the headliner material behind the panel board to create a transitional seam that is flush with the bottom edge of the metal headliner retainer. Apply glue along the edge of the pillar near the window. Pull and smooth the headliner material over the panel board and press it into the glue to secure the material in place.

The back half of the headliner is worked from the door opening to the rear window. Apply glue to the tack area above the quarter window and attach the headliner section by section as you move to the rear. Snug up the seams of each section first and then smooth out the panel material along the top of the quarter window.

The sail area of the headliner is just behind the quarter window. A lot of fabric is here and the key is to keep the material taut and smooth without overstretching it. Overstretching the fabric causes the headliner to pucker. You want the material to look smooth without it scalloping between the seams. The curvature of the sail area makes it difficult to staple the headliner fabric to the package tray tack strip, so it is usually best to just use glue along the bottom edge of the sail area and shape the material into place. Do the same to the other-side sail area.

Look over the installed headliner and make any adjustments necessary before you give it a quick steam to remove any remaining wrinkles. Make additional adjustments to remove stubborn wrinkles that may remain.

Finishing Touches

At this point your headliner should be installed and wrinkle free. Now is the time for finishing touches. Begin to reinstall the garnish moldings around the windshield, rear window, and along the sides of the roofline. It is always easier to hold the garnish molding in place and locate the garnish molding screw holes with the regulator tool prior to inserting the screws. Do not overtighten the garnish molding screws as this causes the moldings to dimple and ruins the look of the interior.

Continue to install the rearview mirror, sun visors, and garment hooks.

Dome Light

Before the dome light can be mounted to the ceiling it must be connected to the new dome light wires. Feel through the headliner to locate the dome light wires and make a small slot in the headliner material to expose them. Be very careful when cutting this slot so that you do not cut into the dome light wire.

Make sure that the slot is in the correct place and that it is not too large, because the base of the dome light must conceal the cut edges of the hole. Expose the dome light

CHAPTER 5

attachment tabs in the roof rail by pressing the headliner material down around them, and cut the material with a razor blade to allow the tabs to emerge through the material.

Connect the wires to the dome light and then fit the fixture in place. Secure the base of the dome light to the roof of the car with its screws or metal tabs. Install a new bulb in the fixture before covering the base with the dome light lens.

Inspect the finished headliner for wrinkles and fingerprints. Clean and make any adjustments necessary. Now it is time to fit a new package tray in the rear window area. Take care when you install the package tray so that you do not create wrinkles in the sail areas.

Making a Headliner from Scratch

Measuring

1 *Bonded Dacron has been glued to the inside roof of the car and serves as an insulation layer blocking outside heat and noise. When the headliner is installed, the friction caused by the bows touching the Dacron helps hold the headliner in place.*

2 *Accurate measurements are needed to create the new headliner. To get the measurements the headliner bows must be set in place, and they need to be aligned both vertically and horizontally square from front to rear.*

118   AUTOMOTIVE UPHOLSTERY AND INTERIOR RESTORATION

HEADLINER

3 *The length of each bow is measured from side to side. These dimensions determine the width of each panel at the seam. All the measurements are recorded to create a legend card. The legend card becomes the pattern for the new headliner.*

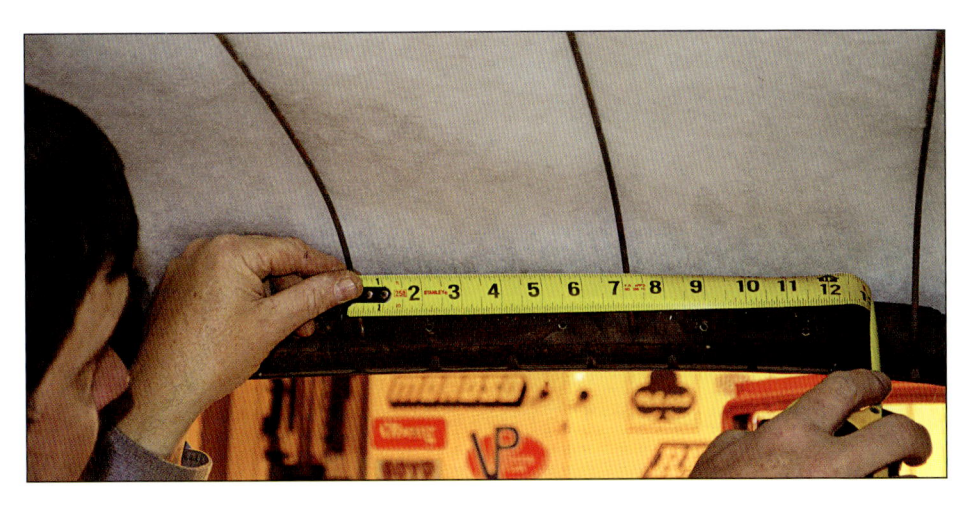

4 *Panel measurements are now taken between each bow starting at the center line. Additional measurements are made every 6 inches from the center line outward to the roof rail. The lines should run straight, but record any variations in the panel width.*

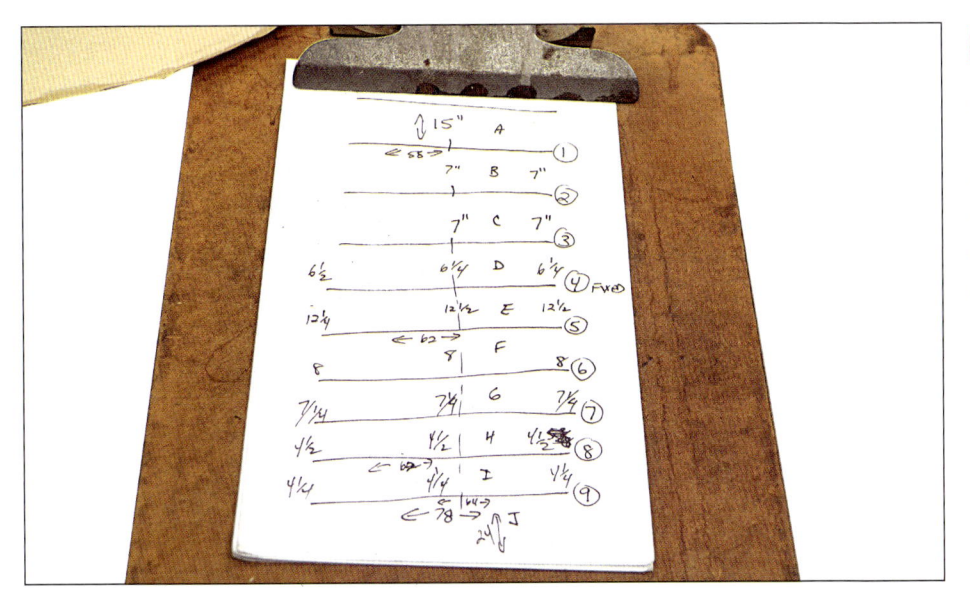

5 *This is what a legend card looks like when all the measurements are recorded accurately. The legend card is the pattern for the new headliner, and by following the measurements on the legend they will be turned into a headliner that fits perfectly.*

AUTOMOTIVE UPHOLSTERY AND INTERIOR RESTORATION

CHAPTER 5

Stitching

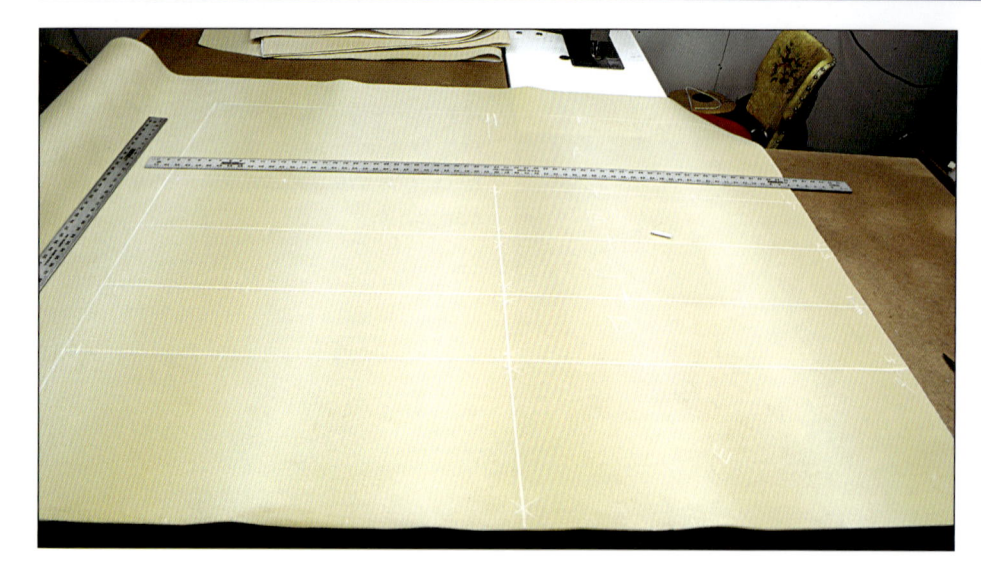

1 The headliner material was laid out face down on the workbench. Measurements from the legend card have been chalked onto the back of the headliner material along with the panel name and number. Each panel is cut and stacked, waiting to be sewn together.

2 At the sewing machine the panels are lined up edge to edge and a listing fabric is placed under the headliner material. The panels are sewn together with a 1/2-inch seam allowance. The witness marks along the seam help to keep the panels aligned properly.

3 Steady and straight stitching is the key to a sharp-looking headliner. The headliner material is not stretched or pulled as it is sewn. The sewing machine does all the work as the material is guided under the presser foot and needle.

Sewing and Installing Windlace

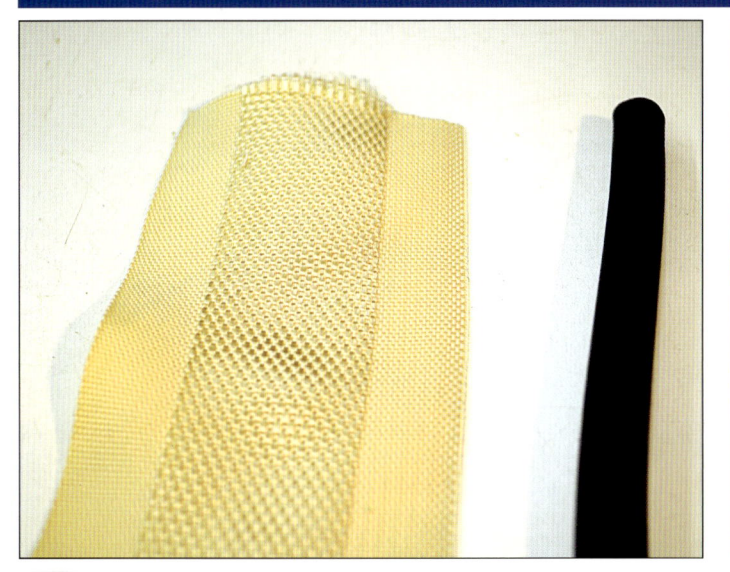

1 Windlace is made from a decorative cover material sewn over a rubber core. The purpose of the windlace is to hide the gap between the door and the door opening. When installed properly, the windlace gives the cab of the car a finished appearance.

2 The correct choice of sewing feet makes the task of sewing windlace easier. Here are a variety of walking feet: a large 1/2-inch welt foot, a right zipper foot, and the needle foot from a double-welt foot set. They all serve a purpose and are great sewing accessories.

3 Except for the larger size core material, sewing windlace is similar to making welt for a seat cover. A decorative windlace cloth is sewn over a 1/2-inch rubber core with a right zipper foot. The wider selvedge of the windlace is attached around the door opening.

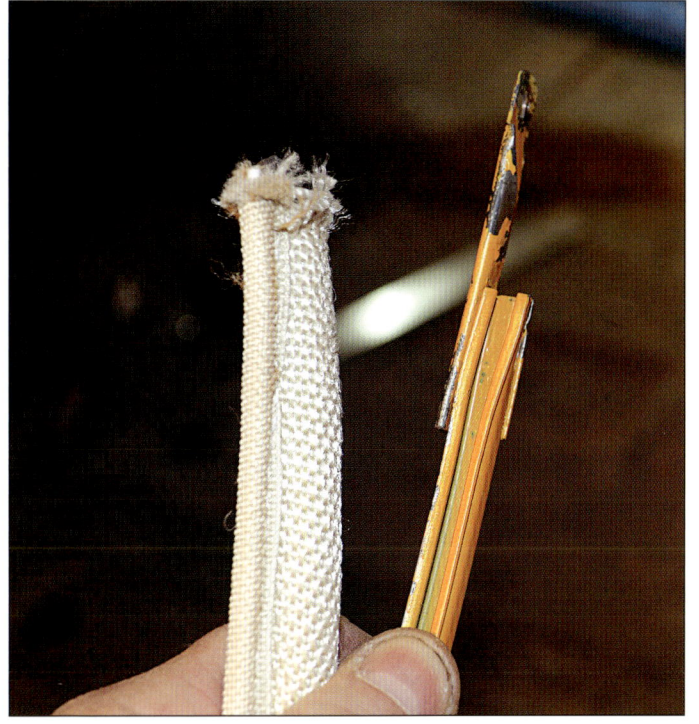

4 This project requires an additional 30 inches of 3/32-inch cord to be sewn into the selvedge edge of the windlace. This special bead is used to hold the windlace securely in the channel on the front edge of the kick panel retainer.

5 A small flat-blade screwdriver is used to help turn the selvedge edge of the windlace over a 3/32-inch cord. The needle foot from a double-welt-cord foot set is used to sew the cord tightly in place. It is a slow process to keep everything tight and even.

6 Install the windlace into the kick panel retainer by simply sliding the small cord through the channel on the front side of the retainer. The windlace should extend from the bottom of the retainer by at least 3 inches. The retainer is then installed and secured with screws.

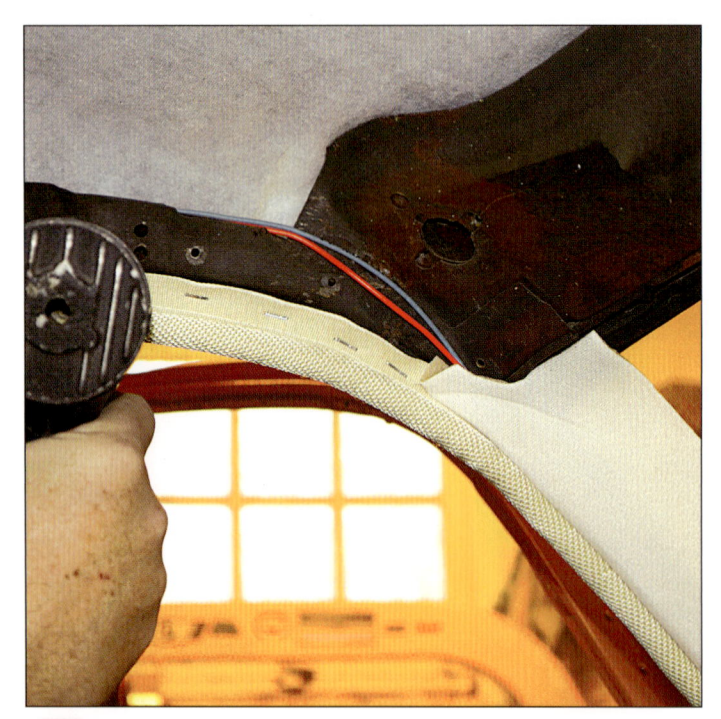

7 The windlace is held in place along the edge of the door opening by stapling it to the underlying tack strip. The windlace is positioned with the sewn seam tight against the door opening. A light tension is put on the windlace as it is fastened to keep it from wrinkling.

8 The metal headliner retainer is installed over the door opening by securing it to the side rail with screws. The metal triangular fingers of the retainer hold the tucked headliner material tightly in place along the edge of the windlace.

HEADLINER

Installing the Headliner

1 Headliner bows are now inserted into their corresponding headliner listings. Each bow is centered in the headliner and the listing fabric is trimmed back about 1 inch from the end of the bow, which exposes the ends for installation into the roof rail.

2 This project has a fixed center bow that is mounted directly to the cross brace in the roof. The center bow of the headliner is pre-fit so that the listing fabric can be trimmed to expose the bow. This allows the headliner to be installed without wrinkles.

3 The listing fabric that was removed allows the metal spikes to be bent around the headliner bow to hold the bow firmly in place. This allows the headliner to hang smoothly without restriction giving the headliner the ability to move for a wrinkle-free appearance.

4 The bent end of each headliner bow is inserted into its corresponding mounting hole located on the left roof rail of the car. To achieve an even tension on the headliner, the bows are set from the center bow forward and then from the center to the rear.

AUTOMOTIVE UPHOLSTERY AND INTERIOR RESTORATION

CHAPTER 5

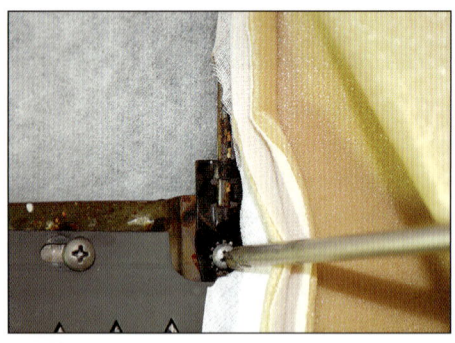

5 The straight end of the bow is set into a mounting clip that is attached to the right roof rail. The bow is raised to a vertical position before the set screw is tightened to keep the bow in place. A slight tension is put on each headliner panel as the bows are set into place.

6 The suspended headliner is centered with equal amounts of fabric along the edges. Any residual wrinkles in the panels were removed by tugging lightly on the seams. The bows are all set with even tension on the panels and straight seams.

7 Glue is applied to the center of the windshield tack strip to hold the headliner material in place. The headliner is attached by pressing the fabric into the glue. The headliner is worked from the center point outward 3 inches at a time.

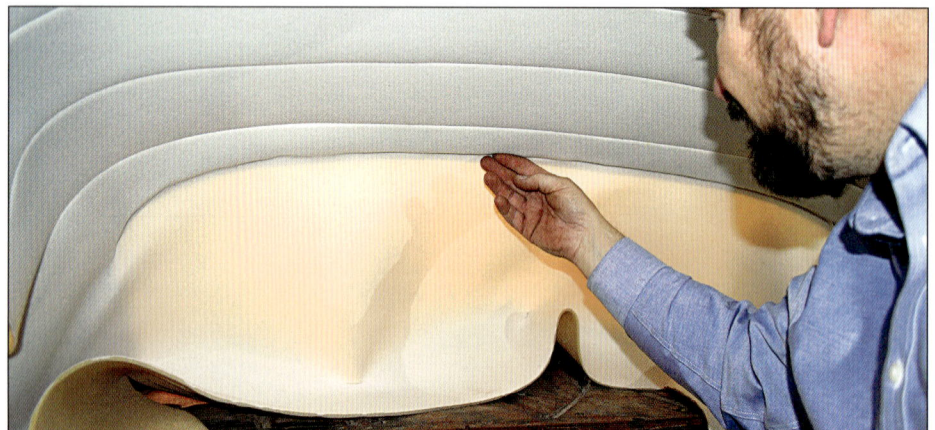

8 The rear panel of the headliner is attached in the same manner as the front panel. By attaching the material at the center point above the rear window the material can be worked to the sides a few inches at a time. The headliner material is kept taut and wrinkles are worked out as it is installed.

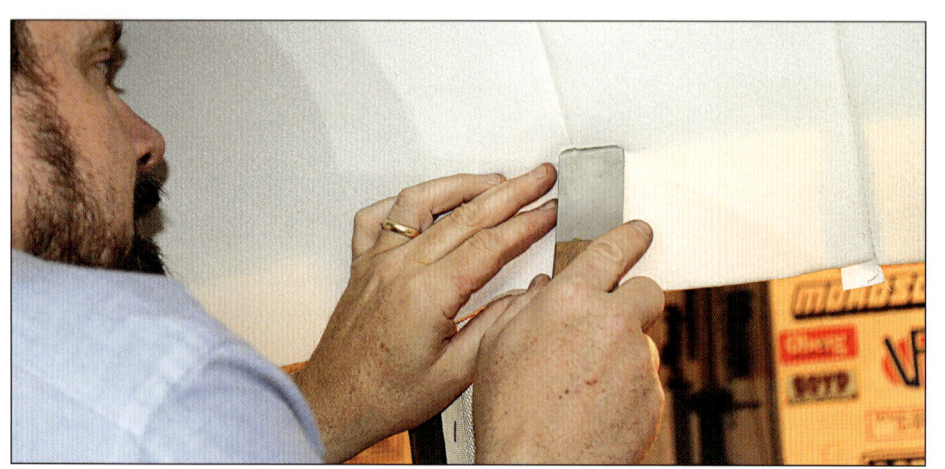

9 Attaching the headliner over the door is done with a headliner tuck tool. This tool is used to push the material under the metal retainer so that the triangle fingers can hold headliner material securely in place. The seams are tucked first to set the correct tension of the panel.

124   AUTOMOTIVE UPHOLSTERY AND INTERIOR RESTORATION

HEADLINER

10 Excess headliner material has been cut away to eliminate bulk from building up behind the retainer strip. After the headliner is trimmed there is enough room for the remaining headliner material to be hidden.

11 Finishing the edge of the headliner is done by gently tucking the remaining headliner material up and behind the retainer strip. The edge of the headliner should meet the windlace tightly and have a clean, tailored appearance.

12 Finishing the "A" pillar requires some gluing and folding. Glue holds the leading edge of the pillar fabric along the windshield gasket. The top edge of the pillar material is folded over to create a smooth transitional seam in the material.

13 The "B" pillar is covered in matching headliner material. A separate piece of headliner material is cut and then stapled face down on top of the windlace of the "B" pillar tack strip. This material is folded and glued into place.

AUTOMOTIVE UPHOLSTERY AND INTERIOR RESTORATION   125

CHAPTER 5

14 A piece of panel board is cut to the size of the pillar as a smooth backing for the pillar material. Staples are used along the leading edge of the panel board to secure it into the windlace tacking strip. This creates a finished edge along the windlace.

15 A transitional seam is made at the top of the "B" pillar by folding the headliner material behind the panel board. Finish the pillar by stretching the material over the panel board and gluing it to the trailing edge of the pillar.

16 The rear half of the headliner is secured, snugging the seams and gluing the headliner material to the tack strip above the quarter window. Glue is used to hold the bottom of the sail area taut to the lower edge of the package tray.

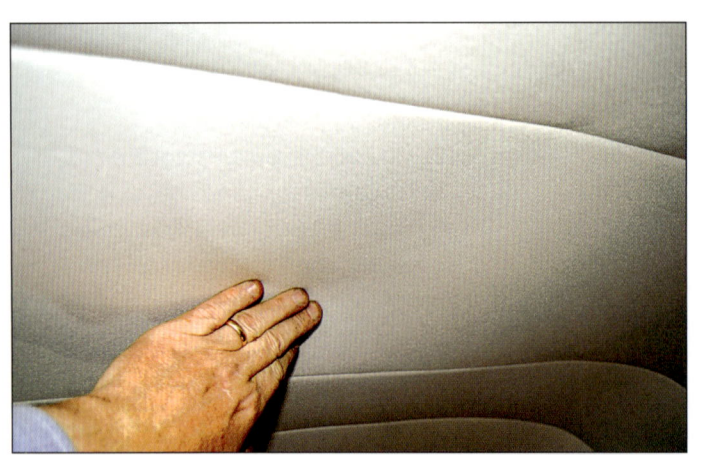

17 The dome light wires are located by feeling through the headliner. Exposing the wires requires making a small hole in the headliner material. Take care not to cut into the dome light wires when you are making the hole in the headliner.

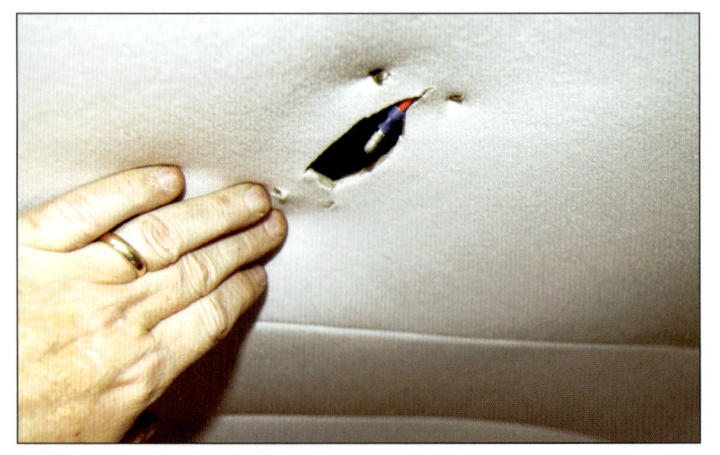

18 Feel for the dome light mounting tabs under the headliner material and make small cuts in the headliner to allow the tabs to poke through. The dome light needs to conceal any cuts that are made, so always start by making small cuts in the headliner material.

126   AUTOMOTIVE UPHOLSTERY AND INTERIOR RESTORATION

HEADLINER

19 *The dome light wires are reattached to the dome light base before it is positioned over the mounting tabs and pushed into place. Twisting the mounting tabs holds the fixture tightly to the roof brace. Snap the lens cover over the base to complete the installation.*

20 *After a quick steaming, the finished headliner has been checked for wrinkles and spot cleaned where needed. Installation of the newly recovered sun visors has also been completed, leaving just the package tray to finalize the project.*

Headliner: Installation Variation

Cars from the late 1920s to the late 1930s that have a smaller rear window and a rubber gasket around the glass require you to trim the curtain panel so that it allows about 2 inches of material around the inside of the glass. Insert a headliner tuck tool under the rubber gasket and gently pry up and apply glue to the metal underneath. Tuck the headliner fabric under the rubber gasket and into the glue. Continue around the window, alternating a few inches at a time from side to side. It takes a little time and patience to do this, but the result is a clean and tight headliner. Let the glue set before you trim the headliner fabric from around the rear window. After the glue has set, trim the excess material within 1/4 inch of the rubber gasket and then tuck the remaining material under the rubber to conceal the cut edge.

The sides of the headliner are attached starting with the center seam and working forward along the roof rail. A headliner tuck tool is used to push the headliner fabric between the metal retainer and the windlace. Work the seams first and then smooth the panel material by allowing the material to slide in from the backside of the tuck tool. The triangle fingers hold the headliner in place so glue is not used on the retainer area of the headliner. Do not push too tightly on the headliner material as this causes the headliner to pucker. You just need to keep the headliner tension even and the fabric smooth as you work your way forward.

After the headliner has been tucked into place it is time to trim away some of the excess material. Trimming the headliner material back relieves the bulk and allows room for the remaining material to be concealed behind the retainer. Carefully cut back the headliner material to within 1/4 inch of the seams and bottom of the metal retainer. Do not cut the stitching in the seams.

The raw edges of the headliner are hidden from view by tucking the remainder of the headliner material under the metal retainer. Be careful that you do not tighten the headliner any more when finishing the edge. The headliner material should look smooth and even along the edge of the retainer; it should fit tightly against the windlace. ■

Sun Visor

Such a simple device, yet it has helped drivers operate their vehicles safely for decades. Originally the sun visor was a metal hood-like accessory that was attached to the outside of the car over the windshield or windscreen, designed to block the glare of the sun to keep it from obscuring the view of the road for the driver.

In the mid-1920s, when cars

AUTOMOTIVE UPHOLSTERY AND INTERIOR RESTORATION

CHAPTER 5

became enclosed, the sun visor was placed inside the cab just over the windshield so that it could be flipped down when needed.

As car interiors evolved, so did the styling of the sun visor. Pivoting mounts allowed sun visors to turn and swivel to shield the sun on the side window and give the driver a safer experience. Styling and function came together when manufacturers added a vinyl grip panel to the leading edge of the visor. The vinyl helped keep the sun visor material from wearing through due to repeated handling when it was adjusted. The added vinyl panel also helped the sun visor stay cleaner while adding a more ornate look. Vanity mirrors were added eventually to increase function. Many sun visors today come with illuminated mirrors and a slide-out feature to block out more glare.

Construction

A typical sun visor is constructed of an inner core made of a heavy fiberboard with a metal spine designed to hold the visor support rod. On later-model sun visors the spine may have an attached pin that is inserted into the support bracket.

The outside of the sun visor is typically covered in a matching headliner material over a thin cotton padding and lightweight cardboard.

The edge of the sun visor was finished with a double-folded vinyl bias tape with the ends of the binding capped off with chrome tips. The modern sun visor is self-edged or turned and sewn instead of relying on the bias binding.

Restoration

Begin by removing the support rod from the sun visor. Disassembly starts by simply twisting and pulling the support rod free from the sun visor. Recondition the sun visor bracket by cleaning away any corrosion. Make sure that the pivot joint works well and then repaint the sun visor bracket. After the paint has cured use a drop of light machine oil on the pivot joint to keep it moving freely.

If the sun visor has an attached support pin that is inserted into the pivot bracket the disassembly process is a little different. First remove the tension screw from the pivot bracket.

Place a thin flat-blade screwdriver in the end of the pivot bracket closest to the spine and gently tap the screwdriver into the slot to drive the pivot bracket away and free from the sun visor pin. This action safely separates the pivot bracket from the sun visor. Absolutely do not twist or pry the sun visor bracket open as this causes the casting to break.

To rebuild the sun visor it must be disassembled. The decorative binding tips are removed by prying them open with a small flat-blade screwdriver to release them from the binding. The stitching on the binding is cut with a sharp razor blade and the binding can be pulled away from the cover board. Remove the cover board from the inner core of the sun visor. Once everything is cut apart, set the pieces aside so that they can be referenced later when you lay out the new sun visor.

Inspect the inner core for cracks and damage. If any problems are found with the core it needs to be replaced.

The core can be removed from the spine by lifting the staples that secure it in place by prying them up with the aid of a screwdriver. Pull out the staples and carefully remove the spine without bending it.

The determined thickness of the old core is 1/8 inch and a new core is cut from a piece of Masonite. Using the old core as a pattern, trace along the edge of the core onto the new material and cut it out with a jigsaw. A fine-tooth woodcutting blade is fitted to the saw to prevent shredding the Masonite.

Cut slowly along the pattern line to free the new core. Sand and smooth the edges of the new core before installing the metal spine.

Fit the metal spine to the new core and drill 1/8-inch holes through the spine and core, making it ready for riveting.

Use a pop rivet tool and 1/8-inch aluminum rivets with 1/4-inch grip range and a backer washer to secure the spine to the core. Smooth the rivet by hammering it flat on an anvil with a ball-peen hammer. Also make sure that the metal spine is securely attached to the core. Insert the visor support rod into the spine to ensure that it fits snugly and not too tight. Make any adjustments at this time by either bending the support rod slightly or making a dimple into the metal spine. The sun visor should be able to rotate up and down on the support rod and hold its position without binding.

Place the sun visor core on a sheet of visor tag board and trace around the perimeter of the core. Rotate the core to the other side and complete the tracing. With a ruler measure and add 1/2 inch to the outside of the visor tracing to allow for sewing. Cut the new visor cover board from the sheet and turn it so that the outside is facing up on the workbench.

The spine of the cover board must be scored so that it can be folded around the spine of the core smoothly and evenly. To begin the process, locate the center point on the spine and with the aid of a straightedge, score the cover board with an upholstery regulator. Move the straightedge 1/16 inch from the center and make three additional score marks on both sides of the center score mark.

Original Design

With the cover material laid out face down on the workbench, spray a light, even coat of glue on the outside of the cover board and the backside of the cover material. Place the cover board on top of the cover material, turn the cover board over, and press the cover material evenly, smoothing out any wrinkles that may have formed. The cover material is now ready to be trimmed to the size of the cover board and then set aside.

Now cut the decorative finger grip panels from vinyl, and using the original visor cover as a template, make an index mark on the outside edge of the backside of the cover board so that the vinyl panel can be aligned for sewing. Place the vinyl panel facing up and set the cover board on top facing down. Align the vinyl with the index marks on the cover board and sew the pieces together. Repeat the process for the other vinyl panels.

Turn the cover board over, apply glue to the backside of the vinyl pieces, and fold them over to create the finger grab area on the surface of the cover board. Apply glue to the inside edges of the cover board and tuck in the wrap material on the notched front and rear of the cover board. Position the core inside the cover board with the metal spine tight to the crease in the cover board. Now fold the cover in half and pinch the glued edges together to hold the inner core in place.

Edge Binding

The edge of the sun visor is finished with a double-folded 3/4-inch bias binding. Binding can be purchased or made from matching interior material for a unified appearance. To make the bias binding for the sun visors the vinyl is marked on the bias (diagonally) of the material. Cutting vinyl material on the bias helps reduce the stretching of the material.

Mark out a strip of matching vinyl 1¼ inches wide and 10 inches longer than the distance around the open edge of the visor. Make reference lines 1/2 inch in from each edge.

Cut the vinyl binding strips and apply glue to the inside of the binding. Now fold the outside edge of the vinyl over and up to the reference line, pressing into the glue. The finished binding should now measure 3/4 inch wide with two folded edges.

The binding is sewn to the edge of the sun visor with a "C" folder or binding appliance. The binder is attached to the sewing machine and adjusted to allow the double-folded binding to flow through the binder at a right angle or perpendicular to the needle bar of the sewing machine. The right-angle binding attachment allows the binding to be applied to the raw edge of the sun visor by following close to the inside and outside curves of the sun visor. This operation is best done on a cylindrical or post sewing machine but can be done on a standard sewing machine.

The ends of the binding are trimmed and the raw cut end of the binding is capped with a decorative chrome tip. The metal tip is fitted to the visor and crimped in place with smooth-jawed pliers.

The sun visor is now ready for the support rod to be inserted and then it can be installed in the car. Use a twisting motion as you insert the support rod into the spine of the sun visor. Be sure that the bracket has a full range of motion before installing the sun visor into the car.

Installation

At the front of the car, feel under the headliner material for the main access hole in the header panel. There should be a large hole that the visor pivot bracket fits into, and there should be smaller screw holes for mounting the bracket to the car.

Once you are sure of the sun visor bracket mounting location, carefully cut a small "X" to allow for the mounting of the sun visor bracket. Observe that there may be a left and right sun visor bracket due to the curvature of the car's roofline. It will become obvious to you when you swing the sun visor to the side. The spine of the sun visor should remain level.

Using a regulator, locate the mounting screw holes and secure the bracket to the header panel of the car with the proper size mounting screws. Support the sun visor while the screws are being installed to avoid damage to the pivot bracket. The pot metal may break due to the weight of the sun visor hanging on a single screw. Prevent additional potential damage by not overtightening the mounting screws.

After the sun visor is securely in place, the tension screw can be adjusted so that the sun visor stays in position without drooping and yet can be moved up and down easily.

CHAPTER 5

Re-Creating a Sun Visor

1 The foundation component of a sun visor is a ridged core with an attached metal spine. A decorative cover surrounds the core and is finished with a bound edge. All of this hangs on a swivel support bracket that mounts to the ceiling of the car.

2 The first part to be removed from this Ford sun visor is the support bracket. Simply twisting and pulling the metal rod from the spine accomplished this. The simple design was practical and inexpensive to produce.

3 General Motors used a support bracket that accepted a sun visor with an attached pin that inserted into the bracket; it was secured with a tension screw. Separating the bracket from the sun visor begins by removing the tension screw.

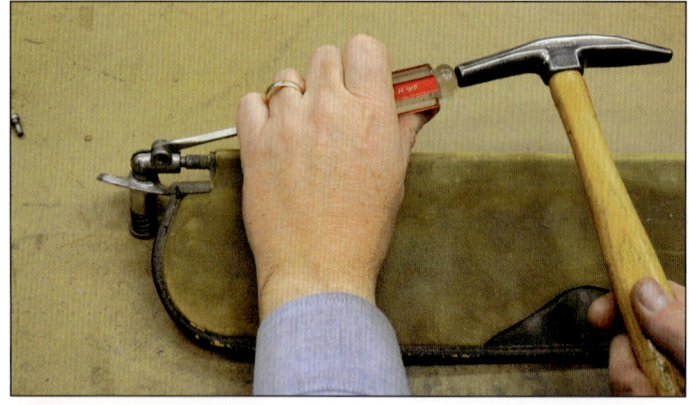

4 The sun visor bracket can be removed easily without causing it any damage by lightly tapping it off with the aid of a screwdriver. The pot-metal casting will definitely break if it is pried open to release it from the sun visor.

5 The raw edge of the bias binding on a sun visor is finished with a decorative metal tip. These small metal clips must be removed prior to the binding. A small screwdriver is used to pry them open to release them from the sun visor.

130 AUTOMOTIVE UPHOLSTERY AND INTERIOR RESTORATION

HEADLINER

6 The outside edge of the sun visor is covered with a sewn-on bias binding used to conceal the raw edge of the sun visor cover materials. A fresh razor blade is used to cut the stitching on the binding free from the outside edge of the sun visor.

7 The heart of the sun visor is the inner core and it must be in good condition to operate properly. Since this inner core is cracked and shows signs of damage, it must be replaced with a new piece of fiber board.

8 The metal spine of the sun visor is attached to the fiber board with industrial staples. A screwdriver is used to lift the staples so that the spine can be removed. Care must be taken when removing the spine so that it is not damaged.

9 The integrity of this inner core has been compromised and is not suitable for use in a restoration. The damaged inner core of the sun visor makes a good pattern by tracing its profile onto a new piece of 1/8-inch Masonite fiberboard.

AUTOMOTIVE UPHOLSTERY AND INTERIOR RESTORATION

CHAPTER 5

10 A jigsaw is used for cutting the new inner core. The saw is fitted with a fine-tooth blade to help avoid tear-out on the Masonite fiberboard. The saw is adjusted to run at a higher speed, which makes a smoother cut.

11 The new inner core is cut from the Masonite by running the blade on the outside of the pencil line. After the new inner core is cut out, the edges are filed smooth and sanded to a slight taper along the outside edges.

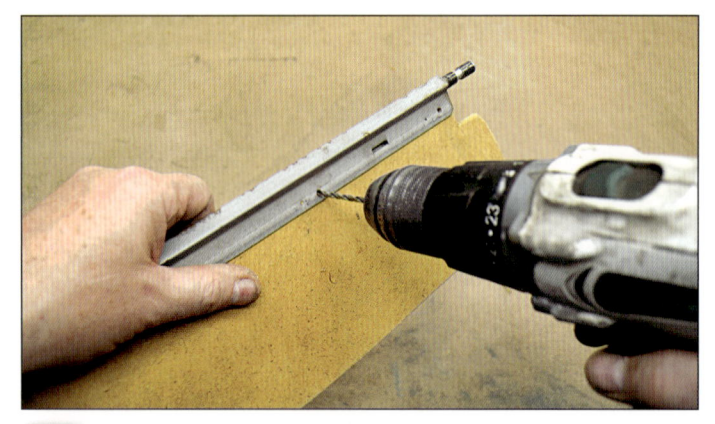

12 The original metal spine is fitted onto the new inner core. To secure the spine to the core it must be drilled and riveted. The 1/8-inch holes are drilled every 2 inches into the metal spine so that pop rivets can be inserted.

13 The metal spine is riveted in place with 1/8-inch aluminum pop rivets instead of the original industrial staples. After the rivets are set the visor is placed on an anvil and the rivets are hammered flat to reduce the bulk of the rivet.

14 A new cover board is created by tracing the profile of the inner core onto a piece of lightweight cardboard. This task requires rotating the inner core from one side to the other to get the whole profile.

132 AUTOMOTIVE UPHOLSTERY AND INTERIOR RESTORATION

HEADLINER

15 An extra 1/2 inch is added to the perimeter of the cover board before it is cut from the tag board. The extra material is needed to extend the cover board beyond the inner core; then you can finish the sun visor by sewing on a decorative binding.

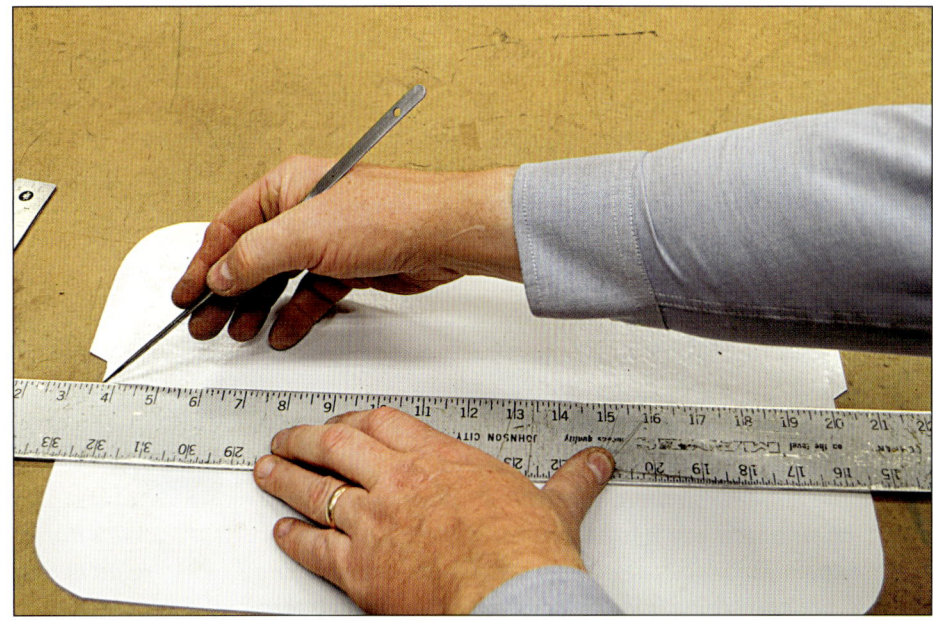

16 The spine of the cover board is prepared for folding by scoring the cardboard. This allows it to fold cleanly over the spine of the inner core. A straightedge and upholstery regulator aids in achieving sharp, clean folds.

17 A light coat of glue has been sprayed on the cover board before it is set onto a piece of cover material. The cover material is then worked evenly over the glued surface of the cover board until all the wrinkles are smoothed out.

18 The cover material is trimmed flush along the edge of the cover board except for the notched ends. Turning the end cover material inside gives the sun visor a finished look when the cover board is folded.

19 Reference lines are made on the new cover board by using the original cover board as a guide. The reference lines help with the alignment of the finger grab material so that it can be sewn in place accurately.

AUTOMOTIVE UPHOLSTERY AND INTERIOR RESTORATION   133

CHAPTER 5

20 *The finger grab panel is set face to face under the cover board and it is lined up with the index marks made earlier. The pieces are then sewn together by stitching along the reference line from the backside of the cover board.*

21 *With the cover board face up on the workbench, glue is applied to the underside of the vinyl so that it can be folded over for finishing the cover board.*

22 *The sun visor cover board is prepared for assembly by spreading glue to the inside edges of the cover board. The glue holds the cover board together after the inner core is placed inside.*

23 *The inner core of the sun visor has been centered inside the cover board with the spine tight to the fold and even margins all around. The cover board is folded over the inner core carefully, locking it in place as the edges are aligned.*

134 AUTOMOTIVE UPHOLSTERY AND INTERIOR RESTORATION

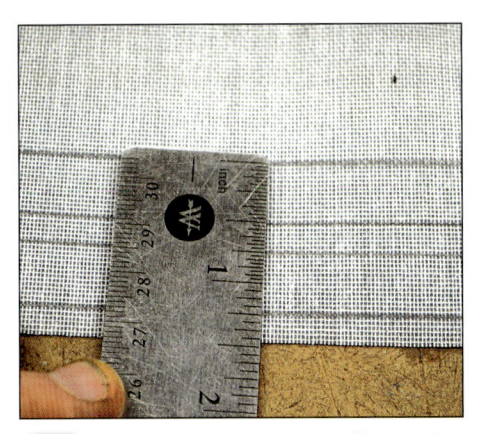

24 For strength and stability, strips of vinyl are marked and then cut on the bias of the matching material. Reference marks are made on the underside of the bias binding to indicate how far to fold over the edge of the vinyl.

25 Before the edges of the vinyl can be turned, glue is applied to the inside edge. The outside edges of the vinyl are now folded inward to the reference marks and pressed flat, leaving you a binding with a finished size of 3/4 inch.

26 The sewing machine has been set up with a right angle "C" folding binder. The binder is used to apply the bias binding smoothly and evenly over the top and bottom of the raw edge of the sun visor while it is sewn in place.

27 After the binding has been sewn in place the ends are trimmed off and the raw edges of the binding are hidden with a decorative metal cap. The small metal cap is set into place on the edge of the visor and crimped with pliers.

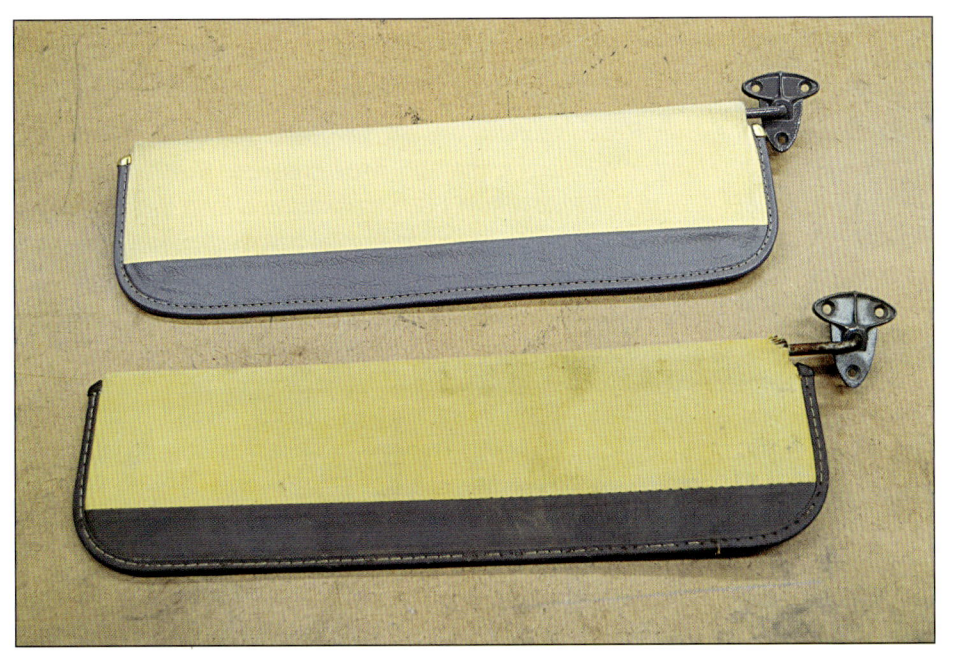

28 The new sun visor is now complete (top) and it looks just like the original (bottom). The reconditioned support bracket has been inserted into the spine of the sun visor and it is ready for installation in the car and many years of service.

AUTOMOTIVE UPHOLSTERY AND INTERIOR RESTORATION

Sun Visor: Modern Design Variation

This example of the modern technique to finish a sun visor is to simply turn the edge and sew the visor closed without binding the edges. Disassembly of the old sun visor and making a new cover board follows the same procedure as the previously described technique. The variation begins with how the cover material is prepared and applied to the cover board.

Measure the cover board to locate the center point on the outside edge. Make a mark on the spot to reference the placement of the finger grab. Lay the cover material face down on the workbench and place the cover board on top.

The outline of the cover board is traced onto the backside of the cover material along with the center reference marks. Remove the cover board and add 1/2 inch to the outside of the line on the cover material. Cut out the oversize piece of cover material on the new outside line.

Cut new decorative finger grabs from matching interior vinyl with an additional 1/2 inch of material along the leading edge. The finger grabs are folded in half to locate the center reference point on the leading edge. The reference point for the finger grab material is now marked at the fold. This point helps with the alignment on the cover material. Now spray the backside of the vinyl with a light coat of glue.

The vinyl finger grabs are set in position by aligning them with the index mark on the surface of the cover material. Turn the cover material over and lightly glue a piece of muslin to the back of the finger grab area. The muslin is used to back the stitching of the finger grabs. Now sew around the outside perimeter of the vinyl finger grabs with a fine stitch to secure them permanently in place. Trim the muslin close to the stitching and then place the cover material face down on the workbench.

If the sun visor is padded it is best to use a layer of modern foam-backed headliner fabric instead of cotton. The 1/8-inch foam on the headliner fabric is neater than cotton and easy to work with. Apply a light, even coat of glue to the outside surface of the cover board and attach the padding and trim it flush with the edge of the cover board. Center the padded cover board over the cover material and make sure that there are no wrinkles in the finish. Apply glue around the inside edge of the cover board and then trim the cover material to 1/2 inch from the edge of the cover board.

Finish the notched end of the cover board by having the cover material diagonally cut into the corners of the cover board and the cover material folded tightly inward. Evenly turn the cover material inside the cover board and press it into the glue. Smooth the material so that it lies flat against the cover board when it is sewn together.

With the cover board open, brush an even coating of glue along the top of the material that was folded inward over the outside edges of the cover board. Insert the core into the cover board with the pin end exposed and the spine tight to the fold in the cover board.

The cover board is now folded in half over the core. Take care to evenly align the edges of the cover board so that the edges of the vinyl finger grabs are in alignment with each other. Press the glued edges firmly together to hold the inner core in position.

Place the rear edge of the sun visor under the presser foot of the sewing machine. Use a wide stitch to sew the sun visor cover together. The wide stitch prevents the cover board from tearing out and it helps with the thickness of the visor materials. The stitching should be within 1/4 inch of the wrapped outer edge of the cover board. After sewing the sun visor, the ends of the thread are tied off at the beginning and last stitches. This completes the sewing of the sun visor.

Inspect the mounting hardware for cracks and damage. Replace damaged castings with original hardware if possible. Reproduction hardware is not always as good as the original hardware for fit and finish, if it can be found. The original hardware can be re-plated and repaired, but at great cost. This is the reason care is taken not to damage the old hardware when removing or reinstalling it.

Reconditioning the old hardware begins by degreasing and cleaning the sun visor brackets. Polish the visor pivot brackets with #0000 steel wool and then use a quality chrome polish to protect the metal from further oxidation. A little rubbing can reveal a gleaming treasure.

Install the visor support rod end into the pivot bracket. It may need to be gently tapped onto the rod end with a plastic mallet, but do not force the casting or pry it open. Replace the tension screw in the pivot bracket and tighten the screw enough to keep the visor from turning. Do not overtighten the screw as it can always be adjusted later.

This self-edged sun visor is becoming more popular with restorers due to the simplicity of the turned edge over the cost and difficulty of setting up a binding attachment.

HEADLINER

Creating a Turned-Edge Sun Visor

1 A center point is established on the leading edge of the cover board to indicate the positioning of the decorative vinyl finger grab. This feature is added to the cover material prior to it being glued in place on the cover board.

2 The cover material has been placed face down on the workbench and marked with the outline of the cover board plus an extra 1/2 inch to create an oversize piece of material. The extra material allows for wrapping of the cover board.

3 New finger grabs have been patterned and cut from the coordinating interior vinyl. Reference marks have been added to the new vinyl finger grabs, which help with their placement. A light coat of glue is applied to the backside of the vinyl to help hold it in place while it is sewn in place.

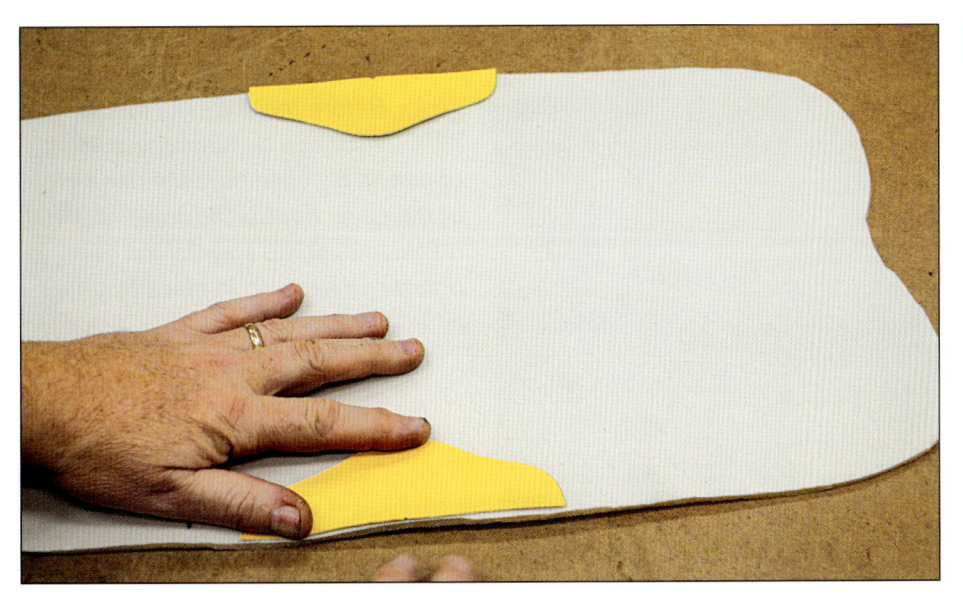

4 Before the vinyl finger grabs can be sewn onto the cover material they are aligned with the index mark in the center of the cover material. A small piece of muslin material is placed under the cover material as a backer to hold the stitching.

AUTOMOTIVE UPHOLSTERY AND INTERIOR RESTORATION

CHAPTER 5

5 The vinyl finger grab is now sewn permanently in place to the surface of the cover material with a small stitch along its perimeter. To reduce the underlying bulk, the muslin backer is trimmed back to the stitching of the finger grab.

6 The cover board is prepped for assembly by spraying the outside surface with a light coat of glue. At this stage of assembly, padding can be added to the cover board before the cover material is applied.

7 The cover material is placed face down on the workbench and the cover board is carefully set in place with an equal amount of material overhanging the edge of the cover board all around. The cover material is checked for wrinkles as it is smoothed into place.

8 Before the edges of the sun visor can be turned, a coating of glue is brushed onto the perimeter of the cover board. The cover material is folded over the edge of the cover board and secured in place by glue.

AUTOMOTIVE UPHOLSTERY AND INTERIOR RESTORATION

HEADLINER

9 The cover material at the notched end of the cover board is cut diagonally into the corners of the notch and turned in. The rest of the cover material in now folded over the edge of the cover board, producing a smooth, finished edge.

10 Before the cover board can be sewn it must be assembled with the inner core. Glue is brushed onto the outer edge of the cover board and allowed to get tacky. The glue holds the folded cover board together after the inner core is set in place.

11 Fold the cover board over the inner core. Be sure to align the vinyl finger grabs and outer edges of the sun visor evenly and press the glued edges together. The inner core should now be firmly held in place with the pin end of the spine exposed.

12 The sun visor is now ready to be sewn closed. The cover is sewn together with a wide stitch and a 1/4-inch reveal beginning from the pin end of the sun visor and continuing to the front end. After sewing, the ends of the threads are tied off.

AUTOMOTIVE UPHOLSTERY AND INTERIOR RESTORATION

CHAPTER 5

13 *You can see the difference a little polishing can make on the old hardware (left). Clean and polish the sun visor brackets and tension screws with #0000 steel wool and a good chrome polish to protect them from further corrosion.*

14 *The sun visor brackets are tapped back onto the pin end of the sun visor. Tensioning screws retain the brackets. The screws are set with only slight tension and are adjusted once the sun visor is installed into the car.*

15 *The finished sun visors are ready to be installed and they look great. With the simplicity of this modern variation, more sun visor restorations today use the turned or self-edged method rather than the traditional bound method.*

AUTOMOTIVE UPHOLSTERY AND INTERIOR RESTORATION

HEADLINER

Installing a Sun Visor

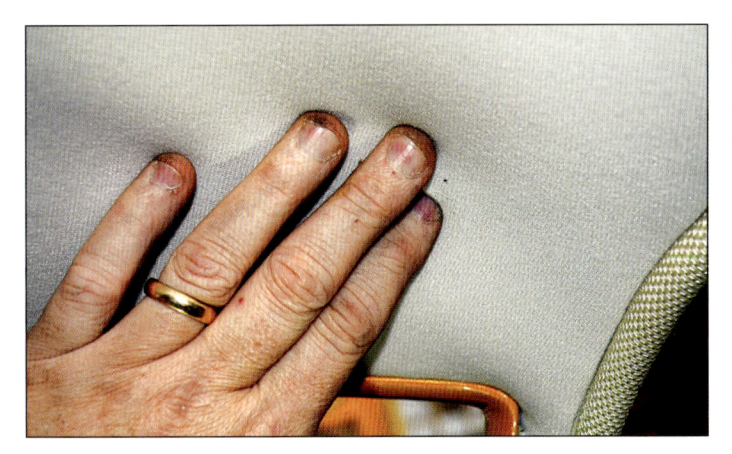

1 The final step is to mount the sun visor in the car. Locating the sun visor mounting holes can be a little bit of a challenge. Feel for the mounting hole underneath the headliner material before you cut into the headliner material.

2 After locating the sun visor bracket mounting position, a small opening is cut into the headliner material. This opening allows the sun visor's mounting bracket to rest correctly on the header panel of the car.

3 The sun visor bracket can now be fitted to the roofline and secured with the correct mounting screws. The weight of the sun visor must be supported while the screws are tightened. This protects the sun visor bracket from damage.

4 The last thing to do to the sun visor is adjust the tension screw. When the tension is adjusted properly, the sun visor stays in place without sagging or binding.

AUTOMOTIVE UPHOLSTERY AND INTERIOR RESTORATION

CHAPTER 5

Package Tray

The flat interior area behind the rear seat and up to the rear window of a car is known as the package tray or parcel shelf.

Notorious for being covered in "fun fur" and cut up to mount 6 x 9 speakers, the package tray is not just a great place to put packages, but it made a convenient place for the driver to store his or her hat while driving.

I recall a story that my dad told me long ago about the trips he had taken in the family 1931 Ford with his sister and mother. He had to lie in the package tray as a seven-year-old child because there was not enough room for him to sit on the seat of the Model A. The package tray can be used many ways, but what do you do when it becomes damaged from the sun, water, and previous owners with a Zen for to loud music?

The metal shelf provides a foundation for the fiberboard liner. The liner may have been made of a textured Masonite or heavy cardboard with a matching color coat. Other liners are fabric or vinyl covered to complement the car's interior. To help block road noise, early cars used a tarpaper insulator under the fiberboard liner. To improve on the insulation of the cab and increase sound dampening properties, later-model cars used a thin jute pad under the package tray.

Before investing time and materials into fabricating a new package tray, it is in your best interest to repair any issues with water leaks and rust due to a worn or damaged rubber window seal.

This is typical of what the car owner did to the package tray in the 1970s: upgrading the sound system with 6 x 9 coaxial speakers and adding fun fur to the package tray. The appearance of this package tray makes it hard to believe this is a 1962 Cadillac.

The underlying rear deck of this 1950 Buick will be the home for a new package tray. The metal shelf is not only a foundation for the package tray but a structural element of the car as well, separating the trunk from the cab.

Making a Pattern

I consider the package tray replacement the final step of a headliner restoration. If the original package tray is intact it may make a good pattern for the new one. I usually make a new pattern to ensure an exact fit. I use the cardboard from shipping boxes since it is abundant and makes an excellent patterning material because it is so easy to cut and manipulate.

Basic measurements are gathered by measuring the depth and width of the metal package shelf. This measurement gives you a starting point to rough cut the first piece of cardboard for the package tray

HEADLINER

A pattern of the package tray must be created before final materials can be cut. The patterning process starts by taking measurements of the package tray area. These measurements are used to precut cardboard pieces for the pattern.

Scribing the profile of the rear cab onto the cardboard is done with a marker. The cardboard is trimmed and checked for fit. This process of marking and trimming continues until the pattern fits the package tray area correctly.

pattern. It is not necessary to make the pattern from one solid piece of cardboard. Several smaller pieces of cardboard are actually easier to work with.

The first piece of cardboard is set in place on the metal package shelf. A marker is used to scribe the profile of the rear cab and window area onto the cardboard. The cardboard is then trimmed to fit the contours of the rear cab. Small amounts of cardboard are cut away until the new pattern fits the profile of the rear window area.

Additional pieces of cardboard are scribed and fitted into the pattern to fill in areas that need extra pattern material or may have been trimmed short. The edges of the added pieces of cardboard are traced onto the pattern with reference marks for alignment. Masking tape is used to hold the new pieces in place as the scribing and cutting continues. Work the cardboard until the new package tray pattern fits perfectly.

Mark the underside of the pattern along the leading edge of the package shelf to indicate the profile of the leading edge of the package tray.

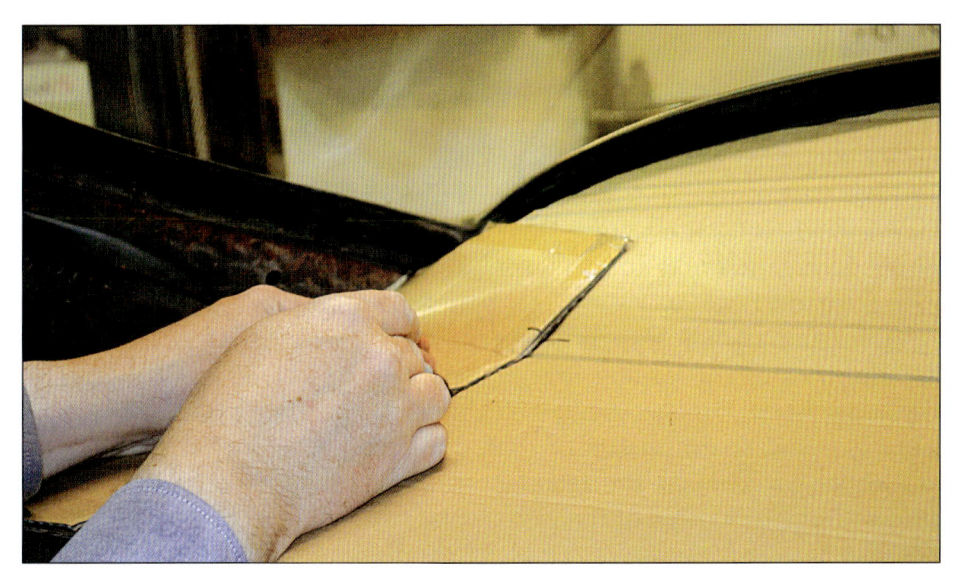

Voids in the pattern can be filled with additional pieces of cardboard. Smaller pieces make the patterning task much easier. The pieces are marked for position and taped together to form a continuous pattern.

AUTOMOTIVE UPHOLSTERY AND INTERIOR RESTORATION

Building a Package Tray

The completed pattern is now brought to the workbench and placed on top of a new sheet of waterproof panel board. The perimeter of the pattern is traced onto the panel board. The edges of the new panel board should be smooth. Fix any wavy or irregular lines in the traced outline before the new package tray blank is cut.

The best way to cut the panel board is with a utility knife fitted with a fresh blade. Cut just outside the line that was traced to remove the bulk of the panel board and do the final cutting with heavy-duty scissors.

When the package tray is wrapped, the thickness of the vinyl increases the size of the package tray. This causes trouble when the package tray is fit into the car. To correct the potential problem, the outside edges of the package tray blank must be relieved by 1/16 inch along the outside perimeter. When this is done, the finished package tray fits properly and lies flat after it is installed in the car.

The leading edge of the package tray needs to be fitted with a 1-inch-wide band that is used to retain an anchor strip. The anchor strip provides a decorative edge on the front of the package tray as well as a way to hold the package tray in place. You will eventually finish the ends of the anchor strip by folding and then gluing them under the package tray.

An additional piece of panel board is cut 1¼ inches wide by the length of the package tray. The anchor strip retainer is now aligned 1 inch back from the front of the package tray and temporarily stapled in place to hold it while it is scribed to fit the front edge of the package tray. After the profile of the front edge of the package tray has been scribed to the anchor strip, remove the staples and retainer strip. Trim the retainer strip back to the scribed line. Relieve the front outside edges of the package tray by 1/16 inch and the depth of the anchor strip to allow for the thickness of the vinyl that will be applied later. Now that you have all the raw components cut, it is time to finish the package tray by wrapping it with a cover layer of matching vinyl.

Roll out the vinyl face down on the workbench and place the package tray blank face down on top of the vinyl. Mark and then cut the vinyl cover material 1 inch larger than the package tray blank. Also cut an anchor strip of vinyl 4 inches wide and 2 inches longer than the width of the leading edge of the package tray. Spray a light coat of glue to the face of the package tray blank and onto the backside of the vinyl cover material.

The package tray blank is positioned over the vinyl with an even amount of vinyl material on all edges. Turn the package tray over and apply even pressure to the surface of the vinyl, pressing it into the glue. Work from the center outward to remove any bubbles or wrinkles before the vinyl is secured to the package tray blank. Trim away the excess vinyl along the leading edge of the package tray so that it is flush with the panel board blank.

Place the anchor strip of vinyl face down along the leading edge of the package tray. Now lay the scribed band of panel board on top of the anchor strip and align the retainer strip with the front edge of the package tray.

Temporarily staple the retainer strip in place with 1/2-inch wire staples. The staples are there only to hold the retainer strip in position as it is being sewn. They are removed as the anchor strip is sewn to the package tray.

With the sewing machine set to a wide stitch, remove the first few staples and begin to sew the retainer strip and vinyl anchor onto the package tray with a 3/8-inch reveal. This locks the retainer strip in place on the package tray. Continue sewing and removing the temporary staples as you go. If you do not remove the staples, the surface of your sewing table may be scratched as they are dragged through the sewing machine. Sew off the panel board and on through to the end of the vinyl strip.

To finish the package tray the edges are turned under and glued in place. Turn the package tray over and apply glue to the outside edges of the panel board and along the backside of the excess vinyl.

Turn the vinyl over the edge of the package tray, making sure that it is pulled tight and that it lies flat and smooth all the way around the perimeter of the package tray. Relief cuts can be made in the curve if necessary to minimize any puckering of the vinyl.

Apply glue to the outside ends of the anchor strip and wrap them to the underside of the package tray.

This finishes the package tray construction. It is now ready for installation.

Installing a Package Tray

A layer of jute padding is first cut and fitted to the surface of the metal package shelf before it is glued in place.

The package tray is installed over

HEADLINER

the jute pad by simply sliding the assembly in place. Garnish moldings hold in some trailing edges of the package tray while others are tucked under the rear window rubber to hold them in place.

The front edge of the package tray is secured in place by applying glue to the anchor strip and to the front of the metal package shelf. The anchor strip is then pressed into place to hold the package tray secure.

Creating a Package Tray

1 The cardboard pattern is traced onto a sheet of waterproof panel board. Before the new package tray can be cut out of the panel board, imperfections in the tracing are smoothed out. The new package tray blank is then trimmed to the cut line.

2 The outside edge of the package tray must be relieved by 1/16 inch to compensate for the thickness of the vinyl material that is applied and wrapped around the edges of the panel board. The front edge is not affected by the cover material.

3 A 1-inch retainer strip is fitted to the front edge of the package tray to secure the anchor strip. Index marks are made at the leading edge of the package tray to line up the anchor strip so that it can be scribed accurately to fit.

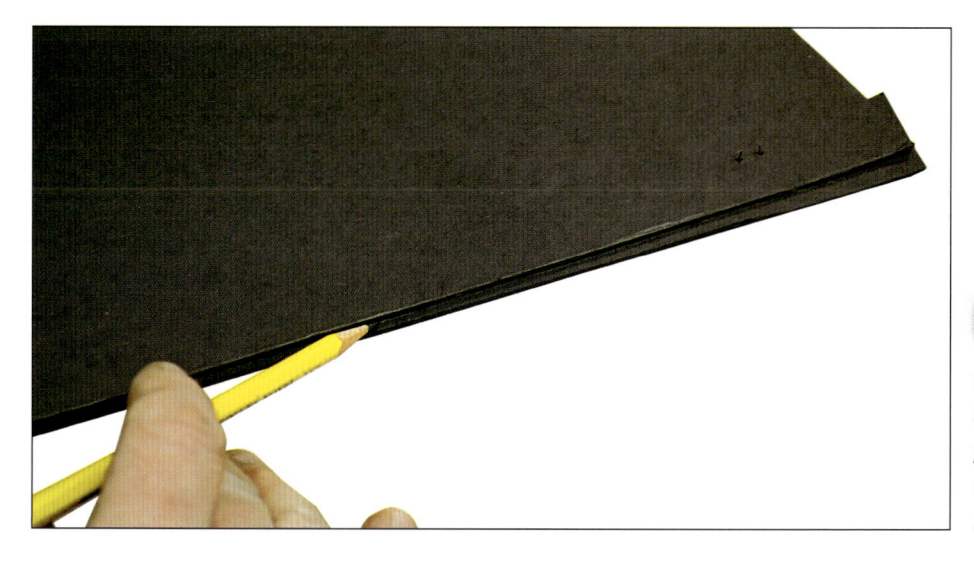

4 The retainer strip is cut, aligned, and temporarily stapled in place on the leading edge of the package tray. The profile of the front edge of the package tray is scribed onto the retainer strip so that it contours to the leading edge of the package shelf.

AUTOMOTIVE UPHOLSTERY AND INTERIOR RESTORATION

CHAPTER 5

5 The vinyl cover material for the package tray is rolled out face down on the workbench. The package tray profile is marked on the vinyl and cut 1 inch oversize for the package tray. An additional oversize piece of vinyl is cut for the anchor strip.

6 The vinyl material is secured to the package tray blank with a light coat of glue. The glue is sprayed onto the vinyl and panel board. The package tray is then set into position on the vinyl, allowing an equal amount of material to be exposed around the perimeter.

7 Smoothing the vinyl from the center outward helps remove any trapped air bubbles and wrinkles in the package tray. After the surface has been smoothed over, the vinyl at the leading edge of the package tray can be trimmed flush with the edge of the panel board.

HEADLINER

8 At the front of the package tray is an anchor strip of vinyl that holds the package tray in place. A retainer strip secures the anchor strip. The retainer strip is temporarily stapled into position until it is sewn permanently in place.

9 Sewing the retainer strip to the package tray secures the anchor strip in place permanently. A wide stitch preserves the strength of the panel board and prevents the materials from perforation tear out.

10 The edge of the package tray is wrapped to give it a finished appearance Glue is applied to the outer edges of the package tray and overhanging vinyl. The vinyl is folded over the edge of the panel and held in place by the glue.

11 Finish the edge of the package tray by pulling the vinyl taut as you turn over the edge and press it into the glue. Make small relief cuts to allow the vinyl to lie flat on the backside of the package tray.

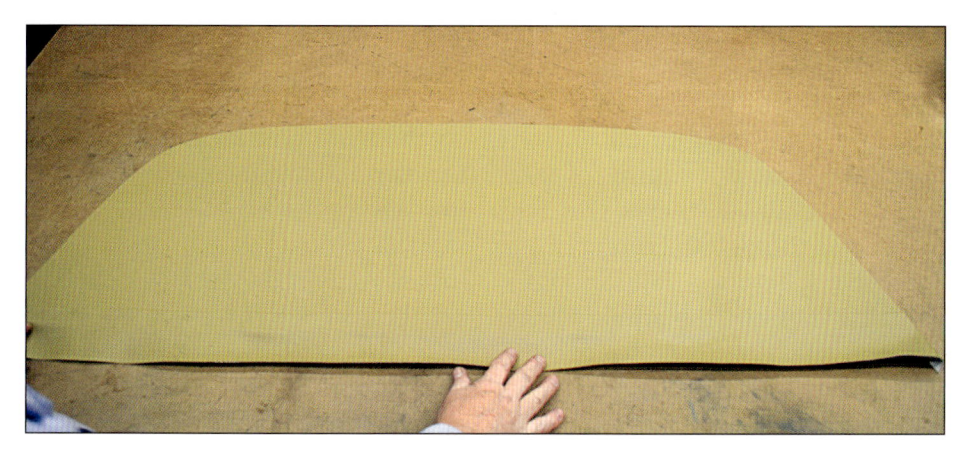

12 Each end of the retainer strip is folded over and glued in place on the backside of the package tray. The surface of the vinyl along the edges must be flush with the contour of the package tray. The completed package tray can now be installed in the car.

AUTOMOTIVE UPHOLSTERY AND INTERIOR RESTORATION   147

CHAPTER 5

13 The package tray is fit into position over the metal package shelf. The rear edge of the package tray is tucked up to the window and is held in by the window garnish molding. Care is taken so that the sail areas of the headliner are not wrinkled or distorted.

14 To keep the package tray in position, glue is brushed onto the backside of the anchor strip and along the front edge of the metal package shelf. The anchor strip is pulled down and pressed into the glue to hold the package tray securely in place.

Package Tray: Variation

Since the package tray is the most convenient and ample place to install speakers, it then ends up with the look of those ugly plastic grille covers, which is just an unacceptable accessory for any restoration. The best alternative is to incorporate blind speaker grilles into the package tray, creating an unmolested and clean original appearance.

The speakers should be flush mounted underneath the metal package shelf. The mounting hardware must be countersunk into the metal, leaving the surface of the package shelf unobstructed. When done correctly, the installed package tray lies flat and smooth.

During the process of patterning the new package tray, mark the location of the speaker cutouts. Trace your package tray pattern to the panel board and cut the speaker holes in the new package tray blank.

The cover material is laid out as usual except that the speaker area is marked so that it can be perforated.

The process of perforating the vinyl cover material is not difficult, but it is time-consuming. It only takes a few minutes to produce the pattern for perforating. The actual perforating takes time and patience. ■

The Grille Pattern

Speaker grilles came in two basic shapes, oval and round, and the shape is generally determined by the size and shape of the speaker. Other shapes and patterns can be used for the blind grille. It is up to you and the owner of the car to choose the pattern.

On a plain piece of paper, start with the square dimensions of your speaker and divide the box in half with a line through the center of the speaker area both vertically and horizontally. These are the primary lines. Now divide each quarter section with two additional diagonal lines. These are the secondary lines. If you do the math and measure correctly, the diagonal lines are equal distances from the center mark.

The perforation pattern is nothing more than dividing each line in 1/2-inch increments from the center point of the design outward. As the pattern expands, fill in the gaps with additional supplemental lines

AUTOMOTIVE UPHOLSTERY AND INTERIOR RESTORATION

HEADLINER

and points. You may notice with this radial pattern that the dots in the circle closest to the center almost touch each other. Do not punch a hole in the first round of the supplementary lines or the center will fall out.

Now that the pattern is complete, tape it to the speaker area on the face of the vinyl. Place a scrap piece of panel board under the pattern area to support the vinyl while it is being perforated.

With a 1/8-inch round punch and a heavy hammer, place the punch over the center point in the pattern and make a hole through the vinyl. Punch the primary vertical and horizontal holes first. Then move on to the secondary lines and punch the holes. Finish with the supplementary lines.

After the vinyl has been perforated it becomes weak and prone to warping. To correct this potential problem the vinyl needs to be supported. Gluing a piece of polyester fabric to the underside of the vinyl not only supports the vinyl, but it helps keep dirt and debris from settling on the speaker.

To bond the material to the vinyl, turn the vinyl face down on the workbench and spray a light coat of glue onto the vinyl. Press the fabric into the glue and smooth out any wrinkles. Once the vinyl is bonded to the package tray blank the grille is stable and resists warping.

The package tray is assembled by gluing the cover material to the face of the blank after lining up the perforated speaker grilles with the speaker cutouts on the package tray blank. Finish covering the package tray the same way as a standard one. The completed package tray is now ready to be installed.

Creating the Grille Pattern

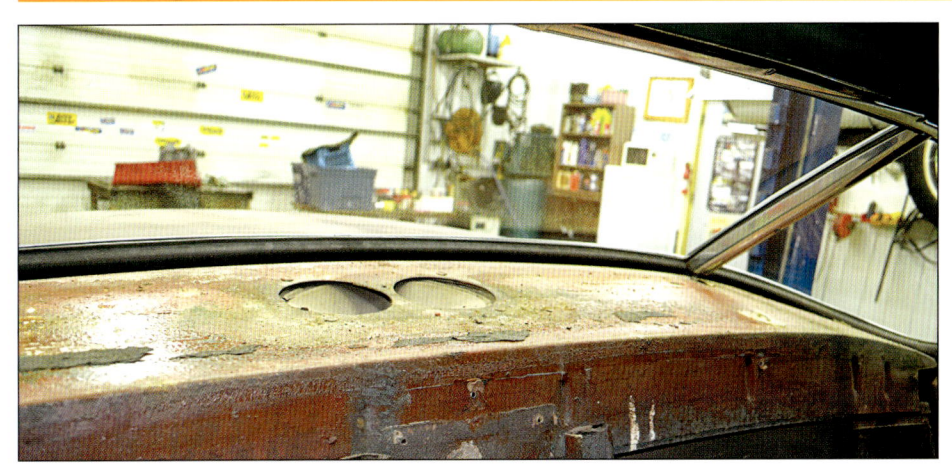

1 *The old package tray has been removed and the package shelf is cleaned in preparation for the new package tray. A new rear speaker is mounted to the underside of the metal package shelf, leaving the surface smooth and unobstructed.*

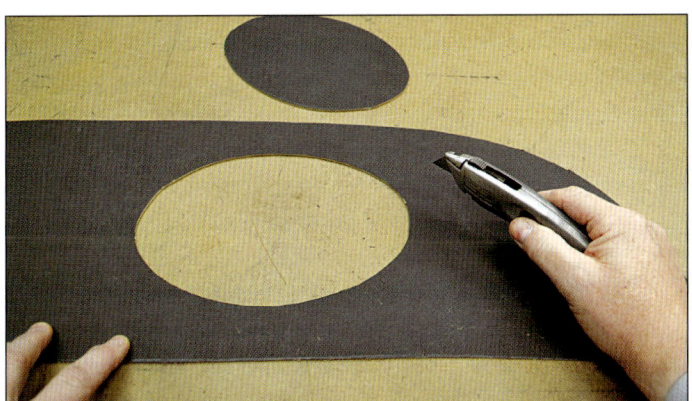

2 *A new package tray blank has been patterned and cut from a sheet of panel board. The speaker locations were marked and are now cut out of the panel blank to allow the full sound to come through without being muffled.*

3 *Coordinating interior vinyl is cut to the size of the new package tray and then set into position over the package tray blank. The speaker locations are chalked onto the vinyl to indicate where the blind speaker grilles are positioned.*

AUTOMOTIVE UPHOLSTERY AND INTERIOR RESTORATION

CHAPTER 5

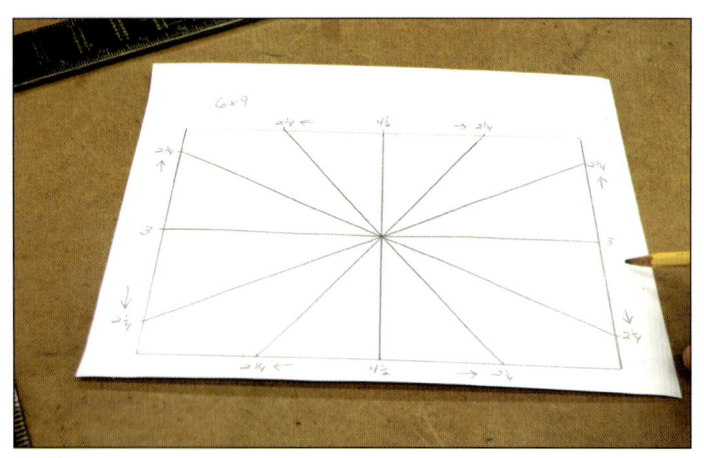

4 *Layout of the speaker grille design begins with a carpenter square and a sheet of paper. Simple measurements and basic math are used to create the foundation markings that yield a symmetrical grille design.*

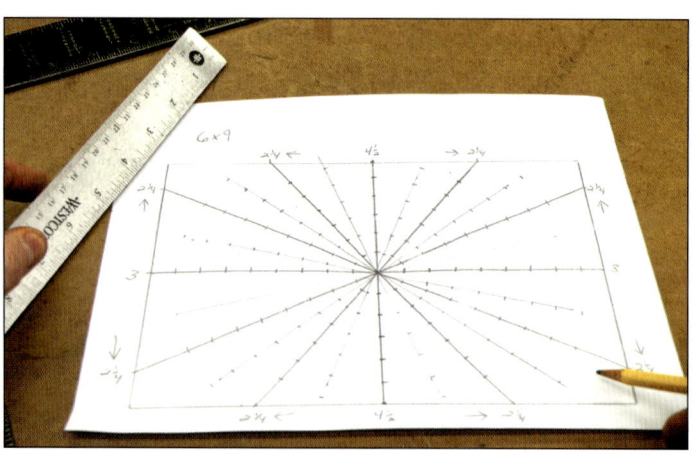

5 *Supplemental lines are added to fill in the open spaces of the speaker grille pattern. Working from the center point outward, the pattern lines are marked at 1/2-inch intervals to indicate where the perforations will be made.*

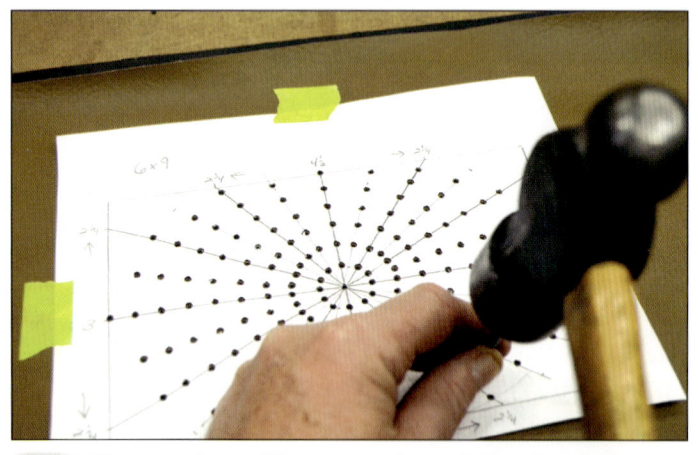

6 *The speaker grille pattern is positioned over the speaker area on the vinyl cover material and taped down. Perforations are made every 1/2 inch from the center point outward with a 1/8-inch round-hole punch and a heavy hammer.*

7 *Now that the vinyl has been perforated, it is prone to warping and needs additional support. A piece of polyester fabric is glued to the underside of the perforated speaker grille. The thin material will help prevent the speaker grille from warping and tearing out.*

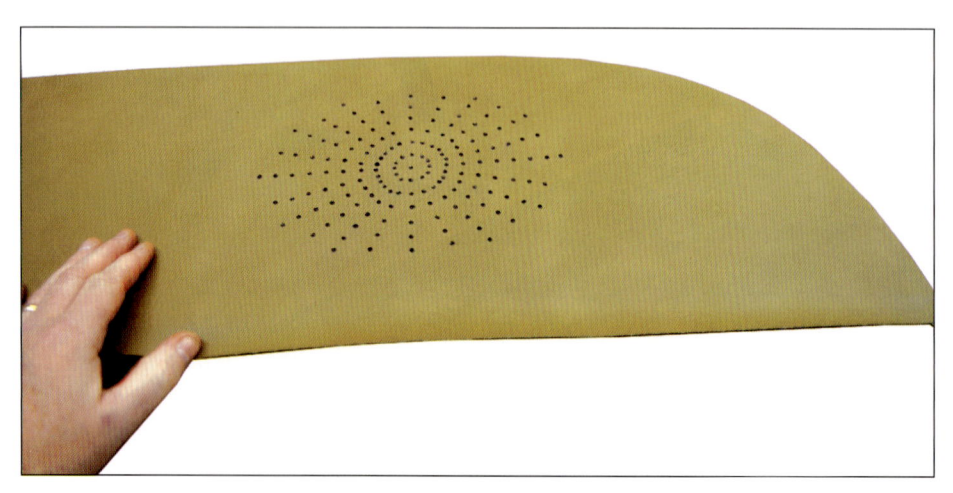

8 *Glue the perforated cover material to the package tray blank, taking care to align the speaker grilles over the speaker cutouts in the package tray blank. The edges of the assembly are finished as usual and the finished package tray is ready to be installed in the car.*

AUTOMOTIVE UPHOLSTERY AND INTERIOR RESTORATION

CHAPTER 6

CARPET

Open-car interiors were exposed to the elements and were often fitted with rubber mats for durability. Square-weave wool carpet was often used in prewar cars, and although it was a luxury item, it was reserved to the rear passenger area while the driver's compartment still had a rubber mat.

It wasn't until after World War II that an abundance of lower cost materials and modern fibers started to dominate the auto industry. Carpet was being made from polyesters and nylon, which proved to be more durable than natural fibers, and the synthetic fibers could be produced in vivid colors and variations in weave. The most popular choices for modern automotive carpets are loop and cut pile.

Early car carpets were not much more than a rug cut to fit the flat floor of the car. The raw edges were bound with a bias cotton material to prevent unraveling of the yarn, giving the carpet a clean, finished edge.

As cars evolved and body panel manufacturing processes became more mechanized, the auto carpeting process changed also. Cut and sewn carpets fit the contours of the stamped metal floors, and this gave the interior a much more tailored look. Modern carpet is produced by press molding the carpet to fit the contours of the car floor. This process proved to be cost efficient and the final result was a smooth and shapely carpet without seams.

It's not just what is on the surface of the car floor that matters. What you do not see is the carpet pad and sound deadener, and they matter more. Without the underlinings, the carpet job does not look as nice or perform as well.

Early autos used different types of material for sound deadeners to mute out the tinny sound reflected to the car floor from the tires and road. Tar-coated paper was laid onto the surface of the floor and the carpet was applied on top of the tarpaper. Other asphalt products were used as sound deadeners inside the car, but they were found to be a bit messy

Removal of the old carpet and pad can reveal some interesting surprises. After a good cleaning, inspect the floor for damage and repair any rust and hydraulic issues you find. Now is also the time to weld seat belt anchors to the floor.

AUTOMOTIVE UPHOLSTERY AND INTERIOR RESTORATION   151

when they melted and migrated into the upholstery due to the high temperatures a car interior reached.

Modern automobiles use a butyl rubber–based product that works well at deadening road noise and is a lot more stable under high-heat situations.

Over the top of the sound deadener you find a jute fiber material used as carpet padding. This carpet pad softens the surface of the metal floor, helping to protect the carpet from damage, and it also helps insulate the cab from noise and extreme temperatures.

Most auto carpet pad is made of jute fibers and recycled materials and they are spun and woven into rolled matting that can be easily cut and shaped to fit the contours of the floor. Household re-bond carpet pad is made from reclaimed foam rubber. This is not a desired product for automotive use because of its ability to hold water, which in turn causes the metal floor of the car to rust away.

Project Assessment

Reproduction carpet sets are not available for most of the cars I work on. When I do get a project for which a premade carpet set is an option, I rely on Auto Custom Carpets for the most accurate reproductions available. I buy my cut carpet yardage from them as well.

The first step to putting carpet in a car is to evaluate the condition of the floor and get some measurements. Remove the remaining carpet and pad from the car and then give the car a thorough vacuuming of the floor area. Inspect the floor for rust and holes. If the floor is not sound it must be repaired before any work can be done. Do not just throw a patch over a rotten floor and expect it to hold. The floor needs solid metal for safety and to keep dirt and water from coming into the cab of the car.

If you want seat belts, now is the time to weld in the seat belt anchors. Choosing to do these repairs later requires removal of the carpet and padding. Always degrease the floor and then prime any bare metal to prevent future rust.

Before work starts, you should also know that it is always easier to pattern the carpet with the accelerator pedal removed from the floor. Some car models do not allow you this luxury. It may be best to leave the pedal alone if the attaching bolts are rusted. Creating more work for yourself is not the goal. Working around an obstacle may take a little more effort, but it gives you fewer headaches in the long run.

Measure the length of the floor from the firewall to the rear seat riser and from sill to sill to get the rough dimensions of the car floor. These measurements help you determine the amount of materials needed for the project. The basic materials needed to carpet a car are carpeting, padding, edge binding, heel pad, and a dimmer grommet. Other options that you might consider are adding seat belts to the car and sound deadener to the floor. Also check the condition of the firewall pad to see if it needs to be replaced. It is a safe bet that it is rotten and dried out or missing altogether.

Place an order for all the materials you need to complete the project. When you have all the materials on hand you can schedule the project and begin the work.

The floor of the car should be clean and free of any dirt and oil to ensure a good bond from any applied materials.

Now is the time to apply any sound deadener material to the floor.

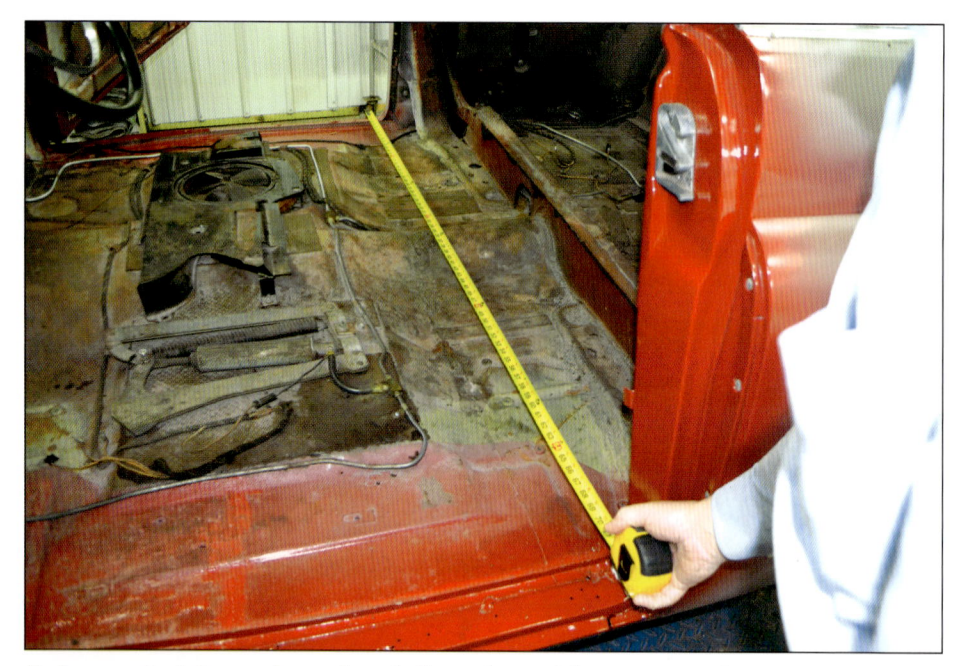

Before materials can be ordered, the cab must be measured to ensure enough carpet and padding is on hand to complete the job. Measuring from front to back and side to side allows you to calculate the correct amount of materials needed.

CARPET

Dynamat is the most recognized brand most car people use. Other brands are available; however, you must be careful what you buy. Some car owners want to save money and purchase asphalt-based products from the local home improvement store. The asphalt melts under extreme heat and causes staining to the interior. Always use a proven product.

The Pad

Jute pad is used as an underlayment for the carpet. Auto carpet pad is available in several weights and thicknesses and is glued in place to keep it from bunching up under the carpet.

I like to add small pieces and strips of jute pad to the depressed areas of the floor and around wires and hydraulic lines to help smooth the surface and build the floor up to allow the carpet to lie evenly.

Once the floor is built up, roll out a piece of jute carpet pad and begin to trim it to fit the general shape required. Use a heat-resistant contact cement to bond the pad to the surface of the floor to keep the pad from moving and shifting. A pressure spray pot or cup gun can be used to apply the glue to the floor and carpet. Aerosol spray cans are usually not well suited for this application, but they can be used.

If the car has a master cylinder access in the floor, do not glue the pad to the floor in this area so that the carpet can be easily lifted to service the brakes in the future.

There should be no obstruction or binding when the carpet pad is laid around the pedals. Make relief cuts up to the pedals and cut away enough material so that the carpet pad lies flat and smooth around the pedals without interfering with their safe operation.

Now is the best time to cut away the pad that is covering the seat belt and seat mounting holes. Cut away and remove enough pad material to expose the threaded hole while the pad is still exposed. This step will save you a lot of grief later when you are ready to install the anchor bolts.

The stamped floor of the car is full of ridges and depressions. Adding pieces of jute carpet pad to these low areas helps level the floor so that the carpet can lie smooth, which reduces wear.

To conceal and help protect the hydraulic lines and wire loom that run across the floor of the car, a second layer of jute carpet pad is built up around the obstacles. Glue is used to keep the jute pieces in place.

CHAPTER 6

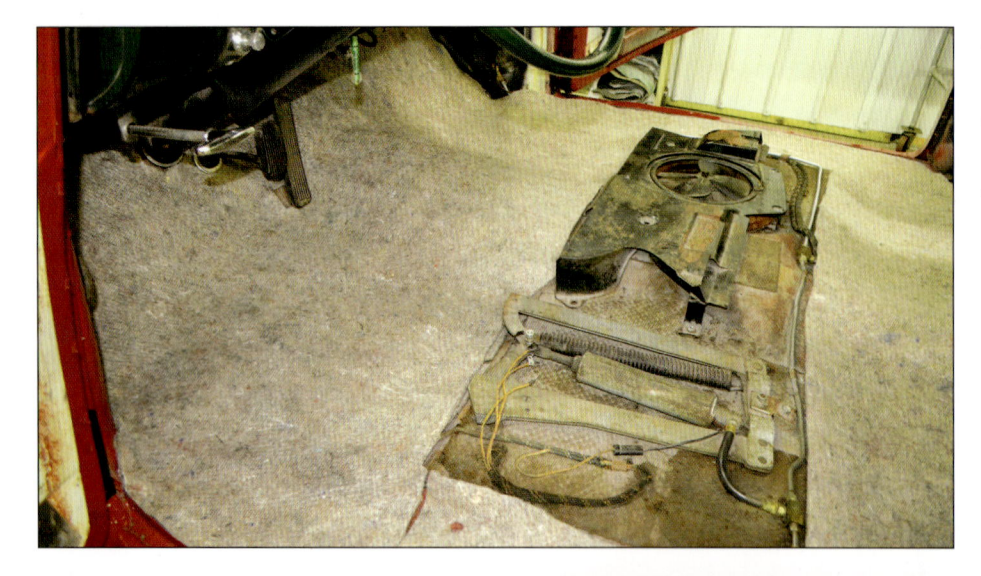

Cutting the jute pad to fit the floor is necessary to prevent obstructions to pedals and promote safe operation of the car. Once the carpet pad is trimmed and fit the carpet can be installed.

Jute padding is used to cover the floor. The padding doesn't just support and soften the carpet, it helps insulate the cab from extreme temperatures and deadens road noise.

Carpet Measurements

After the floor of the car has been leveled and the carpet pad has been glued in place, it is time to measure for the carpet pieces. A typical carpet set is usually done in two pieces to make handling and installation of the heavy carpet much easier. Some cars, such as Corvettes, have multiple pieces that make up the carpet set.

Rough cut the rear section of carpet from the roll of carpet that was ordered and set the carpet in place. When working a carpet on a contoured surface, always start with the center of the carpet and work your way to the outside edges. This way the carpet pulls inward evenly and yields the best results. Smooth the carpet out and try to get it to lie as flat and even as possible over the transmission tunnel.

With the carpet fitted smoothly over the transmission tunnel and onto the floor, press the carpet tight to the floor line and chalk the contour line from the flat floorpan up along the edge of the transmission tunnel where the carpet begins to bunch. This must be relief cut on both sides of the transmission tunnel so the carpet can lie smooth without any wrinkles.

It is a good practice to trim away the carpet pad from around the seat mounting holes before the carpet is installed because the thick jute pad is much easier to cut before it is glued in place. Also, don't forget to cut around the seat belt anchors.

154   AUTOMOTIVE UPHOLSTERY AND INTERIOR RESTORATION

Cut along the chalk lines to allow the carpet to conform to the contours of the floor and transmission tunnel. Only make a single cut line on each side so that the carpet lies smoothly on top of the transmission tunnel. The carpet should now lie nicely with the top of the cut edge over and with the floorpan carpet under. Notice that the lower carpet is longer and the overlap covers the carpet pad, which makes a smooth looking carpet.

You need a reference mark where the rear carpet piece ends. Chalk the leading edge of the carpet onto the carpet pad. This reference line tells you where the front and rear sections meet.

Now measure from the firewall back to the rear carpet edge. Add 4 inches to that measurement and cut a piece of carpet for the front section.

Fit the Pedals

Fit the newly cut front carpet section into place and then fold the front of the carpet section back onto itself with the folded edge at the base of the accelerator pedal. Chalk out the width of the pedal and then draw two parallel lines 3/4 inch apart so that you have a rectangle on the backside of the carpet.

Cut the carpet to create a rectangular hole just big enough to fit around the accelerator pedal. You want the carpet to cover the area around the base of the accelerator without any floor or ragged edges showing. Now carefully lift the carpet over the accelerator pedal and slide the carpet to the base of the pedal. Smooth the carpet out, making sure that the accelerator pedal operates with no obstruction. Check the overall fit of the carpet section. There should be an equal amount of carpet at each door opening and the carpet should be overlapping the bottom of the firewall by a couple of inches.

Fold the carpet squarely until it meets the brake pedal shaft. Chalk a reference line in the center of the pedal shaft and then make a relief cut from the top edge of the carpet to allow the carpet to split around the brake pedal shaft. Repeat the same process of folding, chalking, and cutting with the base of the steering column. After making the relief cut, lay the carpet up and around the column.

Now cut away just enough extra material from around the base of the brake pedal and steering column so that the carpet lies flat and smooth under the base of the pedal and steering column. Fold the carpet up to the bottom of the dimmer switch and mark the outside edges. Then fold the carpet to the side of the dimmer switch and mark the top and bottom edges of the switch. Cut a circle inside the square box that you just made for the dimmer switch. Test the fit of the cutout and make any adjustment necessary before fitting a dimmer grommet into the carpet. The carpet should lie smooth and pucker-free at this stage.

Fit the Transmission

The carpet also must be relieved at the top of the transmission tunnel. Smooth the carpet out so that it lies flat across the top of the transmission tunnel. Chalk a line on the carpet running down the center of the upper transmission tunnel to the base of the flared sheet metal.

Pull the carpet tight and smooth it out over the transmission tunnel. Now chalk an arch on the carpet by following around the base line of the transmission flare. Start chalking from the base of the accelerator pedal and continue going up and around to the upper inside corner of the passenger-side floorpan.

Cut the top part of the carpet in a straight line. This relief cut allows the carpet to overlap and lie smoothly over the upper arch in the floor.

The bottom arch can now be cut along the chalk line, giving you two equal flaps. When laid back into place, the contour of the floor causes the lower portion of the carpet to be longer on the bottom with the upper section lying on top. The two upper flap sections should now overlap from right and then left.

Locate the center point on the transmission tunnel and redefine the centerline on the upper overlapping flaps by drawing a new line straight up with chalk. Add witness marks with chalk onto the upper flaps so that they can be aligned and sewn together.

Fit the Heel Pad

To add durability to the driver's side of the front carpet a color-matched heel pad is fit in front of the pedals. Auto Custom Carpets supplied the medium-size heel pad along with the cut carpet yardage. The heel pad is set in place so that it is square to the pedals. The perimeter of the pad is chalked onto the carpet to indicate its position. The heel pad is glued and sewn onto the carpet so that it does not shift after the carpet is installed.

Before removing the carpet the trailing ends of carpet need to be trimmed to the reference line on the carpet pad. The outside edges of the carpet are not trimmed to size at this time. The final trimming is performed after the carpet is sewn and permanently installed. The chalked carpet set can now be removed from the car and set up on the workbench.

CHAPTER 6

Prepping the Carpet

1 For ease of handling, this is a two-piece carpet set. Measurements are made for the front and rear sections of carpet. An oversize piece of carpet is rough cut from the roll of carpet.

2 The rear edge of the carpet is squared up and fitted smoothly over the transmission tunnel and tight to the rear seat riser. Trimming can now begin on the carpet to get it to fit the width and contours of the floor.

3 A contour line is drawn along the side of the transmission tunnel from the inside upper corner of the floorpan to the leading edge of the carpet. Cutting along this line allows the carpet to lie flatter and relieve the bunching.

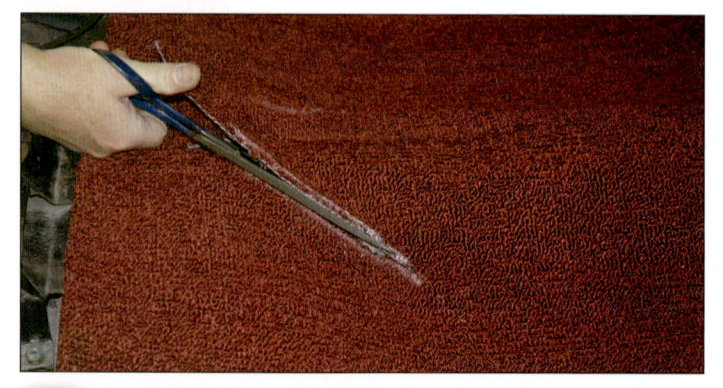

4 A relief cut is made along the chalk line, allowing the carpet to lie flat under the cut line. The carpet can now relax and flow smoothly up and over the transmission tunnel while it stays flat in the floorpan.

AUTOMOTIVE UPHOLSTERY AND INTERIOR RESTORATION

CARPET

5 After making the relief cuts in the carpet you can see how much nicer the carpet contours to the floorpan. Working from the center outward produces an even look to the carpet. Do not trim the outside edges too much now. They can be trimmed properly once the carpet is glued in place.

6 Square up the leading edge of the rear carpet and chalk a reference mark onto the jute padding. This mark helps when the front carpet section is fit. The two carpet sections meet here when they are glued in.

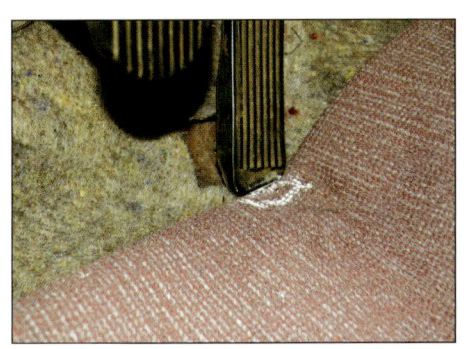

7 The front carpet section is folded and squared up to the accelerator pedal so reference lines can be drawn on the underside of the carpet section for the accelerator pedal. The carpet must fit snugly around the base of the accelerator pedal without binding and still lie flat along the floor.

8 A rectangular hole has been cut into the front carpet so that the carpet can be test fit over the accelerator pedal. The carpet section is checked for fit, making sure there is enough material to cover front to back as well as side to side.

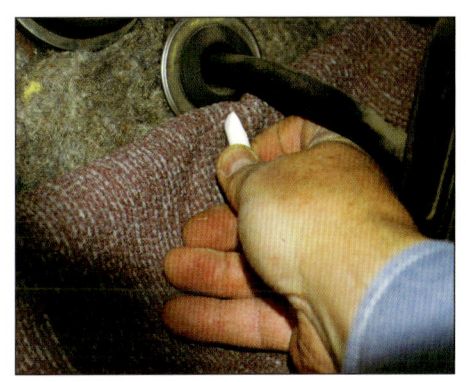

9 The carpet has been folded up to the base of the brake pedal and a chalk reference mark is made indicating where the carpet will be cut to relieve it around the brake pedal. A straight line can now be cut up to the base of the brake pedal.

AUTOMOTIVE UPHOLSTERY AND INTERIOR RESTORATION

CHAPTER 6

10 A relief in the carpet for the steering column is created in the same manner as it was for the brake pedal. The relief cut allows the carpet to be trimmed around the base of the brake pedal and steering column so the carpet can lie flat on the floor.

11 An opening around the dimmer switch was marked and cut carefully, letting the carpet lie flat on the floor. The raw carpet edge of the dimmer switch hole is covered with a rubber grommet, which gives it a neat and clean finished appearance.

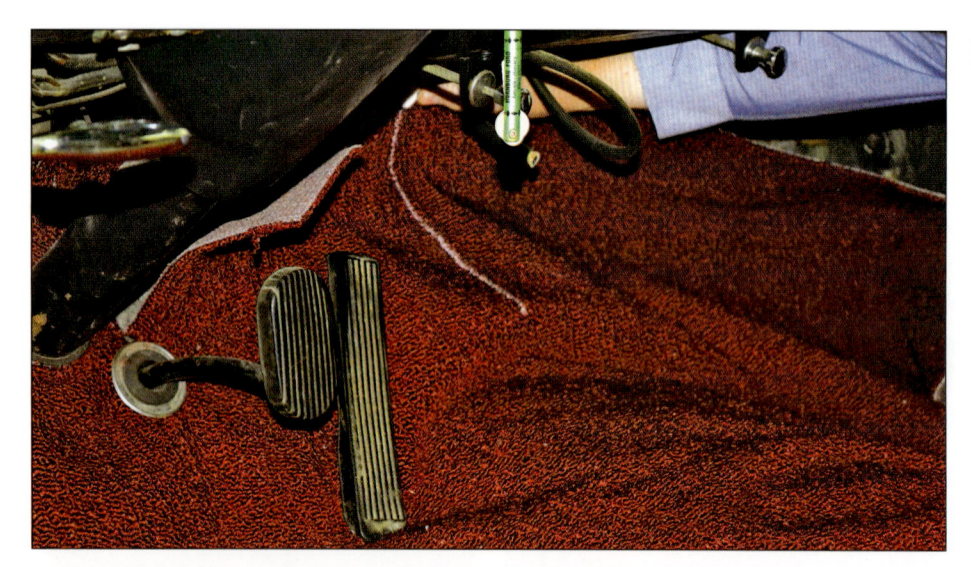

12 The carpet has been smoothed over the upper transmission tunnel and a centerline has been determined and chalked. This centerline will soon be cut to relieve the carpet so that it conforms to the curvature of the sheet metal.

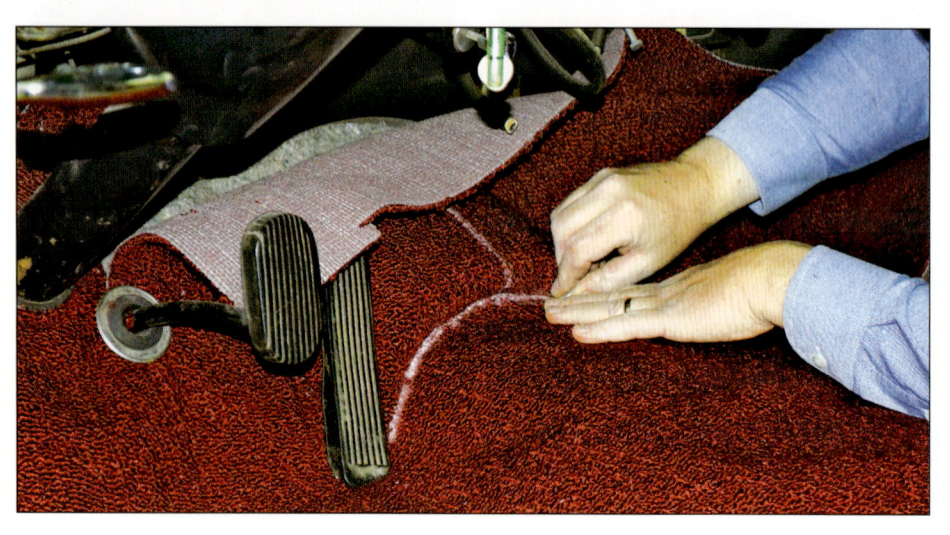

13 The baseline of the transmission tunnel is chalked onto the carpet to form an arch along the bottom of the flare in the transmission tunnel. After this line is cut the bulk of the carpet is relieved and the carpet lies flat and smooth over the curved sheet metal.

158   AUTOMOTIVE UPHOLSTERY AND INTERIOR RESTORATION

CARPET

14 A straight-line relief cut is made along the chalk line in the upper portion of the carpet. This cut divides the upper portion of the carpet in half, allowing the carpet to conform to the shape of the upper transmission tunnel.

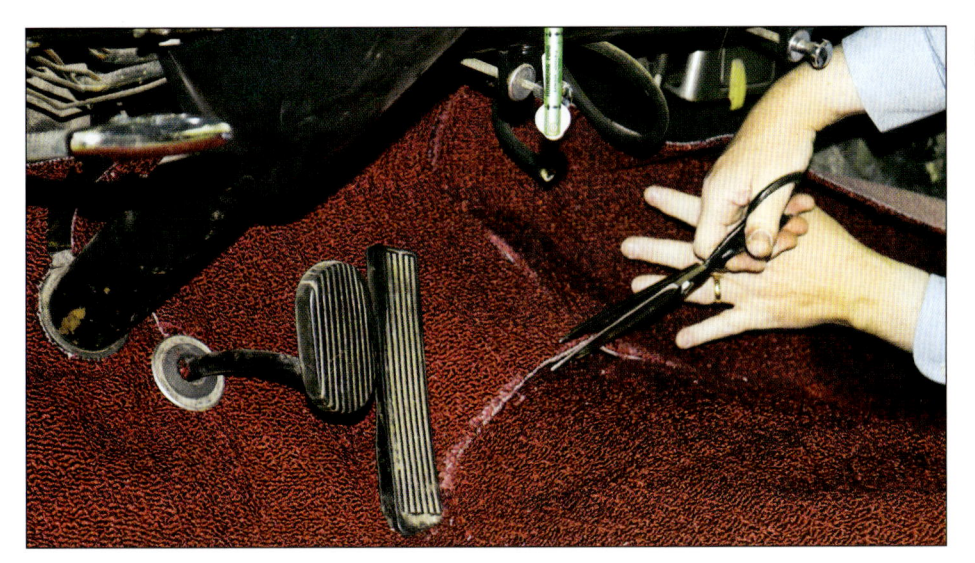

15 The lower section of the arch is cut freeing the upper flaps. The carpet can now be smoothed into position over the transmission tunnel. With the relief cuts made, the carpet should now fit the contour of the floor without any puckering or wrinkles.

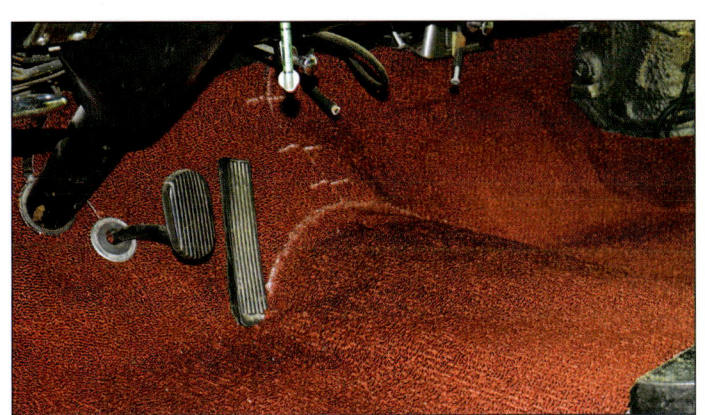

16 The carpet has been relieved and smoothed into place and a new center line is drawn on the upper flaps of the transmission tunnel. Witness marks are added to the upper flaps to aid in the alignment of the panels when the carpet is sewn together.

17 A color-coordinated heel pad is added to give extra durability to the driver's side of the carpet. As a reference for gluing and sewing, the location of the heel pad is marked onto the carpet by tracing its profile.

AUTOMOTIVE UPHOLSTERY AND INTERIOR RESTORATION

CHAPTER 6

Sewing

Before you start sewing the new carpet, a few things need to be addressed. Lay the carpet set out flat on the workbench. Observe that the chalk marks do not line up perfectly when the carpet lies flat on the bench. This is normal, but before it is sewn, some of the lines do need to be evened out.

Trim along the bottom edge of the upper flaps so that there is an extra 1/2 inch of material below the chalk line. This new cut line needs to make a smooth arch. Mark and then trim the centerline of the flaps, allowing 1/2 inch of extra material for a seam allowance.

Now look at the cutout area around the brake and steering column. These should be trimmed to make them rounder, which in turn will allow the carpet to lie flatter and smoother when it is installed in the car. It may be helpful to use an aerosol can as a guide to help round the opening.

The carpet is now prepped and ready for sewing and binding. Binding the raw edge of the carpet is not only decorative, but it keeps the carpet from fraying. Different types of binding can be used to finish the raw edges on carpeting.

Bias binding can be purchased and is available in many colors and materials. Automotive binding is generally made from vinyl. Premade binding usually has one folded edge and is 1¼ inches wide. If you cut your own binding it is best to cut it 2 inches wide and on the bias (diagonal) of the material to help minimize stretch.

Serge binding is done on a special machine that covers the edge of the carpet with a yarn-type thread. This looped edge is found on many vintage cars and on floor mats.

Begin sewing the center seam on the upper flaps. Align the witness marks and sew a straight seam from the bottom to the top of the flap. Once this section is rejoined the bottom edge should form a nice smooth arch with equal distances from the center seam.

Edge Binding

Only the edges of the carpet that show receive a binding. All other edges that are concealed by the carpet or trim are not bound.

The bottom edge of the arch receives a binding to keep the carpet from fraying. Place a 2-inch strip of vinyl face up under the face-down carpet and align the edges. Turn the starting edge of the vinyl in by 1/2 inch and begin sewing the binding with a 1/2-inch seam allowance. Splay the center seam selvedge apart so that the seam lies flat when the carpet is installed. Continue sewing until you are about 1½ inches from the end of the arch. Trim off the vinyl binding 1/2 inch past the end of the arch and then fold the vinyl back onto itself so that the end of the binding has a turned edge finish. Continue sewing to the end of the arch and then turn the carpet face up.

Now fold the vinyl strip tightly over the raw edge of the arch and sew through the face of the vinyl binding, creating an even and smooth top stitch with a 1/8-inch reveal. Bind the trailing ends of the front and rear carpet in the same way. Also bind the rear edge and the top edges of the center relief cuts on the rear carpet section. The lower edge of the transmission tunnel does not get bound.

Heel Pad

The heel pad is next to be sewn. This is a thick and heavy amount of material to put under the sewing machine presser foot, so it is best to bond the heel pad in place before sewing to ensure that it stays in the correct position.

Spray glue to the underside of the heel pad and then spray glue onto the surface of the carpet inside the chalked heel pad line. Set the heel pad in place and press into the glue for a good bond. Once the adhesive has set the heel pad is ready to be sewn to the carpet. You may struggle to get the carpet and heel pad positioned under the presser foot of the sewing machine, but it must lie flat and smooth so that the sewing machine can do its work.

Begin at the center top of the heel pad and sew around the edge of the heel pad in a clockwise direction. Work slowly and do not force the work. The needle must be able to go straight up and down to lock the stitches in place. The needle will break if it deflects from the carpet being pulled. Walk the needle around the corners of the heel pad and finish the sewing with a backstitch when you reach the beginning stitches.

Inspection

Lay the carpet out on the bench and inspect the work. The seams should be tight and the binding must lie flat without twisting. Remove any stray threads and glue overspray that might have been missed. Not all the edges of the carpet need to be bound. The sill plates cover the outside edges of the carpet and the front edge is tucked under the firewall insulation pad. The inside edges of the carpet are typically not bound because they are not seen after the seat has been installed.

Sewing the Carpet

1 Upon inspection of the new carpet set, the model reveals that some of the chalked lines need to be straightened and some additional trimming must be done before any sewing. Addressing these issues now gives the carpet a better fit when it is installed.

2 Making the bottom edge of the transmission arch smooth helps improve its look. A 1/2-inch seam allowance is left for the binding. The center seam is also addressed by straightening it out and creating an even seam allowance.

3 Premade bias binding can be used to finish the edges on most carpet sets, but I prefer to make my own binding from the matching interior vinyl. Strips of vinyl are cut 2 inches wide on the bias of the vinyl and they are sewn to the carpet edges.

AUTOMOTIVE UPHOLSTERY AND INTERIOR RESTORATION

CHAPTER 6

4 The center flaps on the carpet are sewn together to form a continuous arch over the top of the transmission. The center seam of the carpet is sewn carefully together by aligning the witness marks and sewing a straight seam to join the pieces together.

5 A strip of vinyl binding is placed face up under the carpet and sewn with a 1/2-inch seam allowance. The beginning and ending edges of the vinyl are turned in to give the binding a finished end. The selvedge of the center seam is splayed back to make the seam lay flat.

6 The binding is finished by turning the vinyl over the raw edge of the carpet and sewing a top stitch within 1/8 inch of the top edge of the vinyl, locking the wrapped edge on the underside of the carpet.

7 Glue is applied to the bottom side of the heel pad and to the area of the carpet it covers. The heel pad is carefully positioned on the carpet and the glue is allowed to set to keep the pad from shifting position while it is being sewn.

8 Patience and a steady hand are required when sewing through the heel pad and carpet. The thick material is stitched around the perimeter of the heel pad to hold the heel pad in place permanently.

AUTOMOTIVE UPHOLSTERY AND INTERIOR RESTORATION

9 *A final inspection is given to the sewn carpet set, making sure that all the seams are tight and the binding lies flat. Trim any stray threads and clean up any glue overspray that may have been overlooked.*

Carpet Installation

Install the carpet without glue to verify the fit and positioning of the sewn features. If any alterations need to be made, this is the time to chalk up any problem areas and fix them before installing the carpet. The carpet is held in place by gluing it down. This is done a little at a time so that the carpet can be smoothed and worked without causing positioning problems. Remember that a little glue goes a long way to hold the carpet in place, so go easy with it.

With the front carpet section dry fit in place, lift back the heel pad section from the left side over the center and spray glue onto the carpet pad and carpet. Reposition the heel pad so that it lies smooth without interfering with the accelerator pedal. This is the most visual section of the carpet and the heel pad needs to sit squarely in place. The carpet also must be centered in the car. Fold the carpet from the right over the center and spray glue on top of the transmission tunnel for the lower half of the carpet. Pull the carpet back and smooth it into place, making sure that the center seam of the upper section in the center of the transmission tunnel and the binding conform to the contour of the floor. Continue gluing in small sections until the carpet is smooth and wrinkle free. It may also be helpful to use the steamer to relax the carpet into place.

Roll the carpet down from the firewall, spray glue across the leading edge of the floor, and smooth the carpet back into place around the pedals. Carefully lift the bottom edge of the firewall insulation pad and tuck the leading edge of the carpet underneath. Continue fitting and gluing the carpet into the rear of the car by aligning and fitting the center section first and then moving outward to the doors.

Before the seat can be installed into the car the anchor holes for the mounting bolts need to be exposed. Cutting the carpet away is never an easy task and there is always the possibility that the seat bolt can snag a thread in the carpet and cause an ugly run. To avoid this potential problem and make installation of the seat bolts easier, I burn the anchor hole open with a 40-watt pencil-type soldering iron. This cauterizes the fibers of the carpet and prevents them from snagging. It also produces a perfect hole for the seat bolt without any fuss.

With an upholstery regulator, locate the seat anchor holes in the subfloor. Mark these spots, and then with a hot soldering iron poke the tip of the soldering iron into the anchor hole and rotate it for a few seconds. After the soldering iron is removed the anchor hole can be cleared of debris and it is ready for a seat-mounting bolt.

The final step is to fit the sill plates over the outside edges of the carpet. Because they are prone to damage, I do not install them until the seat has been mounted in the car. This is the last part that I install before delivering the car to my customer.

The key to getting the sill plates installed correctly is to not over-torque the screws. The sill plates are made of aluminum, a very soft metal that crushes easily.

Dry fit the sill plates to make sure they fit in the door opening without being touched by the closed door. Chalk the carpet along the inside

CHAPTER 6

edge of the sill plate. Now remove the sill plate. Trim back the edge of the carpet along the sill area, leaving the carpet just short of the screw holes in the doorsill. Do not cut the carpet at the chalk line or it will be too short. Reinstall the sill plate and adjust the flared ends if necessary to fit neatly around the windlace ends.

The windlace should be trimmed to fit just about 1 inch under the ends of the sill plate. Look to see if the screw holes line up correctly or if new mounting holes need to be drilled. If new mounting holes are needed, mark their position and remove the sill plate before you drill.

Again, the sill plates are fragile and the drill chuck will make a dent when the drill bit cuts through. Also check that the carpet is not covering any of the mounting holes. Carefully notch away just enough carpet to allow the screw clear access without snagging the carpet. Do not overtighten the screws. Snug the screws evenly and watch for any distortion of the metal. Avoid the use of a power tool for fastening the sill plates; this is a job for the manual screwdriver.

Installing Carpet

1 *The carpet set has been installed into the car without glue to test the fit. Everything fits correctly and looks good so the carpet installation can proceed. If alterations need to be made they are chalked up and corrected before gluing the carpet in place.*

2 *The carpet is glued into place a little at a time starting with the heel pad. When the carpet is worked in small sections it yields a better fit and minimizes any repositioning after glue has been applied.*

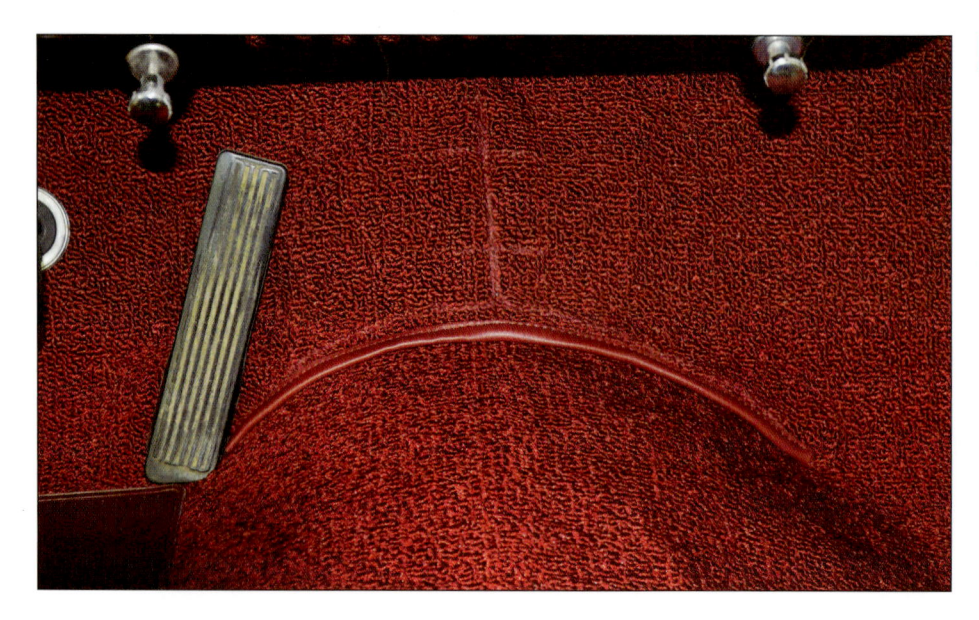

3 *Centering the carpet is crucial. Make sure the center seam is in the center of the transmission tunnel and the arched seam follows the contour of the floor. Working from the center outward always gives you the best results.*

164   AUTOMOTIVE UPHOLSTERY AND INTERIOR RESTORATION

CARPET

4 With all the effort and careful prep work, the carpet conforms perfectly around the brake pedal and steering column. The leading edge of the carpet is now tucked under the firewall insulation for a finished front-edge look.

5 The same installation detail goes into the rear carpet section. Now with the carpet in place, a quick steam helps relax any small wrinkles that may have been missed.

6 A 40-watt pencil-type soldering iron is used to open the seat mounting holes in the floor. The hot soldering iron melts the fibers of the carpet for a clean, snag-free hole for the mounting bolt to pass through.

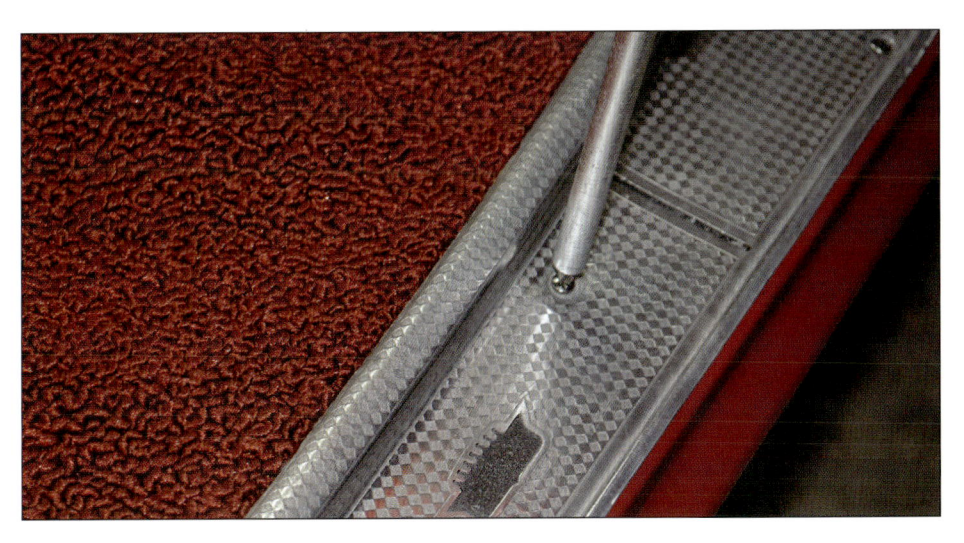

7 The sill plates are fitted to the door openings to complete the carpet installation. When installing the sill plate screws, be careful that the screws are not overtightened; this will cause the soft aluminum to dimple.

AUTOMOTIVE UPHOLSTERY AND INTERIOR RESTORATION

CHAPTER 7

CONVERTIBLE TOP

The very first cars produced evolved from nothing more than modified horse buggies and they were commonly called a phaeton or open car. The term *open* meant that the car was exposed to the elements because they did not have roofs, windshields, or doors. Wood-framed folding tops had already been in service for many years on horse-drawn carriages, but by the early 1920s cars became more refined, and as the cabs were covered with an attached fitted roof they were also sealed with glass to keep out the dust and rain. The option of a folding top became a popular and nostalgic way to open up the car, making it more versatile and appealing to the motorist. These cars that converted from closed to open were referred to as cabriolets.

Consider the elaborate engineering that goes into the design and function of the convertible top frame: side rails with crossmembers all spaced and hinged to allow for compression and expansion while being covered with a canvas fabric to protect the occupants from the sun and rain. Simply stated, all the components of the frame must manually fold and stow away easily without damaging the canvas fabric or bending any of the components that make up the convertible top frame.

Style led to luxury and auto manufacturers started to add power-assisted control to their convertible tops. With the push of a button the top folded into the top well without the driver leaving the seat.

This feat is accomplished by means of a simple hydraulic system made up of a small electric pump that pushes fluid through hoses into pressurized cylinders for the convenience of an unassisted lowering and lifting of the top.

Inspection and Evaluation

The restoration processes involved in bringing a convertible

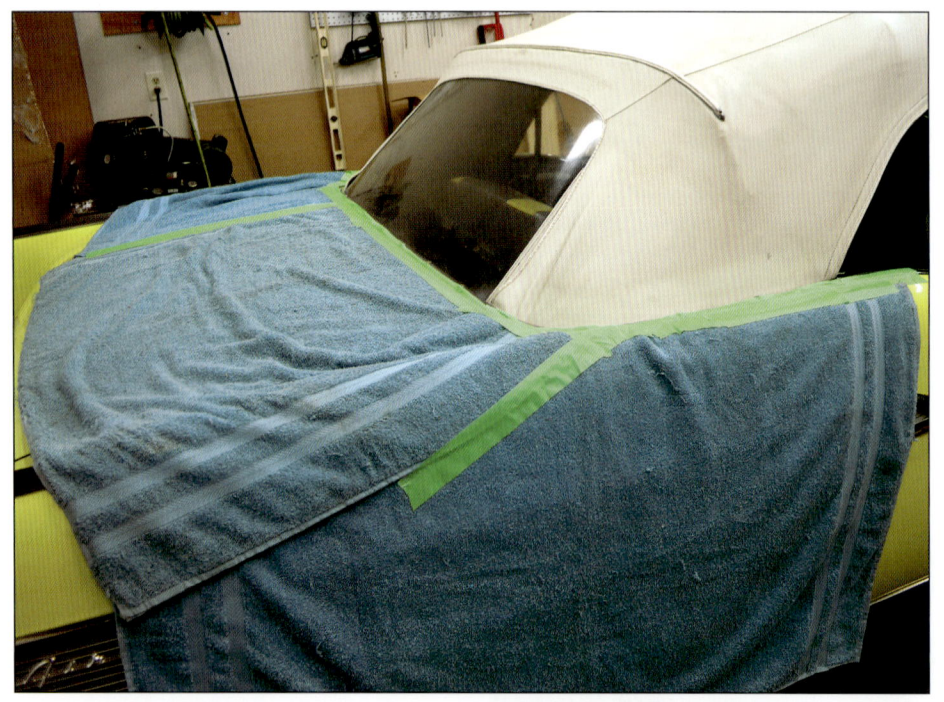

The rear of the car has been draped with packing blankets to protect it. This way you can work on the top without worrying about scratching the paint. Use painters' tape to attach the padding so the paint is not harmed when it is removed.

166   AUTOMOTIVE UPHOLSTERY AND INTERIOR RESTORATION

top back to peak operation are not simple. Convertible tops are the most difficult part of a car to upholster. Many moving parts must function properly without interfering with other frame and top components.

Be wary of taking on a convertible-top project without first surveying its condition. Hidden problems can lead to costly repairs. With this thought in mind, be sure to verify that the top works correctly before beginning a restoration.

Convertible tops operate either manually or by power with a hydroelectric system. The manual tops used heavy assist springs to counterbalance the top and make it easy for just one person to raise or lower the top. It is very important to check that the assist springs are still serviceable; if they are weak or damaged they should be replaced.

Power tops require a lot more maintenance than the manual tops. Early-model convertibles had hydraulic pumps located under the hood of the car as an accessory to power the windows, seat, and convertible top. The old systems prior to 1953 were typically filled with brake fluid and it was pumped to the various locations through metal lines that tend to leak at every joint and fitting. Visually inspect these lines, hoses, and fittings for leaks. If these parts need replacing or service it can become costly in a hurry. The car owner should also be made aware that a brake fluid system should be drained, flushed, and refilled with transmission oil to prevent paint damage from the leaking brake fluid.

The top should go up and down and fold into the well without binding. Start by looking for damaged or bent parts. Pay close attention to the many indicators that help you evaluate the true condition of the project. Normal wear is to be expected due to age and the effect of the elements, but rips and tears, on the other hand, are telltale signs that there is a problem with the top frame. When the top is in motion it should move smoothly and evenly. Listen to the pump motor and observe if the top can go up or down. If the motor runs, but the top does not move, this may indicate that the system may be just low on hydraulic fluid. Lack of any motor noise could be a bad switch or blown fuse. If one side of the frame is lifting uneven with the other it may be due to physical damage. Look for binding due to worn bronze bushings in the frame joints. Also be aware of any bent or broken rails and cross bows.

Check for the presence of bumps under the top material of the front header bow. Irregularities here indicate that rust or corrosion is present and this may lead to a replacement or major reconditioning of the header bow.

It is worth the effort to inspect each potential convertible top project so that you have an accurate estimate. The inspection can also lead you to the conclusion that the job may be beyond your skill set and you may want to pass on the project. Trust me when I say that some projects are just not worth the frustration or the money to contract, while many other projects are challenging and bring you the most satisfaction when you turn a piece of junk into an award-winning jewel.

Removal and Adjustment

Before work begins on the car you need to protect the paint from accidental damage that can occur while replacing the convertible top. Drape protective pads over the rear quarter panels and trunk lid prior to starting the work. Use painters' tape to secure the pads to the car. Regular masking tape may lift the finish when it is removed and that ends up causing an expensive paint repair. Try to tape to the stainless belt line molding if possible. This also reduces the risk of paint damage.

Begin the process of removing the top by starting with the removal of the side rail rubber weather stripping. The weather stripping may be attached with screws, threaded studs with split washers and retaining nuts, or it may be held into a stainless-steel retainer by friction and glue. Cut back any retaining flaps that may be glued to the frame to gain access to the attaching nuts. Remove the weather stripping from the roof rail. Now, unlatch the top from the windshield and lower the top halfway to reveal the front weather seal. Remove the screws and metal retainer strips from the rubber seal and set the screws and retainers aside to be reused upon reassembly.

Originally convertible tops were attached to the folding frame with tacks. Tacks take more time and effort to install and they cause a lot of damage to the frame and tack strips. The modern method of securing a top is to use galvanized or stainless-steel staples. They are faster to use and hold better than tacks without tearing up the tack strip.

Secured to the underside of the header bow is a fiber tack strip that the top and weather seal are attached to. Remove the staples from the front weather seal and then remove the top material from the front tack strip. If the tack strip has deteriorated or it has been torn up from staples it must be replaced with a new one.

Move to the rear bow and with a #1 Phillips screwdriver remove the screws from the wire-on welt tips covering the ends of the wire-on welt trim that is stapled across the rear bow. Pry open the wire-on welt trim and pull the staples to free it from the top. The attachment of the rear section of the convertible top is not standard on all cars. Some tops are attached to the outside beltline of the car and others are secured on the inside of the well area.

Beltline tops have an exposed edge that is finished with a wire-on welt trim, or a stainless molding held on by threaded fasteners from the inside of the car. Tops that are attached to the outside beltline can be removed by taking off the associated trim that covers the edge of the top and then removing the staples or tacks that hold the top to the tack rail.

Prior to removing the top from the rear of the car it is helpful to make reference marks of the curtain openings and pads onto the tape holding the protective padding to the body. These marks help serve as a guide on the repositioning of the top when the new one is fitted to the car.

If the rear section of the top is fastened to a tack rail that is bolted into the well area behind the rear seat, you must access the tack rail by removing the rear seat of the car. Start by moving the front seat all the way forward to give you more access to the rear seat. To remove the bottom seat cushion, simply push in on the bottom front edge of the seat and lift the seat up and out of the car. The rear seatback is attached to the car by sheet-metal screws and/or metal tabs that need to be removed or straightened to release the seat frame from the car. Be careful when exiting the car with the seat cushions so that you do not snag or damage any other interior components.

After the rear seat has been removed from the car, lift up the well liner that is glued or screwed to the rear seatback support mount and using a 1/4-inch-drive ratchet and socket remove the sheet-metal screws that are holding the tack rail to the car body. Be careful that you do not drop any of the sheet-metal screws into the side cavities of the body because they are difficult to retrieve. The top can now be lifted out of the well area and the staples holding the top to the tack rail can then be removed. After all the staples and hardware have been removed, the old top material can be removed from the car.

What you should have still attached to the top frame is the rear curtain and top pads. Some cars have an extra set of pads or webbing in the rear to help shape the top. These pads also need to be removed and replaced with new pads. Mark their position for reference on the masking tape just as you did for the top position.

The top edge of the rear curtain is secured to the rear bow with staples. Remove these staples, take the rear curtain out of the car, and set it aside for future reference.

The rear of the top pads can now be unfastened from the rear bow by pulling the staples that secure them to the rear bow. Visually inspect the rear bow tack strip for signs of damage and deterioration. If the tack strip is in poor condition it must be replaced.

The top pads are also attached to the header bow with staples. Body tape should cover the staples. This tape protects the top from being rubbed by the staples. Peel off the protective tape to expose the staples that are securing the pad to the underlying tack strip and remove the staples from the pad. Inspect the tack strip for deterioration and damage.

The convertible top pad is filled with cotton padding and is sealed to hold the padding inside. Open the pad and remove the pad filler material. The pad is attached to the cross bows by staples or small screws and washers. Remove the fasteners that are holding the pad to the bow and discard the pad; it will be replaced with a new pad. If any of the screws have broken off in the bow they need to be drilled out and re-tapped before the new pads can be fitted. At this point the convertible top frame should be free of all top materials.

Inspect the top for any worn or damaged parts. Operate the top up and down and listen for any popping or clicking irregularities that may indicate worn bushings or loose joints. Also inspect the pump, hoses, and lift cylinders for leaks and wear. Service to the hydraulic system should be done at this point by replacing any worn or failing components as necessary before installing the new top.

One of the cross bows on this frame is bent and needs to be removed from the top frame so that it can be straightened. Unbolt the bow from the frame so that it can be repaired. If you do not have the skills to make the repair then you should bring it to a body shop and have it straightened by a qualified technician. You do not want to risk damaging the bow further or ruining it since replacements are getting very hard to find.

CONVERTIBLE TOP

Removing and Adjusting a Convertible Top

1 Simplify removal of the rubber weather strip by cutting away the attaching flaps to gain access to the attaching nuts. Lowering the top halfway takes tension off the top, allowing you to easily remove the attaching screws and nuts from the frame rail.

2 Under the header bow is a tack strip that the top material and weather seal are attached to. The weather seal is detached from the header by removing the staples that hold it in place. The top material is also removed from the header tack strip.

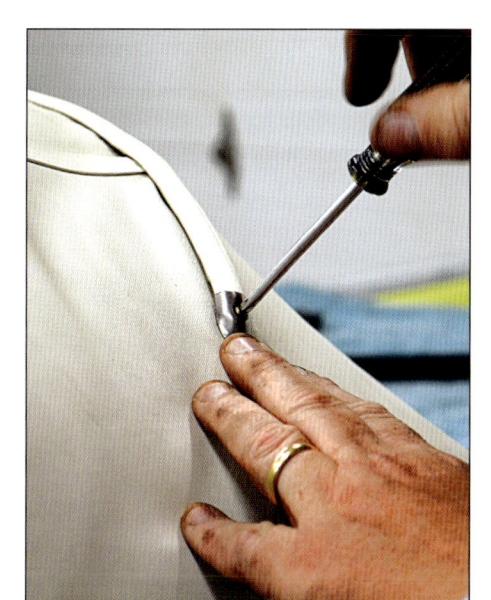

3 A #1 screwdriver is used to remove the stainless-steel tips on the rear bow that finish off the wire-on welt. The wire-on welt is opened and the staples are removed, detaching it from the rear bow. The top is also detached from the rear bow by removing the staples holding it in place.

4 The top of this 1949 Chevy is attached to a tack strip along the beltline on the outside of the car. The rear tack strip is located under the stainless trim, which is removed by unscrewing the fasteners on the inside of the car.

AUTOMOTIVE UPHOLSTERY AND INTERIOR RESTORATION

CHAPTER 7

5 Reference marks of the old top curtain position are made prior to the top being removed from the car. The marks are made on the masking tape that is holding the protective padding. These marks help with the positioning and installation of the new convertible top.

6 Access to the rear tack rail of this 1957 Chevy is through the well area of the car. The rear seat has been removed from the car to gain better access to the rear tack rail. This makes it much easier to remove the attaching hardware.

7 The rear tack rail is bolted to the body of the car under the well liner. The curtain and convertible top are attached to the rear tack rail. The tack rail is secured to the body with #14 sheet-metal screws and/or 1/4–20 machine bolts.

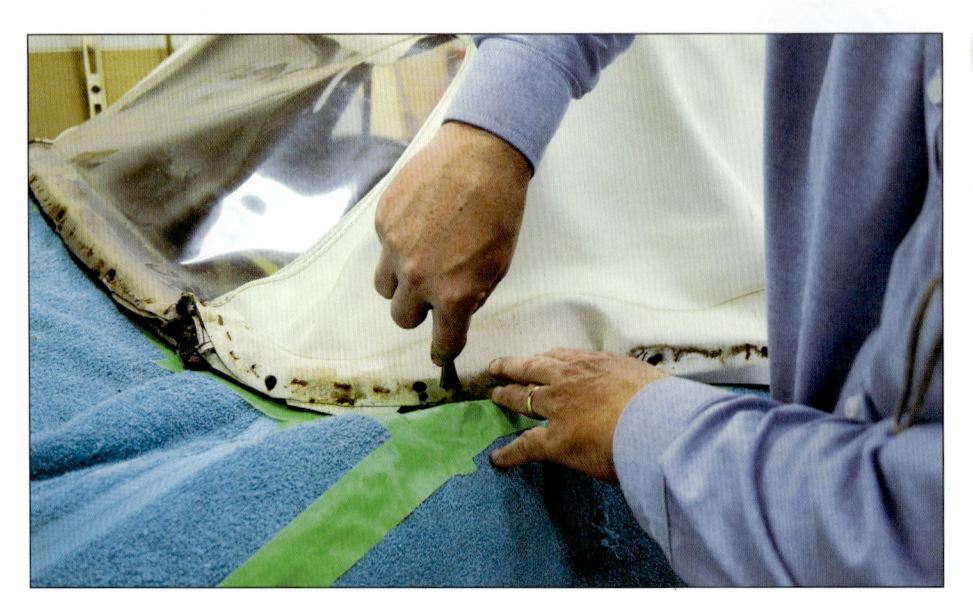

8 The rear tack rail has been unbolted from the well area of the car. The exposed staples can now be pulled from the top material. This releases the sail area from the track rail and the convertible top can now be removed from the car.

170   AUTOMOTIVE UPHOLSTERY AND INTERIOR RESTORATION

9 The remaining components of the convertible top are the pads and rear curtain. The bottom of the curtain is removed from the rear tack rail along with the staples holding the top of the curtain to the rear bow. Once the curtain is free from the rear bow the curtain can be removed from the car.

10 The protective convertible top pads are no longer serviceable and must be replaced. Staples are pulled from the end of the top pad that is attached to the rear bow. The pad will be thrown away and replaced with brand-new materials.

11 The leading edge of the pad is attached to the header bow by staples. Under the protective tape are staples that need to be pulled so the pad can be removed. The tack strip can now be inspected for damage and wear.

12 Inside the pad and under the padding are four or five small screws that hold the pad to the cross bows. The screws and washers are removed but saved to secure the new pad to the top frame. If a screw has broken off in the bow it must be repaired before the new pad is fit.

CHAPTER 7

13 *After removing the pads it was discovered that the center bow is bent. This bow must be removed and straightened before any more work can be done on the top. Inspect the entire top frame for other damaged or worn parts.*

Header Bow Servicing

Most of the time there is some rust or corrosion on the header bow that needs to be addressed. Ford used aluminum for many of its top frames and header bows, while General Motors made its top components from steel. The best way to service the header is to unbolt it from the top frame and work on the header while it sits on the workbench.

With the header bow on the bench you can easily strip it down for cleaning and repairs. Visually inspect the header bow to evaluate what needs to be done. This bow must be repainted and the tack strips replaced.

In a case of the header being rusted or damaged beyond a simple repair you need to secure a new replacement header bow. If one is not available for your model car it may be necessary to have a metal shop repair your old header bow or fabricate a new one for you.

Begin the disassembly by removing the latch handles, guide pins, and footman loop from the header bow. Since these are all chrome-plated pieces they need to be cleaned with #0000 steel wool and then a chrome polish to protect the parts from further corrosion.

Remove the worn tack strip from the header by lifting the metal tabs that secure it in place. Straighten the retainer tabs with pliers and if any of the tabs are broken or rusted away they can be replaced by welding a new tab in place. The top is secured to the bottom tack strip and it must be able to take the strain of the top as it is raised and locked to the windshield. The top may fail if the tack strip is not secured tightly to the header bow. On many cars, a weather strip retainer is screwed to threaded studs. Run a tap through each stud to chase the threads, ensuring that they are clean so that the new screws go in without binding.

Turn the header over and remove the pad tack strips by lifting the metal tabs holding them. If industrial staples hold the tack strips, rivet the new tack strip in place.

Thoroughly clean and sand the header to remove any rust and corrosion. Use body filler to smooth out any dents or imperfections and then prep, prime, and paint the header in a nice satin black. Allow the paint to fully cure before you reassemble the header bow.

To protect the newly repainted header bow from scratches while it is being worked on, cover the workbench with a protective pad. Place the header on the workbench and replace the underside tack strip with a new one by fitting it into the header and securing it in place by hammering the metal tabs down. On aluminum headers the best method to secure the tack strip is with aluminum rivets. Punch or drill holes in the tack strip prior to fastening as this makes for a tighter and more secure fit.

Install all the reconditioned chrome pieces on the header and tighten them down. Be careful that you do not over-torque the screws as they can easily break off.

CONVERTIBLE TOP

Reconditioning a Header Bow

1 The header bow has been unbolted and removed from the car and placed on the workbench to be reconditioned. Inspection of the bow reveals that there is no rust or damage, but the tack strips are worn out and need to be replaced.

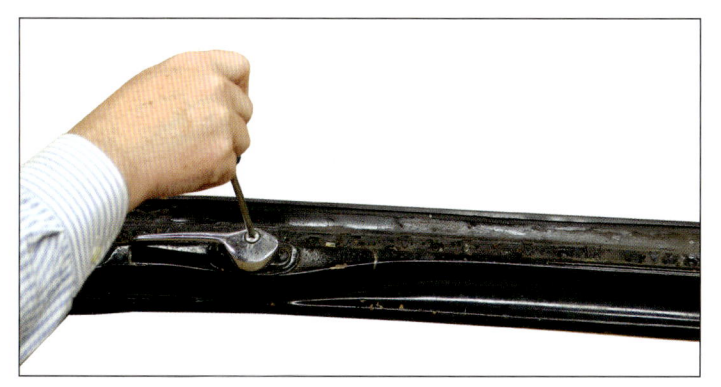

2 Removal of all the chrome pieces from the header allows you to get a better paint finish on the bow. Once removed the chrome pieces can be cleaned with #0000 steel wool and protected with chrome polish to make them look like new again.

3 The header bow tack strip is worn and must be replaced. Lifting the retaining tabs frees the old tack strip from the header. The header bow is now ready to be reconditioned so that a new tack strip can be installed.

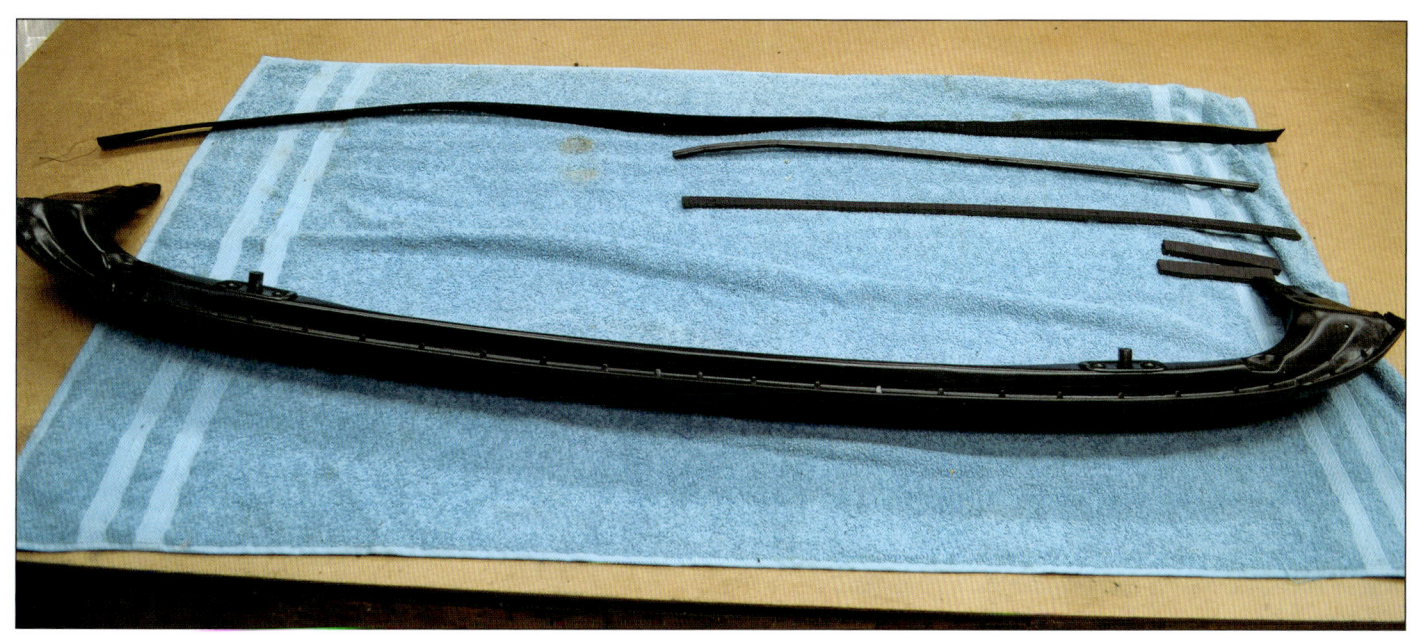

4 This header bow has been cleaned, sanded, and repaired and has been given a new coat of satin black paint. A protective pad has been spread out on the workbench to prevent the header bow from scratches while it is being serviced.

AUTOMOTIVE UPHOLSTERY AND INTERIOR RESTORATION

CHAPTER 7

5 *After the paint has cured on the reconditioned header bow, install new tack strips. The tack strips are set into a recessed channel and small metal tabs are hammered onto the tack strip to lock them in place.*

6 *With the installation of the chrome latch handles, guide pins, and foot man loop, you have now finished the reconditioning phase of the header bow. The header bow will be reinstalled on the car after the top frame is repaired, cleaned, and painted.*

Frame Servicing

Make any and all necessary repairs to the top frame before proceeding with the installation of the top. Once the top is installed it is very difficult to make any additional adjustments to the frame due to the tension caused by stretching the top and pads.

Often you find that some of the screws that hold the pads to the bows have been broken off and left as is. These must be drilled out and re-tapped to 6-32 before the new pads can be fitted. Failure to repair the broken screws results in a pad that may slip out of place, and this may damage the new top.

Replace worn or damaged rear bow and tack rail tack strips with new ones. Tack strip comes in different sizes and materials. The original tack strip material was made of a dense paper and is the preferred choice for holding tacks or staples. The modern choice for tack strip is a dense rubber that is generally available in two sizes for the front and rear bow. The factory-installed tack strip is held in place by industrial staples. When replacing these tack strips, use sheet-metal screws or rivets. Be sure that the tack strip is tight and secure so that it does not pull loose or wrinkle.

Adjustment of the top frame and glass is vital for the top to fit properly. The top frame must work flawlessly before fitting the top. The side rails should be straight and fold up and down evenly. You should not hear any clicks, pops, or snapping sounds when the top is operated. Moving the tensioning arm up or down adjusts the tension of the top. Loosening and moving the header bow adjusts the header. It takes a little time to get the top to perform correctly and there is no excuse for not

The cross bows on the convertible top frame need servicing. Several of the pad screws are broken off and need to be extracted. The process includes re-tapping the bow to accept new pad screws. This is always a stressful process, but it is vital to fix the bow correctly.

174 AUTOMOTIVE UPHOLSTERY AND INTERIOR RESTORATION

CONVERTIBLE TOP

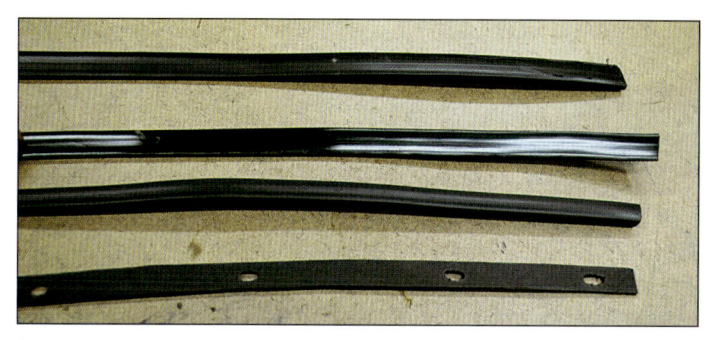

Several choices for tack strip material are available for use on a convertible top frame. The modern replacement rubber tack strip is available in three sizes. From top to bottom: 3/4 x 1/8 x 50 feet, 5/8 x 1/8 x 50 feet, and 1/2 x 3/8 x 50 feet. The bottom tack strip is an original-style paper fiber.

getting it right. After the top frame is adjusted all the nuts and bolts should be checked and tightened to ensure that they do not loosen up or slip.

For the door and quarter glass to fit properly, install the new rubber weather strip to the frame side rails and across the header bow of the convertible top frame. The doors should open and close with the glass up touching but not catching on the new rubber. The quarter glass should also raise and lower without interfering with the weather strip. Adjust the door glass if necessary so that the gaps between the glass and rubber are equal all around.

Now that everything is adjusted as best as possible remove all the pieces of rubber weather strip and clean the top frame so that it can be painted.

Frame Painting

The top frame is visible from the inside of the car and it does get its share of scratches and wear. To prepare the frame for paint I wipe the entire frame down with a rag and lacquer thinner. You have to be extremely careful that you do not splash the paint of the car with lacquer thinner. Put the thinner on a rag and rub the top frame down to remove any grease, dirt, and oil. You can use fine-grain sandpaper on any surface that is rusty or where the old paint has chipped to smooth the surface. Wipe the sanded surface with a rag to remove the sanding dust.

Lower the top so that the frame is about one quarter of the way retracted so that you can get fresh paint on all the surfaces of the frame.

Drape the entire car with 1-mil poly sheeting to protect the paint and interior of the car from overspray. Tape around the top frame where it mounts to the body to prevent overspray from entering the car. Spray the top frame with satin black enamel. Give the top frame several light coats of paint so that it does not

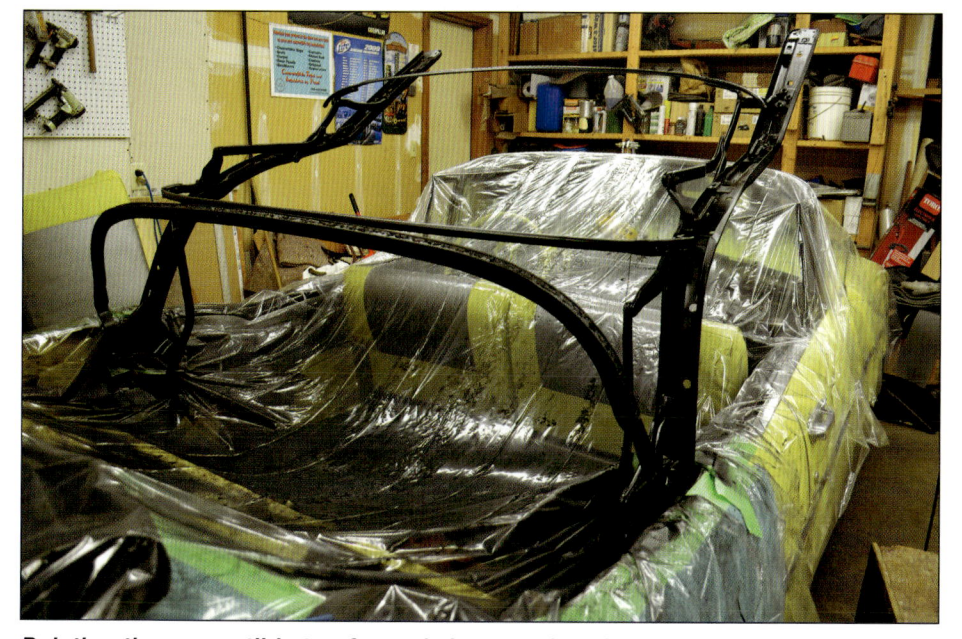

Painting the convertible top frame is just another detail in the restoration process. The frame is repaired, adjusted, cleaned thoroughly, and then painted a beautiful satin black. A sheet of 1-mil poly is draped over the entire car to protect the finish and interior from overspray.

Proper lubrication of the convertible top frame is vital so that it continues to operate without binding. Every moving joint in the convertible top requires a drop of 3-in-One oil. This particular brand of oil works its way into the bronze bushings; it keeps the steel bolts and rivets from rusting.

AUTOMOTIVE UPHOLSTERY AND INTERIOR RESTORATION

run. Make sure to put an even coat of paint on the entire top frame. Allow the paint to dry completely before removing the poly drape. After the paint has cured, remove the poly drape and install the header bow. Raise the top and verify that everything is adjusted correctly.

Lubricate each joint with a drop of 3-in-1 oil. This oil penetrates the bronze bushings and keeps the frame from binding for years to come. Just a drop of oil per joint should be enough. Using more oil only causes a mess from oil dripping from the joint. At this point the top frame should be in proper working order and the pads can now be fitted to the top frame.

Pad Installation

The pads are the first component to be installed on the convertible top frame. The purpose of the convertible top pad is to protect the convertible top from damage by the mechanical frame. A vintage pad is made up of a jute webbing or burlap core material with a thin layer of cotton batting on top that is covered with bow drill fabric. Modern pads are constructed of convertible top material and vinyl with a foam core.

The pads are attached from the header bow to the rear bow on each side of the frame. The rear bow is set at a specific height and it is critical that this measurement is accurately set so that the top fits and operates correctly. To get the bow height right simply measure from the center rear well molding to the center point of the rear bow. The position of the rear end of the pad can be adjusted to raise or lower the rear bow height. To install the pads the leading end of the pad is fit to the header bow and secured with a staple on each edge. The pad is then stretched to the rear bow and temporarily stapled to hold the rear bow in place. Open the pad up and secure the lower pad material to the cross bows with the appropriate fastener (staples or screws). Remove the staple in the rear bow so it can be adjusted to the correct bow height and staple the inside of the pad to the rear bow.

To make the pad functional and give cushion to the top a piece of foam is added to the inside of the pad as the cushion material. Fit the foam snugly to the edges of the pad and fold the pad flaps closed over the foam leading with the inside flap and the outside flap on top. If any air manages to get under the top it flows over the pad and does not cause the pad to balloon up. Apply glue to the edge of the flaps to secure the foam from shifting and staple the ends closed to finish off the pad installation. Measure the rear bow height again, and if everything is correct you can trim the pad flush with the rear bow.

At the front of the pad carefully trim the excess material and apply cloth body tape over the staples to protect the top material from the staples. The modern substitution for cloth body tape is Gorilla tape. The cost is a fraction of the cost of cloth body tape and it holds extremely well. Do not use duct tape to cover the staples because it will fail.

Installing a Top Pad

1 *Rear bow height is critical for a convertible top to fit properly. It is determined by measuring from the middle of the well area's chrome molding strip up to the center of the rear bow. The bow height is adjusted by modifying the length of the pad at the rear bow.*

CONVERTIBLE TOP

2 To prevent the convertible top pad from moving out of position it is opened and the bottom layer of the pad is secured to the cross bow with #6-32 screws and washers or staples. This holds the convertible top pad in place on the cross bow while the top is folded.

3 The purpose of the convertible top pad is to protect the top from the frame. While the pad is open it is filled with a piece of foam to cushion the top from the frame.

4 The top pad is enclosed by folding over the inside flap first and then the outside flap. You do it this way so that wind does not get under the pad and cause it to inflate. Seal the pad by gluing the edge of the top pad to the lower pad flap to make a finished seam.

AUTOMOTIVE UPHOLSTERY AND INTERIOR RESTORATION

CHAPTER 7

5 After the convertible top pad has been sealed, excess material is trimmed from the end of the pad. A sharp utility knife blade is run along the inside rear edge of the rear bow tack strip to cut the convertible top pad flush to the bow.

6 After the front end of the convertible top pad is trimmed to fit the header bow it needs to be finished by covering over the staples with protective tape. The tape keeps the staples from damaging the convertible top and it also seals them to prevent corrosion.

Rear Tack Rail

Prior to 1953, most convertible tops were attached to the outside of the car along the beltline to an external tack strip. If the external tack strip has become worn and unable to hold a staple due to age, weather, and previous top replacements, it may be time to replace the tack strip with a new one.

Inside the well area on later-model cars you find the tack rail. This metal band contains the tack strip that the top, rear curtain, and well liner are stapled to and attaches to the body

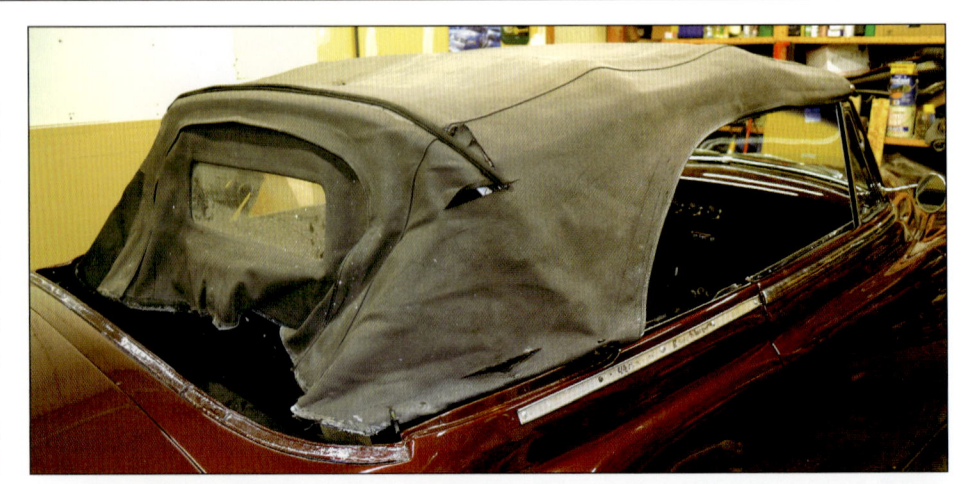

The rear of this 1949 Chevy has a tack rail on the outside of the body. The tack strip material was damaged and badly deteriorated from prior top installations and it was reconditioned with new fiber tack strip material prior to the car being painted.

178   AUTOMOTIVE UPHOLSTERY AND INTERIOR RESTORATION

by 1/4-20 machine bolts or #14 sheet-metal screws. When installing the threaded fasteners into the body I recommend using a 1/4-inch-drive ratchet to avoid over-torquing the fasteners and prevent the bolt holes from becoming stripped out and leaving the rear tack rail loose.

Well Liner

Inside the car behind the rear seat is the top well. This open storage space for the folded top is separated from the trunk space by a well liner. Up until the mid-1950s the well area was integral to the car's interior and it was fully upholstered, making it another finished component of the car.

Later-model cars had a well area that was separated from the trunk by a bag-like structure that attached to the rear tack rail and was fastened to the rear seat mount by glue or trim screws.

On these later-model cars the convertible top is mounted inside the body of the car, so they were also equipped with a rain gutter inside the well area.

The rain gutter is a metal or plastic trough that is welded or screwed in place just below the tack rail. The purpose of the gutter is to channel water out of the car through weep holes located in the floor of the car just in front of the rear wheels. If the rain gutter is damaged or missing you should repair or replace it at this stage before the new top is installed. Without a functioning rain gutter the car is prone to rusting from water seepage. Also located behind the rear seat and in the well of these later-model cars is the hydroelectric pump that powers the convertible top. Hoses attached to the pump run through the well to hydraulic ram cylinders on both sides of the car.

This well liner is an upholstered compartment in the rear of the 1949 Chevrolet. Eleven separate pieces make up the well liner. The individual pieces are layered and fastened in place to finish off the well area of the car.

A soft well liner is installed into the well area of this 1957 Chevy, separating the trunk space from the cab area of the car. The well liner is made up of three pieces of vinyl sewn together as one piece. The well liner hangs from the rear tack rail and attaches to the top of the rear seat support.

CHAPTER 7

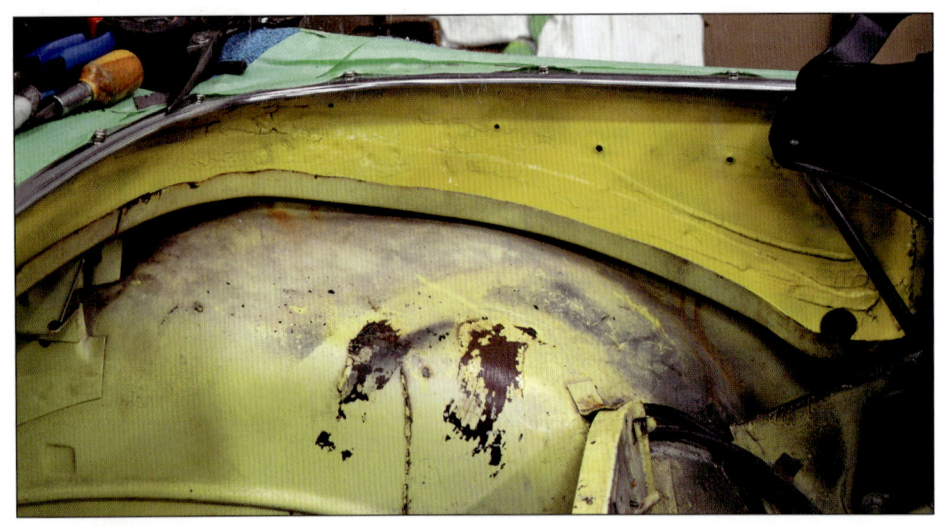

On the inside of the 1957 Chevy well area is a welded-in rain gutter. The rain gutter diverts any water from the car to keep the inside of the trunk dry. Water exits the car through weep holes in the floor that are located in front of the rear tires.

The well liner is attached to the rear tack rail and drapes over the top. When the tack rail is bolted in place the well liner conceals the tack rail, rain gutter, and all the hardware underneath. After the top is installed and the rear tack rail is bolted into the car, all that is seen is the well liner.

To conceal these elements the well liner is hung from the rear tack rail. Start at the center point on the tack rail and staple the new well liner so that it hangs over the top of the tack rail. Reveal the holes for the mounting hardware by cutting away the well liner material.

Rear Curtain

The back window section of a convertible top is called the rear curtain. Many different configurations are possible for rear curtains. Some rear windows are integrated into the top, making it an all-inclusive top while others have the rear curtain installed as a separate element. The window portion of the curtain can be made of plastic or glass. Some glass windows may even have an electronic defroster built in. Vintage convertibles used a double-blank curtain that sported a small glass window that was set in a metal frame.

The rear curtain is attached along the top to the rear bow and it is secured to the rear tack rail that is mounted into the well area inside the car (modern) or it can be attached along the rear beltline on the outside of the car (pre-1953) depending on the car model. Another feature many curtains have is a heavy-duty brass zipper. The zipper can run horizontally across the top of the window, vertically on both sides of the window, or horseshoe around the

The double-blank curtain is a classic look for a convertible top. The rear curtain on the 1949 Chevrolet is made up of a small glass window sandwiched between two pieces of top material. The glass is held in place by a metal frame that is secured by screws on the outside of the fabric.

AUTOMOTIVE UPHOLSTERY AND INTERIOR RESTORATION

CONVERTIBLE TOP

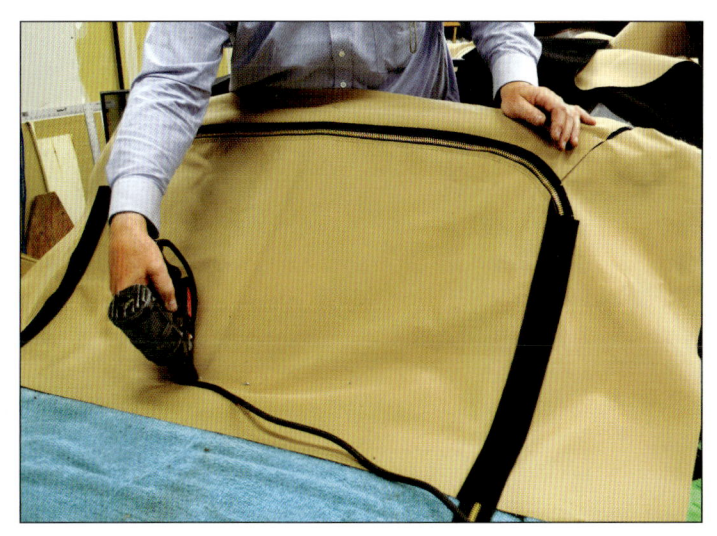

Fitting the double-blank rear curtain of the 1949 Chevrolet is done by temporarily stapling the top of the curtain in the center and at the ends onto the rear bow. The curtain is then stretched and temporarily stapled to the rear tack rail. Adjustments are made to remove wrinkles.

A spacer block is used to raise the top off the windshield, which takes the tension off the back section of the top. After adjustments have been made to the top, the spacer block is removed and additional tension is put on the top, stretching the top tighter for a perfect fit.

window and allow the curtain to be opened up. After the top of the curtain is stapled to the rear bow, stretch the curtain to the tack rail and make a pencil mark along the edge for reference.

Unlatch the header bow from the windshield and place a 2 x 4 spacer block between the header and windshield to relieve tension. Attach the lower edge of the rear curtain about 1/4 inch past the pencil line by stapling it to the tack rail, paying attention that the talon of the zipper is above the tack rail and on the inside of the car.

The modern curtain is attached to the rear bow and then to the tack rail following the install line designated by the top manufacturer. The curtain material is cut away from the tack rail mounting holes before the curtain is placed back into the well of the car. Unlatch the header bow from the windshield and place the 2 x 4 spacer between the header bow and windshield. Bolt the rear tack rail to the body starting with the center bolt and then only using every other mounting bolt. Remove the spacer and latch the top to the windshield. If the rear curtain is too loose it must be removed and adjusted up or down on the tack rail until there is an even tension on the curtain when the top is latched.

At this point you can remove the spacer and latch the top to the windshield. Make sure that the rear bow height is correct, check the fit

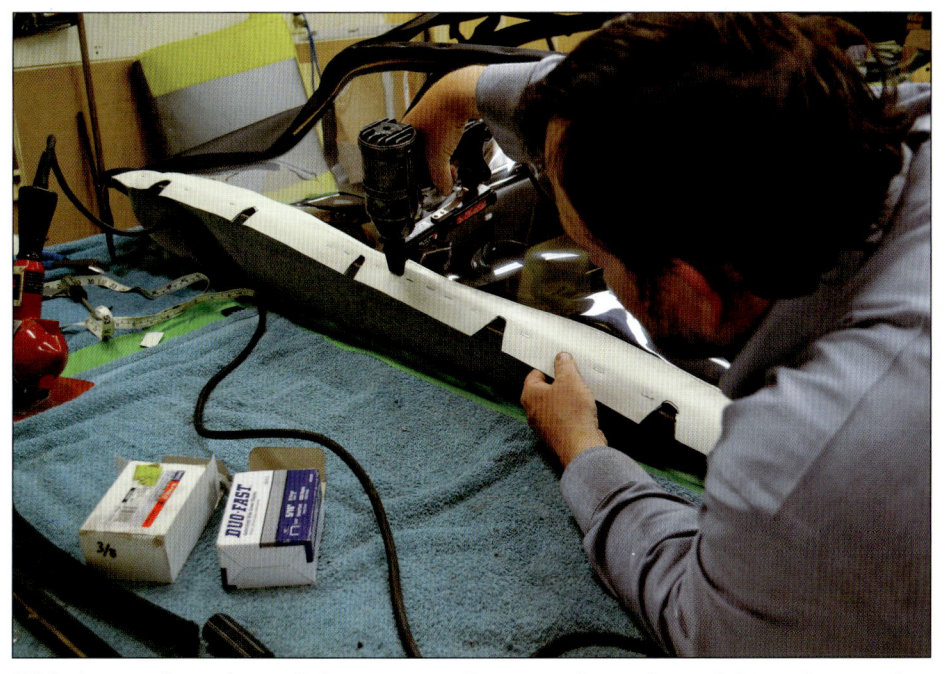

With the tension taken off the top, an adjustment is made to tighten the curtain. The bottom of the curtain is fully stapled to the rear tack rail and material is removed from the lower edge of the rear curtain to reveal the tack rail bolt holes.

AUTOMOTIVE UPHOLSTERY AND INTERIOR RESTORATION

One unique detail of the curtain is the zipper. The sole purpose of the zipper is to allow the window to be opened. The zipper talon should be accessible, so make sure that it is positioned on the top side of the rear tack rail.

Applying heat to a vinyl curtain helps relax the vinyl and allows it to flow and stretch smoothly, giving it a glass-like appearance. Extreme care must be taken when using a heat gun on vinyl so that you do not scorch or melt the curtain.

of the rear curtain, and remove any small wrinkles with a heat gun. Be extremely careful when you use a heat gun to remove wrinkles. Keep the heat gun in motion at all times to prevent excessive heat to any one spot. If you melt or distort the vinyl curtain it must be replaced.

Top Fitment

Once the pads and rear curtain have been installed, the top can be fit to the convertible top frame.

Unlatch the top from the windshield, insert the spacer block to relieve tension on the top frame, and then unbolt the tack rail from the car. Set the new top in place over the rear bow and attach the bound edge of the curtain opening to the rear tack rail where the previous top was attached. Attach the leading edge of the sail to the tack rail at its recommended position.

Now stretch the sail area of the top over the curved portion of the tack rail, and using as few staples as necessary, attach the rest of the sail area of the top to the tack rail. Do not trim the excess material off at this point in the installation, but cut away only a small amount of the top material to allow the mounting bolts through the bolt holes. Bolt the rear tack rail into the well of the car. Pull the top forward until it has just a little tension on it. Do not pull it tight at this point; you just need to get the top to move enough to smooth the sail areas.

Temporarily staple the top to the header at the center, corners, and seams with just a few staples. Latch the top to the windshield for the first stretch and check the fit. You will no doubt experience wrinkles in the sail panels of the top upon the first fitment. To correct the fit, apply a strip of painters tape on the sail of the top just above the beltline and mark on the tape where corrections need to be made.

Unlatch the top from the windshield and put in your spacer block. Remove the rear tack rail from the well and remove the staples necessary to free the top material so that adjustments can be made. Reinstall the tack rail and check the fit for wrinkles. This process may take several tries but continue the process of adjustments until all wrinkles are gone and the top sail areas are wrinkle-free. Recheck the rear bow height and adjust as needed.

Staple the top along the rear bow tack strip between the deck seams to secure the top deck material to the rear bow. Keep the staples straight and evenly space them about 3/4 inch apart.

Stretch

Now make a pencil mark across the front edge of the header bow, unlatch the top from the windshield, and lower the top halfway down to expose the header tack strip. Remove the staples holding the top to the header and pull the top material over the edge of the header bow about 1/4 inch past the pencil mark. Staple the top to the header bow. Now raise the top and latch it to the windshield to give it a good stretch. Check the fit of the top from side to side and make additional adjustments as necessary so that the top deck is smooth and wrinkle-free.

Wire-On

To conceal the staples across the rear bow, use a decorative trim cord called wire-on welt. This is stapled to the rear bow and then folded over to cover all the staples. Wire-on finishes the rear section of the car.

Position the wire-on welt by measuring down 4½ inches from the sealed seam on the top and making a pencil mark on both sides of the top in the center of the rear bow tack strip. Open the wire-on welt with the small bead facing to the rear of the car and begin to staple it in place at the pencil mark. Keep the wire-on welt taut and staple it across the rear bow, covering over the exposed staples in the rear bow. Trim the wire-on welt at the opposite end pencil mark and finish stapling the wire-on welt to the end. Fold the wide portion of the wire-on welt over the staples and secure it by tapping it down with a rubber hammer. Place the metal wire-on welt tip over the cut end of the wire-on welt and attach it with the accompanying screw to hold it in place.

Side Cables

One flaw that exists with convertible tops is that they balloon up and flutter (which is known as buffeting) when driving at higher speeds.

In an attempt to correct this problem of buffeting, carmakers fit a snap to the top side rail to help hold the top tight to the frame, which offered some help but not enough. Another solution was to build in a bow sleeve that secured the top to the center cross bow. In 1961 car manufacturers started to make their tops with a sleeve sewn into the outside edge of the top. They ran a cable through the sleeve and secured it to the front and rear of the frame rail, keeping the top tight to the frame to prevent buffeting.

I add a cable sleeve to every convertible top I install. Electron Top makes all of the tops that I use and they are in my opinion by far the best in the industry for fit and finish. Above all that, the customer service and quality consciousness of the company cannot be found anywhere else in the industry.

To fit the cable to the side rail I unlatch the top from the windshield to relieve tension on the top so that the edge of the top can be turned up to reveal the openings in the cable sleeve. Mark these positions on both sides of the frame rail. The top is then lowered halfway down, relaxing the top from the frame to allow ample access to the frame rail so that a hole can be drilled into the frame rail for a pop rivet.

Locate a place approximately 3 inches from the rear cable sleeve opening, mark it, and drill a 3/16-inch hole into the frame rail. Do the same for the front mark and then repeat this step on the opposite side rail. Raise the top, but do not latch it. Measure the distance between the two holes and make up the universal cable 1/16 inch less than the measurement between the two holes. This gives ample tension on the cable when the top is latched to the windshield. Lower the top halfway down and thread the cable into the cable sleeve with the spring end at the rear of the top.

Insert a 3/16 x 1/4–inch steel rivet through a #8 flat washer and secure the spring end of the cable to the top rail. Secure the front end of the cable just like the rear and then do the same procedure to the cable on the other side of the frame rail with rivets and washers.

Weather Strip

If the top is wrinkle free and no other adjustments need to be made, glue the flaps at the front corners of the top to the bottom of the side rail. Now you are ready to make the front weather seal.

Measure from corner to corner along the front edge of the header to determine the length of the header seal. Take a strip of matching convertible top material 5 inches wide, fold it in half with the outside in, and sew the ends closed at the header dimension. Turn the seal inside out, insert a length of 1/2-inch rubber core into the seal, and sew it closed. Lower the top halfway to expose the header tack strip.

Apply glue to the underside of the top along the front edge of the header and to the selvage of the header weather seal. Take the seal to the header and fit it to the edge of the header beginning at one corner and working your way across the header, pressing the two pieces together and lining up the stitching of the weather seal on the edge of the header. You do not want any staples showing on the outside of the header seal because they would be exposed and prone to rust. It also does not look nice to have staples visible, so to conceal the staples open the selvage and staple inside of the weather seal to secure it to the header bow tack strip. Glue the selvage closed on the header seal to hide and protect the staples from any weather. Trim the weather seal flush with the rear edge of the header tack strip; cut away and remove the top material that is covering the weather strip retainer screw holes.

While the top is still halfway down, attach the rubber weather stripping to the header using the metal weather strip retainers to hold it in position. Now secure it in place with the retainer screws. Mount the front rubber frame rail seals to the frame using the correct hardware and then raise the top and latch it to the windshield. Glue the rear quarter flaps to the vertical frame rail and then attach the rear rubber weather strip to complete the installation of the top.

Now is a good time to give the top a good steam to help it settle in. The top should remain in the up position locked to the windshield for at least a week to help it keep its stretch. Use a clean damp cloth to remove any smudges that may be on the top.

Applying and Fitting a Top

1 Only a few staples are used to secure the top to the rear tack rail for the initial fitting. This helps with the staple removal and repositioning adjustments that will be made after the top is stretched and fit for the first time. Additional staples can always be added later.

2 The top is attached to the header bow by temporarily tacking the top at the center, seams, and corners. These few staples are enough to hold the top in place when it is latched to the windshield to give the top a preliminary stretch.

3 A band of tape across the sail panel is used to mark the places that need to be adjusted to remove wrinkles from the sail area of the top. This process may take several tries to get it just right. The key here is to make small adjustments and not overcorrect the top.

4 Securing the top to the rear bow sets the top so that it can be finished at the header bow. Just a few staples are needed at this stage. More staples are added when the seam is finished with its decorative wire-on welt.

CONVERTIBLE TOP

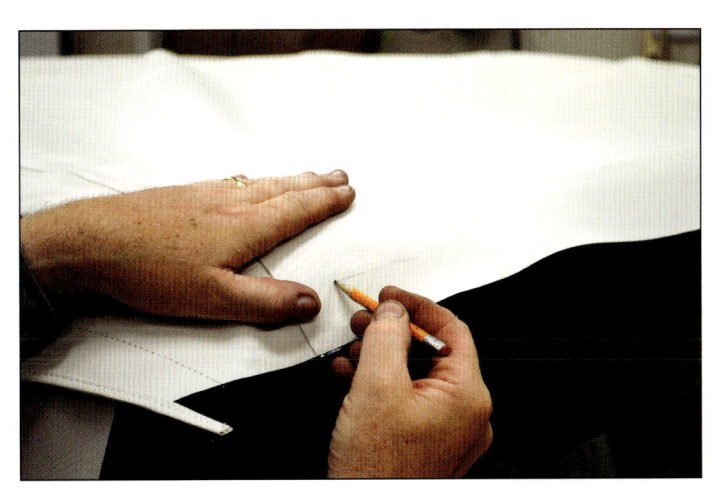

5 The top material has been stretched forward and a pencil line is drawn on the top to indicate the front edge of the header bow. The top is pulled over the header 1/4 inch past this reference line and stapled to the tack strip on the bottom side of the header bow.

6 Reference marks are made 4½ inches down from the sealed seam on each side of the top. This becomes the guide for the placement of the wire-on welt. The end of the wire-on welt begins and ends on these marks.

7 The purpose of the wire-on welt is to conceal the staples across the rear top bow and protect them from the weather. Beginning at the index mark, the wire-on welt is stretched across the rear bow and secured to the bow by stapling it on the inside.

8 A soft mallet is used to fold over the wire-on welt that is attached across the rear top bow. Once the wire-on welt has been folded over it seals in the underlying staples, hiding them from view and protecting them from weather.

9 The finishing touch of the wire-on welt is a stainless-steel tip that seals the end of the welt and completes the wire-on installation. The metal tips are held in place on the rear top bow by a simple screw, adding just a touch of bling to the top.

AUTOMOTIVE UPHOLSTERY AND INTERIOR RESTORATION

CHAPTER 7

10 Convertible tops have a reputation for ballooning and buffeting when going down the road. Manufacturers installed snaps on the frame to help hold the top tightly to the frame. These fasteners seldom worked and were later replaced by cables.

11 The openings of the top bow sleeve are transferred to the frame rail so that the top side cable can be fit. Side cables are a necessary addition to older tops to help keep the top tight to the frame and prevent ballooning and buffeting of the top.

12 Measurements are made from the index marks for the bow sleeve openings so that a hole can be drilled into the frame side rail to secure the side cable with a rivet. Accurate measurements ensure that the cable operates correctly inside the cable sleeve.

13 Measure the cable to the desired length and slide the locking ferrule onto the cable. Create a 1-inch loop in the cable by inserting the loose cable end into the locking ferrule and peen the ferrule closed. Trim off the excess cable, seal the ferrule, and cut the cable end with heat shrink.

14 The side cables are riveted securely to the top frame side rail. A spring is built into the side cable to allow the proper tension to be maintained. Without a spring the side cables can stretch and loosen over time, becoming ineffective.

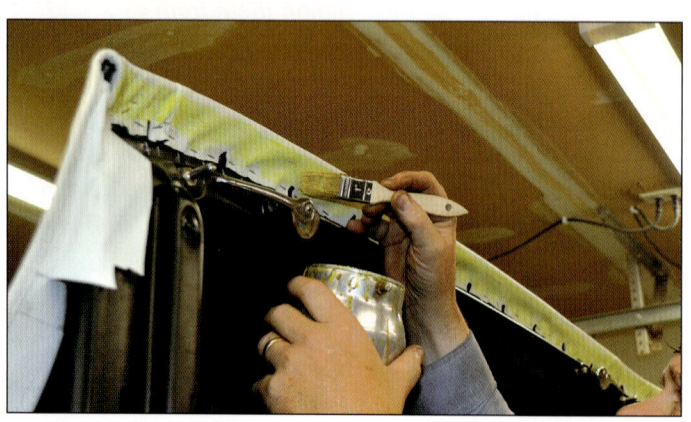

15 The front weather seal is measured to fit the header bow. It is made up of matching top material with a 1/2-inch rubber core and sewn to fit across the front of the header bow. To help with positioning, the weather seal is glued to the header bow.

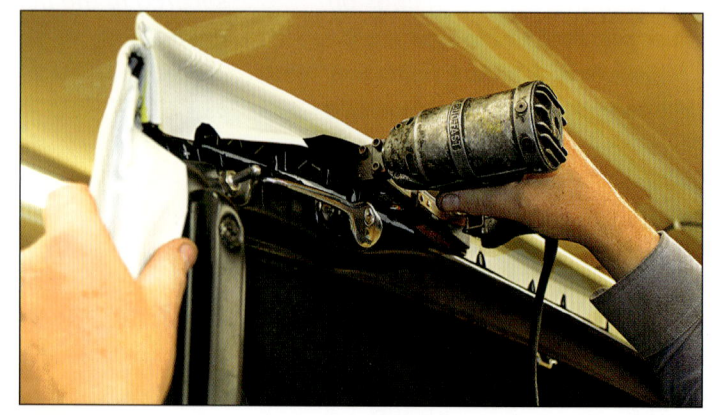

16 To secure the weather seal it is stapled along the inside selvage to the header bow tack strip. This conceals the staples from view and protects them from exposure to the elements. Because it hides the staples, the weather seal also looks a lot nicer when the top is retracted.

CONVERTIBLE TOP

17 Glue is applied to the inside selvage of the weather seal to close it. This is done to keep the staples from exposure to rain and prevent corrosion. The selvage edge of the weather seal can now be trimmed to the edge of the tack strip.

18 The rubber header weather strip is applied to the underside of the header bow and is held in by a metal weather strip retainer. The weather strip retainer also covers the raw edge of the front weather seal and is attached to the header bow with machine screws.

19 The rear-quarter flaps of the top are glued in place to the vertical frame rails to finish the convertible top installation. The rubber weather strip seals are then attached to the frame rails with the correct retaining washers and nuts.

20 Finish the convertible top by giving it a quick steam to remove any small wrinkles, which helps relax the top to fit the frame perfectly. The well liner is attached to the rear seat support and the rear seat is reinstalled. With the protective draping removed from the rear of the car it is ready to enjoy.

Prior Damage Repair

After a few top replacements it is not uncommon for the sheet-metal screws that hold the rear tack rail in place to become loose from wear and stretching of the metal due to over-torquing. Sometimes the original screws have been replaced with larger screws or lag bolts to help with the oversize mounting hole. The incorrect hardware only makes the problem worse and is not a fix but a rather poor solution to a common problem.

The simplest fix is to tap the metal around the screw hole with a small body hammer to shrink the stretched screw hole. This works well most of the time, but only if the hole hasn't been enlarged due to the screw being replaced with a much larger screw. An enlarged screw hole can be fixed several different ways. The first option is to weld the screw hole closed and drill it to the correct size. Another repair technique is to rivet in a new piece of metal with the correct screw hole drilled in it.

In some cases I find that using a Rivnut is a great choice to repair an oversize mounting hole. Use a 1/4-20 steel Rivnut and follow the instructions for proper installation.

AUTOMOTIVE UPHOLSTERY AND INTERIOR RESTORATION

CHAPTER 7

Most of the time a simple repair to a tack rail bolt hole is done by bumping the metal back into place with the aid of a pick hammer. Always try this repair first because it is the easiest and most noninvasive repair that can be made to the car.

Stripped-out tack rail holes that are just too large for conventional repair can be repaired with a Rivnut. It takes a little more skill and a special tool to make this repair, but the result is a solid repair that will last a long time and function normally.

Hydraulic System Servicing

The hydraulic system of a convertible needs to be inspected regularly to ensure that it continues to perform properly. I recommend inspecting the system in the spring before putting the top down and in the fall before storing the car for the winter.

Look at the hose connections and run your fingers over them to check for leaks. Feel the hoses and look for checking or small cracks that form with age. If you see worn or damaged hoses it is best to replace them before they fail.

Listen to the pump for differences in tone as this may indicate that the system may be low on fluid. The system should only be about 75 percent full. Overfilling of the pump causes damage to the system.

Look at the lift cylinder rods. The rods should be shiny and smooth. If they are rusty, pitted, or show signs of excessive oil and dirt buildup then they must be replaced.

Replace Pump and Cylinders

Although repair kits are available to rebuild the hydraulic pump, I recommend that you have the pump professionally serviced or replace it with a new one to ensure that it does not leak or give you future problems; replacing a few seals may not be enough to correct what ails your old pump. Leaking cylinders are not serviceable and they should be replaced with new cylinders. It is also a good practice that if one cylinder is bad you should replace them both because the other one may fail soon.

An upper hose and lower hose run from the pump to each cylinder. The hoses are fitted with brass flared fittings and they thread into the cylinders and pump. Use a flare nut wrench when securing the fitting, being careful to not overtighten the fitting.

Bleed the System

After replacing a component of the hydraulic system you need to bleed the system of excess air so that the fluid can reach all the components and function properly.

Disconnect the rod ends of the cylinders from the top so that they can extend and retract without interfering with the top.

Keep the reservoir on the pump filled to 75 percent while running the

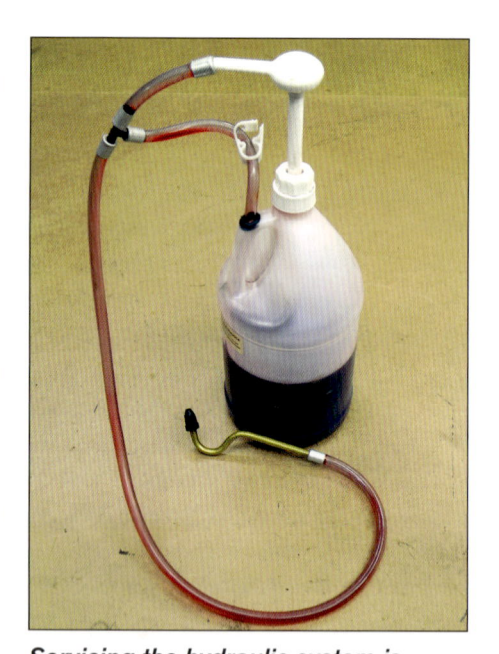

Servicing the hydraulic system is a breeze with the Fluid-Matic. This simple device not only saves time by taking the guesswork out of filling the pump and cylinders, it also eliminates the use of a funnel or syringe for fluid transfer, making it a lot less messy.

pump. Keep the plug out of the reservoir so that the air can escape from the system. This gets messy, so have plenty of rags on hand to catch spills. As the fluid fills the cylinders they go up and down unevenly until they

188   AUTOMOTIVE UPHOLSTERY AND INTERIOR RESTORATION

CONVERTIBLE TOP

The hydroelectric pump is the heart of the power top system. It is a good practice to listen to and inspect the pump visually for leaks; correct any problems as they come up. Neglecting the warning signs of the pump will lead to a costly repair or replacement.

Hydraulic hoses and cylinders need to be inspected visually for leaks. Hoses tend to develop check cracks and leaks at the fittings. The ram cylinders develop leaks at the rod seal. Look for excessive oil and debris on the rams. Any questionable components should be replaced.

have both been equalized with fluid. Do not overextend the cylinder rods as this can damage the cylinders.

Operate the pump in short bursts for 15 to 20 seconds at a time so that the pump motor does not overheat.

After the system operates evenly you can replace the plug in the reservoir of the pump.

Connect the cylinder rods to the top frame and test the function of the top.

If everything works properly you can proceed with the top installation.

To make the job of filling and bleeding the hydraulic system easier I use the Fluid-Matic convertible system fill and bleed tool from Convertible Service. This simple tool allows you to service your hydraulic system without the mess, and best of all, there is no guesswork as to how much to fill the system.

Tack Rail Reconditioning

The tack rail may need to be reconditioned if the fiber tack strip material inside shows signs of deterioration. The process of removing tacks and/or staples tears up the tack strip and after a while it no longer holds a staple securely.

To remove the worn-out tack strip material pry open the metal tack rail to gain access to the tack

The tack strip in this rear tack rail is weather damaged and no longer holds a staple; it needs reconditioning. The tack strip is replaced and the metal tack rail is cleaned and treated to prevent further deterioration.

The tack rail is opened and the old tack strip material is removed and discarded. All signs of rust and corrosion must be removed and the metal must be prepped and painted before it can be reassembled.

A new tack strip has been cut and placed inside the reconditioned metal tack rail. The tack strip has been secured by crimping the metal edges of the tack rail around the new tack strip material. The tack strip material is then drilled out to open the mounting holes.

CHAPTER 7

strip material and remove the damaged tack strip.

Clean the tack rail to remove any rust or debris and paint the metal to prevent further rust.

Insert new tack strip material into the metal rail and cinch the metal casing along the edges to secure the new material in place.

Open the tack rail mounting holes by drilling out the tack strip material. Do not enlarge the holes in the metal; only remove the material inside the hole.

Double-Blank Curtain

Almost all vintage soft-top cars had an applied glass window in the rear. The glass is sandwiched in the curtain and held in place by a metal frame. The windows used can come in many different shapes and sizes depending on the owner's personal choice.

Determine the height and placement of the window by temporarily installing the double-blank curtain in the car and setting the top in place to get a measurement for the window height.

Remove the curtain from the car and lay the curtain out face down and flat on the workbench.

Transfer your measurements to the inside of the curtain and insert the glass pane between the two pieces of curtain material.

Place the front section of the window frame under the curtain so that the glass pane is aligned and sitting correctly inside the frame.

Place the back section of the frame on the surface of the inside of the curtain so that it mates with the front section of the frame and the glass is properly in position sandwiched inside the curtain.

Through the screw holes of the rear frame use a regulator tool to locate the threaded screw receivers in the front frame and begin to insert the screws and tighten them 1/3 of the way. When all of the screws are in place, begin to snug the screws down evenly by alternating from top to bottom and from side to side until the frame is secured around the glass.

Use a fresh razor blade and run it around the inside edge of the frame to reveal the glass. Turn the curtain over and do the same to the front. Be careful not to scratch the glass with the razor blade or slip and cut the outside of the fabric.

Install the finished curtain in the car as normal.

Installing a Double-Blank Curtain

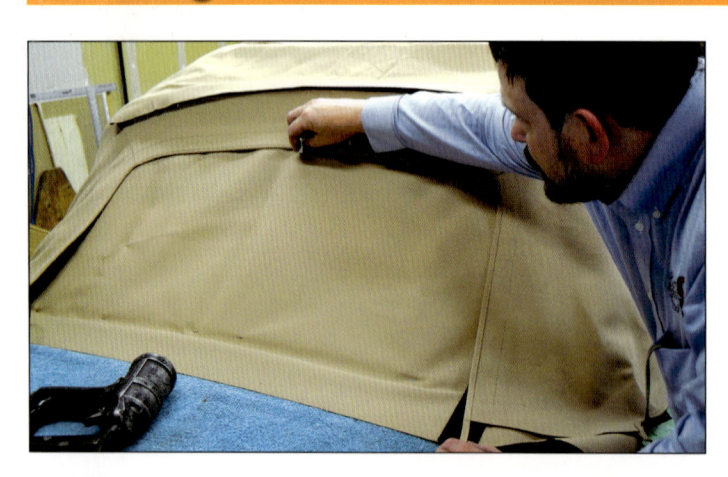

1 *The double-blank curtain is temporarily set and the top material is placed over the curtain. Reference lines are marked on the curtain to aid in locating the window position. The top and curtain are removed from the top frame and the curtain is brought to the bench for the fitting of the rear window.*

2 *With the rear curtain placed face down on the workbench, reference marks are made on the backside of the curtain to aid in the fitment of the glass rear window. The glass window must be level and an accurate layout is important.*

CONVERTIBLE TOP

3 The rear window is made up of an inner and outer metal frame designed to hold a tempered glass window. The frame is held together by small machine screws that sandwich the glass inside the curtain material between the frames.

4 The tempered glass has been positioned within the layout lines on the inside of the double-blank curtain. The front half of the frame is positioned on the outside of the curtain while the back half of the frame is lined up with the front half. A regulator is used to align the screw holes.

5 The frame is screwed together, sandwiching the tempered glass and curtain material inside the metal frame and creating a weatherproof seal around the tempered glass. The screws are tightened a little at a time by alternating across from each other to create an even seal.

6 The curtain material is removed from inside the frame with a fresh razor blade, taking care not to damage the glass or the frame, thus revealing the tempered glass window. The curtain is turned over and the process of cutting away the curtain material is repeated to reveal the window completely.

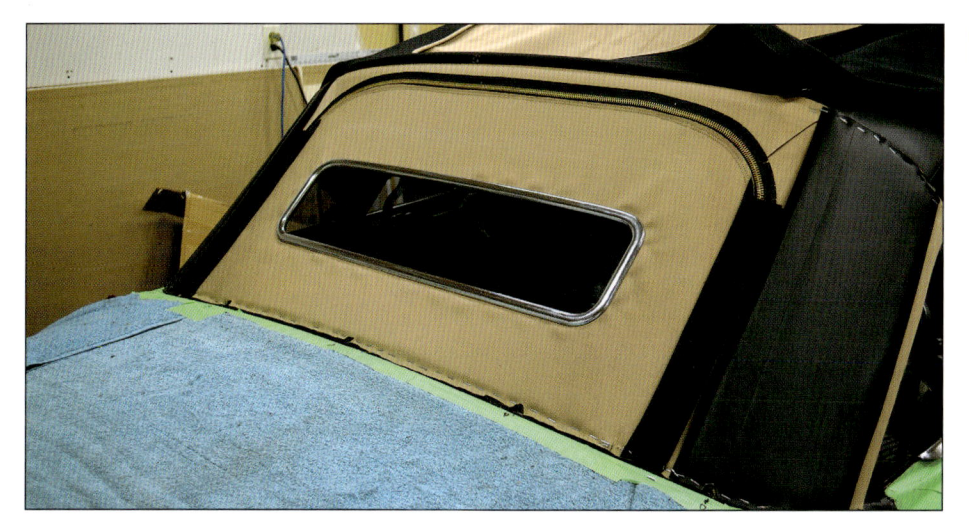

7 This is what the finished rear curtain looks like after it has been installed permanently in a 1949 Chevrolet. Installation of the rear curtain was completed as it normally would be. The new top can now be fitted to the car.

AUTOMOTIVE UPHOLSTERY AND INTERIOR RESTORATION

SOURCE GUIDE

3M
3m.com

ACME Auto Headlining
550 W. 16th St.
Long Beach, CA 90813
acmeautoheadlining.com

Al Knoch Interiors
9010 N Desert Blvd.
Canutillo, TX 79835
alknochinteriors.com

Auto Custom Carpets
1429 Noble St.
Anniston, AL 36202
accmats.com

Auto-Vehicle Parts
P.O. Box 76548
100 Homan Dr.
Cold Spring, KY 41076
auveco.com

Berry's Staple Remover
Lubbock, TX 79423
berrysstapleremover.com

C. S. Osborne
125 Jersey St.
Harrison, NJ 07029
csosborneupholsterytools.com

Coast to Coast Leather & Vinyl
1 Crossman Rd. S.
Sayreville, NJ 08872
coast2coastleather.com

Convertible Service
5126 Walnut Grove Ave.
San Gabriel, CA 91776
convertibleparts.com

DAP
Weldwood
2400 Boston St., Ste. 200
Baltimore, MD 21224
dap.com

Electron Top
126-15 89th Ave.
Richmond Hill, NY 11418
electrontop.com

Evapo-Rust
4801 S Danville Dr.
Abilene, TX 79602
evaporust.com

Fabric Supply
3434 2nd St. N.
Minneapolis, MN 55412
fabricsupply.com

Gorilla Tape
4550 Red Bank Expressway
Cincinnati, OH 45227
gorillatough.com

G.T. Motorsprots
P.O. Box 18308
Reno, NV 89511
plastex.net

HooVer Products
San Jacinto, CA 92582
HooverProducts.com

Hydro-E-Lectric
5530 Independence Ct.
Punta Gorda, FL 33982
hydroe.com

Jiffy Steamer
4462 Ken-Tenn Hwy.
Union City, TN 38261
jiffysteamer.com

Menards
5101 Menard Way
Eau Claire, WI 54703
menards.com

Metro Molded Parts
11610 Jay St.
Coon Rapids, MN 55448
metrommp.com

Parts Unlimited
2801 Interior Way
La Grange, KY 40031
puiinteriors.com

Pyramid Trim Products
576 N. Prior Ave.
St. Paul, MN 55104
pyramidtrim.com

Rochford Upholstery
7624 Boone Ave. N. Ste. 200
Brooklyn Park, MN 55428
rochfordsupply.com

Rust-Oleum
rustoleum.com

Seatbelt Solutions
15835 Corporate Rd. N.
Jupiter, FL 33478
seatbeltsolutions.com

Soft Seal
104 May Dr.
Harrison, OH 45030
soffseal.com

Steel Rubber
6180 Hwy. 150 E.
Denver, NC 28037
steelerubber.com

Trim Parts
2175 Deerfield Rd.
Lebanon, OH 45036
trimparts.com

Seat Belts Plus
1338 Rocky Point Dr.
Oceanside, CA 92056
seatbeltsplus.com

SEM Products
1685 Overview Dr.
Rock Hill, SC 29730
semproducts.com

Wiss Apex Tool Group
1000 Lufkin Rd.
Apex, NC 27539
wisstool.com/scissors-shears

Woodward Fab
P.O. Box 425
1498 Old U.S. 23
Hartland, MI 4835
woodwardfab.com